Equestrian Cultures

ANIMAL LIVES

Jane C. Desmond, Series Editor; Barbara J. King, Associate Editor for Science; Kim Marra, Associate Editor

Books in the series

DISPLAYING DEATH AND ANIMATING LIFE: HUMAN-ANIMAL RELATIONS IN ART, SCIENCE, AND EVERYDAY LIFE
by Jane C. Desmond

VORACIOUS SCIENCE AND VULNERABLE ANIMALS: A PRIMATE SCIENTIST'S ETHICAL JOURNEY
by John P. Gluck

THE GREAT CAT AND DOG MASSACRE: THE REAL STORY OF WORLD WAR TWO'S UNKNOWN TRAGEDY
by Hilda Kean

ANIMAL INTIMACIES: INTERSPECIES RELATEDNESS IN INDIA'S CENTRAL HIMALAYAS
by Radhika Govindrajan

MINOR CREATURES: PERSONS, ANIMALS, AND THE VICTORIAN NOVEL
by Ivan Kreilkamp

Equestrian Cultures

Horses, Human Society, and the Discourse of Modernity

Edited by
KRISTEN GUEST AND
MONICA MATTFELD

The University of Chicago Press
Chicago and London

The University of Chicago Press, Chicago 60637
The University of Chicago Press, Ltd., London

Published 2019
Printed in the United States of America

28 27 26 25 24 23 22 21 20 19   1 2 3 4 5

ISBN-13: 978-0-226-58304-4 (cloth)
ISBN-13: 978-0-226-58951-0 (paper)
ISBN-13: 978-0-226-58965-7 (e-book)
DOI: https://doi.org/10.7208/chicago/9780226589657.001.0001

Library of Congress Cataloging-in-Publication Data

Names: Guest, Kristen, 1967– editor. | Mattfield, Monica, editor.
Title: Equestrian cultures : horses, human society, and the discourse of modernity / [edited by] Kristen Guest and Monica Mattfeld.
Other titles: Animal lives.
Description: Chicago ; London : The University of Chicago Press, 2019. | Series: Animal lives | Includes bibliographical references and index.
Identifiers: LCCN 2018019129 | ISBN 9780226583044 (cloth : alk. paper) | ISBN 9780226589510 (pbk. : alk. paper) | ISBN 9780226589657 (e-book)
Subjects: LCSH: Horses—History. | Human-animal relationships—History. | Horses—Social aspects. | Animals and civilization. | History, Modern.
Classification: LCC SF283 .E67 2019 | DDC 636.1—dc23
LC record available at https://lccn.loc.gov/2018019129

♾ This paper meets the requirements of ANSI/NISO Z39.48–1992 (Permanence of Paper).

CONTENTS

INTRODUCTION

Equestrian Cultures

KRISTEN GUEST AND MONICA MATTFELD

Pictured in textured shades of sepia, the horses of Roberto Dutesco's popular and highly publicized Sable Island photographs both reaffirm and unsettle our conceptions of what it means to be "horse" in the contemporary world. As beings who conjure the prospect of freedom from the constraints of modernity—particularly the effects of progress—Dutesco's subjects speak to the longing of contemporary Western, largely urbanized humans for connection to an authentically wild experience. Though idealized as beings who have successfully "returned to nature,"[1] however, the Sable Island horses are in fact products of modernity: having come to occupy the island off the coast of Nova Scotia as a result of the voyages of discovery and colonization that initiated economic globalization, they become visible for us as a result of technology and are today the focus of lucrative industries related to art, publishing, and tourism.

Though painted almost 250 years before Dutesco's photographs, George Stubbs's iconic 1762 portrait of the racehorse Whistlejacket similarly challenges period understandings of "horse." Depicted in isolation and impressively life-size, not only does *Whistlejacket* communicate a sense of animal selfhood unusual in eighteenth-century depictions of animals, it also suggests the problems posed by modernity's objectification and commodification of equine and human bodies. Like Dutesco with his Sable Island horses, moreover, Stubbs represents his subject as a proto-celebrity, and in doing so he offers an exemplary representation of a species that is unique within the animal kingdom in its relationship and interdependence with humans.[2] Both *Whistlejacket* in the eighteenth century and the unlikely celebrity status of the Sable Island horses today suggest the ways the horse continues to be accorded special status among animals as a being that both shapes questions of meaning and identity for human culture and mediates the ideological relations that frame our experience.

How has our understanding of the horse changed from the century of Whistlejacket, and how has this change taken place in response to the collective effects of modernity? What commonalities continue to link human understandings of the horse in Western culture from the eighteenth century onward? These questions are the subject of this collection, which explores the role and representation of horses in human culture from 1700 to the present in a wide array of geographies and contexts and from multiple disciplinary and theoretical perspectives within the humanities. Taken together, the chapters map changes and continuities in the relationship between humans and horses that have both shaped and been shaped by the forces of modernity. Specifically, they address how horses complicate formulations of identity and otherness central to our historical understanding of human-animal relationships, with an emphasis on the ways this dynamic is subject to our ideas about national identity and social space, our engagement with discourses of science and technology, and our understanding of the ways the relations between status and commodification play out in our real and symbolic relationship with horses. Individually, contributors' investigations of specific equine cultures—from the definition of national identity and heritage in Europe, Australia, and the Americas to explorations of the ways horses figure in distinctively modern genres of the self such as biography and photographic portraiture—prompt deeper understanding of how horses have remained symbolically central to the accelerating culture of modernity.

In taking up this subject we contribute to the ongoing scholarly endeavor that Donna Landry has characterized as the "collective project of rectifying the imbalance between the equestrian saturation of early modern culture and today's marginalization of matters equine."[3] This collection builds on the significant body of scholarship focusing on the horse before 1700, such as Peter Edwards's *The Horse Trade in Tudor and Stuart England* and *Horse and Man in Early Modern England*, Pita Kelekna's *The Horse in Human History*, and Kevin De Ornellas's *The Horse in Early Modern English Culture*, as well as on collections such as Karen Raber and Treva Tucker's *The Culture of the Horse: Status, Discipline, and Identity in the Early Modern World* and Peter Edwards, Karl Enenkel, and Elspeth Graham's *The Horse as Cultural Icon: The Real and the Symbolic Horse in the Early Modern World*.[4] It is also indebted to the broad range of scholarship by eighteenth-, nineteenth-, and twentieth-century scholars of literature, history, art history, and anthropology, which suggests cumulatively that, far from signaling their obsolescence, the declining position of horses in everyday life in modern Western society has amplified their symbolic centrality to human culture.

In addition, this work engages with the diverse effects we have come to understand as the conditions of modernity, tracing the ways the horse participated in, and offered metaphors for, technological change in industry and warfare—as in Clay McShane and Joel A. Tarr's *The Horse in the City: Living Machines in the Nineteenth Century*, Ann Norton Greene's *Horses at Work: Harnessing Power in Industrial America*, Margaret Derry's *Horses in Society*, and Louis A. DiMarco's *War Horse: A History of the Military Horse and Rider*.[5] It also charts the horse's centrality both to emerging discourses of nationalism and gender identity and to the transformation of indigenous cultures, approaches pioneered by Donna Landry's *Noble Brutes*, Monica Mattfeld's *Becoming Centaur: Eighteenth-Century Masculinity and English Horsemanship*, Gina Dorre's *Victorian Fiction and the Cult of the Horse*, Sandra Swart's *Riding High: Horses, Humans, and History in South Africa*, and Peter Mitchell's *Horse Nations*.[6] Building on this body of work, *Equestrian Cultures* examines the ways horse-human relationships in Europe, America, and Australia have crystallized the lived contradictions occasioned by the accelerating forces of modernity while questioning how current understandings of modernity are unsettled by the presence of the horse.

Although this complex force was already clearly evident in the early modern period, the effects of changing human-animal relationships since 1700 have reshaped our understanding of modernity and its effects, from the Enlightenment belief in scientific rationalism, progress, and human perfectibility to the emergent forces of capitalism, technology, nationalism, and globalization. Traditionally, as Anthony Giddens argues, modernity rests on the belief that the world is open to transformation by human intervention.[7] Similarly, as Timothy Mitchell points out, the forces of modernity "divorce 'man' from his surroundings" and emphasize the "principle of human reason or enlightenment, technical rationality or power over nature."[8] Approached through what Susan Nance describes as "the great shift in animal-human and human-animal relationships" inherent to modernity,[9] *Equestrian Cultures* is interested in the ways the cumulative effects of our attempts to transform the world in the service of specific human interests—and the consequent effects on individuals—show themselves particularly in human-animal relations, where they suggest the often unanticipated, and frequently contradictory or colliding, effects of "human intervention."

Moreover, *Equestrian Cultures* is also interested in taking animals seriously while looking to one species in particular in order to move beyond the current state of knowledge that charts a narrative of dislocation and alienation. Within this narrative, and during the period covered by the chapters included here, a change occurred that many scholars have characterized as a gradual and alarming shift in human-animal relationships in response to the conditions of modernity that saw society move from a system heavily dependent on animals to one that objectifies nonhuman life.[10] Within this worldview, if animals are seen at all they are "no longer seen as individual sentient beings but as rows of food-producing elements": as objectified products of human ingenuity and technology rather than as live beings.[11] At least that is usually the argument made for animals in modern Western culture. When scholars shift their focus away from "the animal" or "animals" in general to horses, however, modernity's metanarrative—and the focus of much scholarship on the industrialization of human-animal relationships from the early nineteenth century onward—begins to destabilize. Indeed, we argue, when we consider the effects of modernity acted out on the bodies of horses circulated, exchanged, and physiologically reshaped in the service of human society and culture, a different picture emerges. Horses not only have provided humankind with the labor and animal technology that has allowed us to transform the world, as Sandra Swart and Pita Kelekna variously note, they have also acted as the symbolic vehicles through which we have attempted to make sense of modernity's effects. Horses have helped us both to imagine and describe new technologies and—as with dogs, cattle, and other domestic species—to conceptualize human identity in new ways by reshaping an older concern with aristocratic lineage through the concept of breed and bloodlines. They have also functioned as objects or possessions that denote human status, even as their perceived nobility as animal subjects allows us to ennoble ourselves through our real and imagined relations with them. The horse is thus a complex, often conflicted, figure in human society, one that—as a result of its perceived status as at once an animal object and a humanized subject—blurs the line between human and animal.

If horses allow us to imaginatively ease both the paradigm shifts and the negative effects of modernity, however, they also draw attention to and magnify contradictions implicit in the human ends they are called on to serve. They are, as Isa Menzies and Rune Gade variously suggest in their chapters, uncomfortable residual reminders of the conflicts that arise as a result of the global circulation of human and animal populations. Furthermore, as Susanna Forrest demonstrates in her chapter on the human consumption of horsemeat, the symbolic and ideological functions of the horse in human culture lodge in real animal bodies in ways that unsettle modes of thinking informed by the oppositional logic that has come to be one of the organizing principles of modernity in Western society since the eighteenth century. This book charts some of these conflicts between the horse as human symbol and the horse as a living being whose experience—like ours—has been definitively altered by the conditions of modernity. Recognizing the way horse-human relations have evolved symbiotically, this collection argues that one cannot be understood without the other.[12] Indeed, we contend, animals must walk beside humans in any study that hopes to explore the forces of modernity. Where Mitchell questions the geographic origins and periodizing of modernity, then, this collection—following the work of Nance and others—questions its speciesism.[13]

The scholarship collected in *Equestrian Cultures* brings to the fore what is perhaps the most influential animal in human history and examines the shifting relationship between horses and humans, both as representation and as lived experience. We believe that the ways we vest horses with meaning relate to conflicts central to the human experience of modernity, so that human representations speak both to our aspirations and to the ways we objectify others (and perhaps ultimately ourselves). We also argue that the lived experience of horses that results from these expressions offers insight into the contradictions we experience as human subjects. Unpacking these concerns, and in particular answering the question of how to address the lived experience of the horse, challenges researchers who glean their primary data from human cultures. The chapters included here engage this difficulty by mapping the dialectic relation between symbolic, human formations of meaning and identity and the material conditions of lived experience for both horses and humans that result from these formations.

Taken together, the diverse scholarship collected in *Equestrian Cultures* examines the horse's function as status object, the complexities of equine agency and subjectivity, and the early, often uneven effects of accelerating modernity on the material culture associated with horses in England, Europe, and America. Addressing what we see as three core aspects of modernity that focalize the effects of horse-human relations since 1700, the chapters included here are grouped under three headings: science and technology, commodification and consumption, and national identity. While these groupings highlight key points of thematic engagement within and between chapters, there are also significant points of chronological convergence. For example, chapters by Gade and Menzies suggest the diverse paths of horses relocated to serve the ends of expanding modernity, even as they offer powerful reminders of the divergence between human attempts to romanticize the horse and the lived experience of real horses.

The focus of the first section on science and technology highlights both the horse as a form of technology—as in Donna Landry's chapter on warhorses at Waterloo—and as subject to science and technology. In the opening chapter, Monica Mattfeld places Englishman Richard Berenger's writing about bits in the context of changing ideas about the meaning of horse-human relationships. The two chapters that follow, by Landry and by Sinan Akilli, examine examples of the ways that conflicted human engagements with the horse in nineteenth-century Britain inflect questions about death and equine mortality. Taking up writing about warhorses prompted by the horrors of the battlefield at Waterloo, Donna Landry considers the warhorse as "a walking contradiction: companion species in co-becoming—comrades in arms with humans, but also pieces of technology, both fellow sentient sufferers and implements of destruction." Focusing on representations of horses in Victorian novels by George Eliot and Thomas Hardy, Akilli highlights the importance of the horse as an ambiguously placed presence that unsettles received notions about animals as other through the metaphor of blood relationship. The final chapter in this section, Rune Gade's examination of photographs of American caisson horses by contemporary Dutch artist Charlotte Dumas, hints at the afterlife of Landry's warhorse as a symbol of masculine, military, and national identity. For Gade, Dumas's photographs situate the horse historically both as a subject of technology and as a vulnerable physiological being.

Our second section, focusing on the horse as global commodity, begins at a key moment at the end of the seventeenth century, a moment when the horse's traditional role as partner in the elite art of horsemanship began to be redefined. Examining the construction and artistic program of the elaborate baroque stable at Pommersfelden, Magdalena Bayreuther and Christine Rüppell suggest how the manège horse was situated as an artistic commodity connoting status. The chapter that follows, by Charlotte Carrington-Farmer, shifts attention to the eighteenth-century trade in horses between Maryland and the Caribbean, which bred and circulated horses to serve the sugar industry. Extending Bayreuther and Rüppell's interest in horses as objects signifying elite identity, Jessica Dallow analyzes the connection between breed and discourses of race in nineteenth-century American paintings of racehorses by Edward Troye. Extending this concern with synergies between Thoroughbred racehorses and human identity, Kristen Guest takes up contemporary racehorse biography as a genre that attempts to mediate human anxieties about the effects of commodification on human identity through the imagined experience of exceptional horses.

Our final section focuses on the horse's role in articulations of, and conflict about, questions of national identity. Charting the ways horses are enmeshed in both formations of national identity and changing economic contexts, Tatsuya Mitsuda traces debate about practices in Germany's nationalized breeding industry from the late eighteenth century through the end of the nineteenth. Progressive commodification of the horse sat uncomfortably alongside its status as a vehicle for formulating national identity in the nineteenth century, particularly in attempts to promote horsemeat for human consumption. Taking up a particular instance—a hippophagic banquet held in Kansas City in 1898—Susanna Forrest examines how conflicted human views of horse and human identity coalesce in attempts to challenge this persistent Western dietary taboo. Exploring representations of human-horse relationships in late nineteenth-century France, Kari Weil considers the ways horses mediated attempts to "rejuvenate" French manhood. The context Weil examines represents a significant moment of reengagement with older beliefs about the interconnection of horses, men, and the right to govern, in which modern ideas about the purity of blood were set alongside newer ideas about self-discipline. In the final chapter, Isa Menzies examines the dispute about brumby culls in Australia. Locating the brumby at the center of debates that capture significant anxieties about Australian national identity and colonial heritage, Menzies's work suggests the ways the global circulation of horses in the eighteenth and nineteenth centuries produced unanticipated symbolic and physical effects.

This book is not, indeed cannot be, exhaustive even in its focus on eurocolonial engagements with the horse from 1700 to the present. Instead, we hope that the range of themes and disciplinary perspectives explored here will point out directions for further work by placing a diverse range of scholarship into conversation. Scholarly consensus is finally seeing questions of human-animal relationships and of the "horse" as essential to our understanding of human and animal life. Horses shaped the process and forces of modernity, and those forces shaped them in return. This book thus represents what we hope is only the beginning of more sustained exploration of horses in the modern period.

PART ONE

Science and Technology

ONE

Machines of Feeling

Bits and Interspecies Communication in the Eighteenth Century

MONICA MATTFELD

When Jacques Derrida writes of Bellerophon and his half-brother Pegasus—whom Bellerophon bits and tames—he wonders what it is "[to hold] one's other by the bit? When one holds one's brother or half-brother by the bit?"[1] Bits, those seemingly inert pieces of metal ubiquitous to the riding experience, have over time inhabited the mouths of millions of horses. They are a tool of mastery of man over animal and, at the same time, the technological means of interspecies communication. However, Derrida was correct to question what it meant to use one. What did it mean to place a bit in a horse's mouth, and how did this small piece of technology function in the entwined lives of horses and humans? Expanding on my previous work on the history of horsemanship and masculinity in eighteenth-century England, here I explore the role of technology in the horse-human relationship.[2] I do so by following one of the most vehement debates about riding technology to come out of the eighteenth century—a debate over whether a horseman should use curb bits or snaffles. Focusing specifically on the views of Richard Berenger (d. 1782), master of horse to George III of England, I argue that this change in bitting technology reconfigures a body-based language of riding central to period debates about equine liberty, promoting period insights into human and nonhuman anatomy and riding methodology. Unlike earlier generations of riders who adopted a dominating system of riding, horsemen of the middle to late eighteenth century aspired to ride with feeling; communicating with bodily sensitivity and grace, they opted for a technology that placed the horse's freedom at the heart of their relationship and equestrian semiotics.

In what follows, I argue that placing a bit in a horse's mouth is an enactment of "kinship in technoscience," to use Donna Haraway's phrase.[3] In this formulation of human and animal, both beings come together in a process of "co-evolution" as "companion species," eschewing the subjective singularity of either participant.[4] Often described using the ideal of the centaur, horse and rider are the products of a continuing, reciprocal process of "becoming with" each other through the kinesthetic act of riding. They are also the products of a process that is always cyborg, since riding a horse requires not only finesse, time, effort, and skill but also technologies—such as bits—that shape the horse-human relationship. As Jane Bennett argues, all matter, even the most seemingly inert metal, has agency, "material vitality" that influences all around it.[5] Although small and seemingly utilitarian, I suggest, bits directly shaped the lives of the horses and humans who "intra-acted" with them in complex apparatuses of "mattering." As Karen Barad argues, "matter comes to matter" in the most fundamental of ways, and that mattering shapes both human and animal together.[6] In other words, through the technology of the bit horses and men, animal and human, configure each other to form something new, something composed of all three.

Nerves

In the eighteenth century, bits and bitting practices increasingly came to be understood as intimately connected not only with the rider's body—his hands, legs, and seat—but also with his internal self. To ride with feeling was a matter not only of skill and training, but also of material composition. It was a matter of nerves. Over the eighteenth century scientists were beginning to understand how the human nervous system worked, but with this knowledge came a philosophy of nerves that ranked people on a hierarchy of bodily feeling. It was widely believed that everyone possessed nerves to some degree, but some people had more than others and hence were more sensitive or sentimental. Within a period that popularized sentiment as an ideal masculine virtue, to express more feeling than others increased one's reputation and social standing.[7]

To understand how the nervous system worked, scientists began experimenting on animal subjects. Since antiquity, scholars had looked to animals for insights into the inner workings of the human body, and the similarity between human and animal bodies was widely acknowledged. In the seventeenth and eighteenth centuries, however, as science increasingly became interested in mind, sensibility, and consciousness, the perceived connection between animal and human physiology became ever more problematic.[8] Questions were raised about animals' cognition, their ability to feel pain or emotion, and whether they had souls. Such questions are evident in the work of the influential Swiss physiologist Albrecht von Haller (1708–77), whose work on sensibility and irritability explicitly suggested parallels not only between animal and human bodies, but also between animal and human feelings.[9] Haller regarded his animal experiments as undeniable proof of human bodily function, and he concluded that humans and animals shared enough material similarities to allow for a systematic investigation of the complex question of shared sentiment—a system of feeling that was at once physiological and based on external sensation, but that also was grounded in the mind and the soul.[10]

As Stephanie Eichberg points out, eighteenth-century scholars' denials that animals had souls (in keeping with biblical tradition) was increasingly challenged by evidence that humans and animals possessed analogous nervous systems. For sensationalists, this shared physiological quality not only indicated some form of shared mental ability but also challenged theories about the soul as the ultimate cause of motion.[11] Many scholars began to embrace theories that reduced or negated the question of the soul in an effort to understand how the nervous system functioned as a link between the body and the mind. For them, "mind" or rationality in animals was explained as a neo-Aristotelian "intelligence" inferior to human reason, and animal movements (potentially indicators of thought and hence soul/mind) were dismissed as "patterns of behavior directed by innate images"—a school of thought that would later develop into theories of instinct. More directly, mechanist theories (made famous by René Descartes) simply denied animals any cognitive abilities, claiming that any seeming capacity for reason was a mechanical outward manifestation of external stimuli.

In contrast, sensationalist theory (most famously espoused by John Locke, David Hume, Étienne Bonnot de Condillac, and Erasmus Darwin) "implied no difference between human and animal reason, at least on a theoretical level, for both were thought to be guided by images derived from sense experience."[12] In this theory the "soul" was equated with "mind" as "based on sensory experience alone." For Haller, Ildiko Csengei argues, "sensibility, at least in humans, denoted the feeling capacity of the soul, and was restricted to the nerve fibre. In animals, . . . sensibility could be made visible by causing pain and observing 'evident signs' of suffering."[13] However, the metaphysical understanding of "soul" continued to be debated by sensationalists, among whom "it could not be settled whether "sensation" involved an intervention of the soul/mind or was an exclusive property of nerve tissue."[14] In other words, it was possible for animals and humans to share physiological traits such as the nervous system and to then use that system, and the stimuli it conveyed, both to reason like humans and to demonstrate through their actions the presence of a thinking mind/soul.

While Berenger remains somewhat ambiguous on the subject of equine souls, he, like many famous horsemen before him (including William Cavendish, the first Duke of Newcastle),[15] believed horses had individual and eminently independent minds that were able to express "will," "imagination, memory, and judgment" in much the same way as their riders did.[16] Expressing themselves not only through pain (an equine feeling horsemen were to avoid at all costs) but also through their ability to learn and understand the aids (instructions) of their riders, for Berenger horses seemed to possess rationality and feeling. They had minds and nerves, and as a result they had no trouble expressing their views and communicating with men, with whom they were equally nerved, educated, and rational.

Horses and humans communicate through a shared kinesthetic language system grounded primarily in the material body; thus horsemanship is an art that eschews verbal speech in favor of touch. This system, as Kari Brandt argues, is therefore a "co-creative process" in which both horse and human learn and influence the semiotics of the other.[17] By building individualized systems of "intra-action" iteratively over time, in effect horses and humans co-create each other by coming to know their partners' body and will. This way of knowing and being in a multispecies world is widely acknowledged as the heart of much horsemanship practice today (especially dressage), but it was of increasing importance in the eighteenth century as new scientific and philosophical emphasis was placed on the physiology of bodies.[18] Often understood as searching for and, for the lucky few, achieving "centaur" status, riding was a process of joining with the other to form a single being comprising both human and animal.[19]

To form the centaur, horsemanship as communication between animal and man demanded that each party adopt the bodily language of the other.[20] A properly reciprocal communication between man and animal, often termed "appui" by eighteenth-century horsemen, developed slowly over time and was the result of frequent repetition during training. As Henry Herbert, Earl of Pembroke, argued, "'tis necessary that the greatest attention, and the same gentleness, that is used in teaching the horses, be observed likewise in teaching the men, especially at the beginning. Every method and art must be practised to create and preserve, both in man and horse, all possible feeling and sensibility."[21]

Proper riding, he emphasized, was about reason and bodily feeling between man and animal, a sentiment Berenger highlights. "The horseman works not only upon the understanding, but even upon [the horse's] sense of feeling," he argued, and though the horse was blessed with three senses ("hearing, feeling, and seeing"), only "touch" was useful to "make him very quick and delicate." Only through "touch, or feeling" could the horseman's strongest aids be conveyed; "when he is once brought to understand the aids which operate upon this sense," Berenger concludes, "he will be able to answer to all that you can put him to."[22]

Similarly, he insisted that only through training and practice could a horseman learn the aids and feeling necessary for the reciprocal embodiment of sensibility. Over time, horse and man learned the qualities common to sentimental social deportment—"ease," "freedom," and "grace"—necessary for harmony, without which a body "can never feel that fixed point, that just counterpoise and equality, in which alone a fine and just execution consists."[23] If given justly in good time, he claimed, the aids (or language) of a horseman "will create and call out, as it were, those cadences and equalities of time of which the finest airs [or movements] are composed; measures and cadences which it is not possible to describe, but what every man, who calls himself a horseman, ought to comprehend, attend to, and feel."[24] This idea about the language of horsemanship emphasized a mutual circle of sensitive bodily feeling that led to equality of reciprocal communication. For Berenger this was something every horseman could feel but not describe, for "reciprocal" feeling was entirely body-based, beyond verbal language written or oral.[25]

Technically the horse's entire body was capable of feeling, and hence receptive to aids; however, while a horse's sides and back (the areas in contact with the saddle and the rider's legs) were essential to the communication process, it was the horse's mouth that received the most attention and care. It was here, common wisdom emphasized, that most communication occurred, where a horse could be made or lost, and where the success or failure of a horse in the manège was determined. The mouth was the most heavily nerved, and hence sensitive, part of the equine anatomy and therefore the most easily ruined both by incorrect or insensitive riding and by the rider's choice of bits. Moreover, mouths came in all shapes, sizes, and sensitivities: they could be wide with thick lips but narrow bars (the interdental gap between the incisors or canines and the molars), narrow and long with fleshy bars and a low, hard palate, or deep with thin lips and medium bars but a thick tongue.[26] Each horse, and hence each bitting choice, was therefore unique. Horsemen needed to know what bits would work for their horses, and all bits must be chosen to maximize the pleasure and "delight," or appui, that came with habitually wearing one.[27]

Because of the mouth's sensitivity, it was most receptive to the rider's hands (themselves the most heavily nerved, and hence sensitive, part of a rider's anatomy). As Berenger explained: horsemanship "depends chiefly upon the goodness and quickness of feeling; and in the delicacy which nature alone can give." Nature was fickle, however, and she did "not always bestow" feeling equally. This was a problem because, for horsemanship,

> the first sensation of the hand consists in a greater or less degree of fineness in the touch or feeling. All of us are equally furnished with nerves, from which we have the sense of feeling; but as this sense is much more subtle and quick in some persons than in others, it is impossible therefore to give a precise definition of the exact degree of feeling in the hand, which ought to communicate, and answer to the same degree of feeling in the horse's mouth; because there is as much difference in the degrees of feeling in men as there is in the mouths of horses.[28]

Because the level and functionality of nerves for man and horse differed so much between individuals, what constituted proper appui was indescribable; nonetheless, general conclusions could be drawn for the reader about how bodily feeling could be formed.

According to Berenger a rider's hands should embody three essential qualities: they ought to be "firm," "gentle," and "light." "A firm and steady hand" was one "whose feeling corresponds exactly with the feeling in the horse's mouth." A firm hand was also steady, enabling a "just correspondence between the hand and the horse's mouth, which every horseman wishes to find." Similarly, "an *easy* or *gentle hand*[,] is that which, by relaxing a little of its strength and firmness, eases and mitigates the degree of feeling between the hand and horse's mouth." Finally, "a light hand is that which lessens still more the feeling between the rider's hand and the horse's mouth, which was before moderated by the *gentle hand*." A horseman's hand, put simply, exhibited fine degrees of sensitivity that depend on "being more or less felt or yielded to the horse, or with-held."[29] These vague criteria of nerved feeling could be taught, but the sensitivity needed for the nuances necessary to determine whether the aids were received by the equally sensitive mouth of the horse, and then to modulate the strength of that feeling depending on the messages received through the reins, was ideally innate within the superiorly nerved body of the horseman.

Subtlety, sensitivity, and gentleness were essential for effective appui, and once experienced this clarity and sensitivity in interspecies communication allowed the horseman to "unite" himself "entirely to the animal who carries" him, while the horse could be "quite *together*, and in the hand" of the rider.[30] Frequently understood as dual-natured centaurism, perfection in horsemanship expressed the complete togetherness of body and mind in both horse and rider.[31] For Berenger this embodied centaurism was the ultimate form of perfection, "for there is such an intelligence and harmony between the rider and the horse, that they may, almost in a literal sense, be said to be but one creature; the horse understanding the *Aids* of his rider as if he was a part of himself, and the rider equally consulting the genius, powers, and temper of the horse."[32] Mediating (creating or destroying) this unity between man and horse, however, was the carefully selected bit.

A Bit of History

The history of bits in England is complicated and generally not well known. Donna Landry, in *Noble Brutes*, comes closest to a comprehensive history of bit technology and related debates. She points out that snaffles were probably an invention of the Eurasian steppe and were in heavy use in Asia and among the Celtic peoples of Britain and Ireland for much of human history. However, the curb, with its long shanks and sometimes punishing mouthpiece, was also one of the most popular bits throughout the world. Making its way to Europe during the Middle Ages, the curb quickly became the bit of choice for European and British nobility.[33] This increasing popularity among the aristocracy informed the emergence of a classed and politicized debate about the curb's suitability and use.

Bits were troubling pieces of mechanistic technology that could lead to the destruction of horse and rider, and even of the nation, as Charles I's "Proclamation prohibiting the use of Snaffles, and commanding the use of Bittes for Riding" indicates. The 1627 Proclamation was designed for the express "defence" of "his loving Subjects" and of the "Realme, upon all occasions, and sudden events." Making clear a directive that British men must not "use any Snaffles, but Bittes onely" when riding horses in the army, because "such horses, as are to be imployed for Service, are more apt and fit to be managed by such as that ride them being used to the Bittes, then to the Snaffles," the Proclamation connected the chosen bit's influence (mechanistic action) on the horse (making the horse serviceable) to the continued security, prosperity, and protection of the kingdom from both foreign and domestic interference. Informed by the continental fashion for the curb in period practices and discourse, the Proclamation embraced the idea that men who worked with curbs, and horses that were used to them, possessed both innate and educated superiority in obedience, courage, and fitness for warfare. Snaffles, in contrast, were perceived as completely unsuitable for the defense and maintenance of the kingdom. They were the bit of choice for training young horses, not horses used in war, and were used by men who did not participate in the elite equestrian culture dominant in court circles.[34]

For Charles I, the usefulness of curbs was inarguable, as it was for Thomas Blundeville and William Cavendish, who both provided detailed diagrams

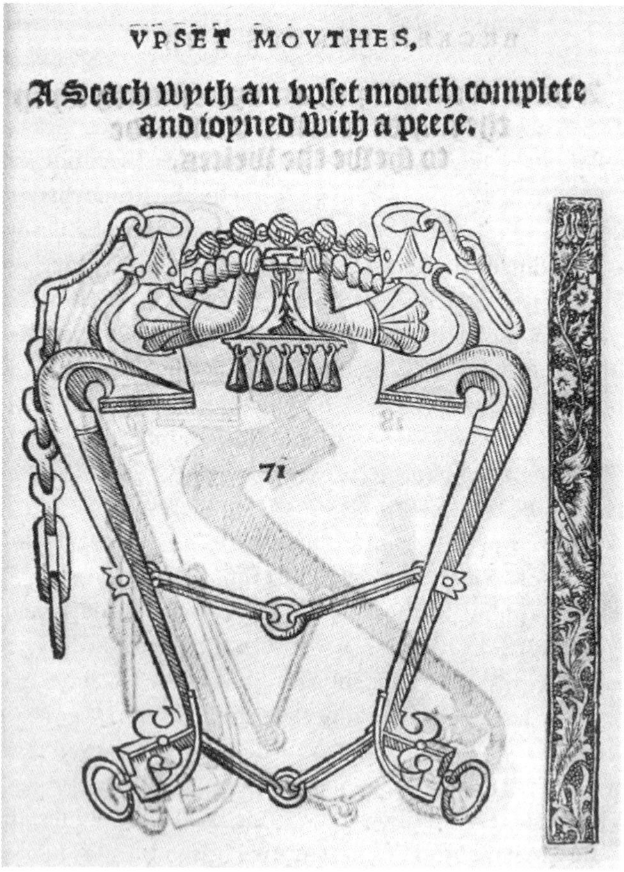

Figure 1.1. "Plate 17 (A Scrach wyth an upset mouth complete and joyned with a peece)." From Thomas Blundeville, *The fower chiefyst offices*. . . . (London: Wylliam Seres, 1566). Image supplied by RCVS Knowledge and used with their permission.

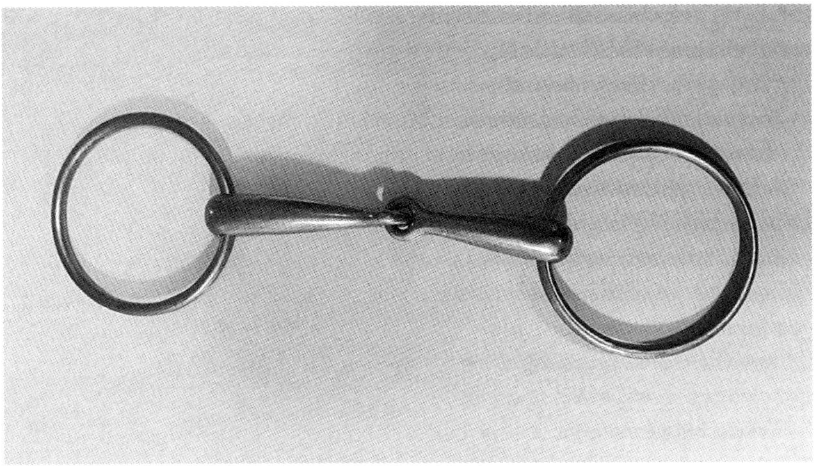

Figure 1.2. Loose-ring snaffle bit.

of ideal curbs in their treatises on riding. In Blundeville's case, in fact, the bigger and more complex the curb bit, the better. These seventeenth- and early eighteenth-century horsemen saw nothing wrong with elaborate bits designed to exert maximum force on the horse's mouth and jaw (fig. 1.1).[35] There was no universal acceptance of all curb designs, however: Cavendish's critique of Blundeville's designs condemns the bits as "completely Abominable" and full of "Tormenting ignorant Follies."[36] Nonetheless, curbs remained his bits of choice, though with lower ports and a simplified design, because they were the most efficient for the art of haute école. Their action on the roof and bars of a horse's mouth invited a shift in balance from the forehand to the hindquarters, resulting in collection and increased control of the horse's overall appearance. For Cavendish the only other bit design available, the snaffle (fig. 1.2), was reserved for men who could not ride, men of old England not versed in the latest equestrian fashion.[37]

Cavendish's views on the curb were standard among most horsemen for much of the eighteenth century. Even though Berenger argues for their use throughout his midcentury work (1771), he broke with tradition in a daring move that affirmed his belief in the sensitivity of a good horse. After spending the greater part of his *History* either praising curbs or taking their presence for granted, the second part of his second volume is dedicated entirely to bits. Here he provides a history of the development and use of curbs, beginning with ancient Rome, and a discussion of their parts and benefits. He then dramatically changes tone:

> An humbler, plain, and hitherto despised instrument, can nevertheless do the feat [or "continue the perfection of horsemanship"]; and that with such certainty, readiness, and ease, that to prefer a *Bitt* to it, seems to be as strange, as to make use of the huge, complex, and intricate machine, called by the ingenious *Hogarth*, a *new Invention* to draw a cork out of a bottle, instead of a common *Screw*; than which, in a good hand nothing can be more effectual. This instrument is called the *Snaffle*; and if ever there was a *Panacea*, or universal medicine, the *Snaffle* is one for the mouths of horses.[38]

While curbs were in theory useful, Berenger acknowledges, in practice they did nothing but make horses go with "their heads between their knees." Men who insisted on adopting the riding methods and equestrian aesthetics of Cavendish or other riding masters were characterized as "generally a blind and servile herd" that "ran headlong into . . . errors." Indeed, he insisted, a head carriage caused by a bit that had been considered integral to a completely trained horse was now considered a false indicator of proper collection, communication, and training. According to Berenger, curb bits did nothing but make the horse go incorrectly and cause him discomfort or pain. Indeed, he suggests, "ancient horsemen understood but very imperfectly the posture in which the horse's head should be placed, so as to influence and direct his motions." Where the curb's action artificially tucked and lowered a horse's head, Berenger argued that the snaffle (and the bridoon, or small snaffle, in the double bridle) could correct problems in equine ways of going. With the mechanistic and jointed action of a snaffle, he suggested, a horseman could raise his horse's head while maintaining the manège outline and movement, thus nurturing sensitive appui and complete control. "To illustrate this," Berenger began, "let the horse be considered as a *Lever*, or poll, when one end is *downward*, or towards the ground, it is certain that the other must be *raised*, and turned upward." With this commonsense approach to riding and bit selection,

> it quickly becomes apparent that if the head of the horse, therefore, is brought *down* towards his knees, it will follow that his *Croupe* must be *raised*, and that it is then impossible for him to be balanced upon his haunches, or to be well in *Hand*; for the hand can have but little power over the horse, while the head is *down*; nor had the horse, when in this attitude, a possibility of *uniting*, or

> *putting himself together*; for this can only be done, by bringing his *Haunches* under him, and making them support the fore parts.

Therefore, he reasoned, curbs were useless, whereas snaffles, with their delicate rising action, were perfect for properly discursive horsemanship.[39]

In calling for the return of the snaffle as the horseman's bit of choice, Berenger was aware that his views were controversial. Even though he was not the only horseman to advocate their use (both Charles Hughes and the Earl of Pembroke sang their praises), doing so separated him from the noble tradition of horsemanship where the curb ruled.[40] Berenger admitted to committing "*High Treason* against the dignity and pretended rights of the bitt," once the legal requirement for men of the army, but now "not being legally entitled to the pre eminence [*sic*] it has so long enjoyed." It was time for a change for the benefit of horses forced to wear the infernal "machines" of previous ages.[41]

Liberating Bits

Berenger's pro-snaffle arguments, as controversial in the eighteenth century as they are in many dressage circles today, were not anomalous among the equestrian elite. Indeed, his comments came at a time of escalating change to horsemanship practice that mandated a change in bit technology. As I argue elsewhere, the late seventeenth and early eighteenth centuries witnessed a sea change in horsemanship practice. During roughly the seventeenth century, the manège and haute école were the dominant forms of equestrian practice among the nation's elite. By the beginning of the English Civil Wars, however, sport riding and racing became increasingly popular. To enable horses to move with the pace and ease required for racing, hunting, or even travel, a more relaxed and stretched-out head carriage was necessary. Alongside this shift in practice there was a shift in the breed horsemen favored and a related change among connoisseurs both in the horse's preferred way of going and in the technology required to bring perfection to the practice.[42]

Before this shift, horses of Eastern bloodlines represented the ideal. Barbs, Arabs, and Turkomans, among other oriental breeds and their offspring, had more upright conformation, offering carrying and collecting power suitable to the extreme movements of the haute école. These were the horses of the social elite and royalty: horses suitable for ceremonial displays of power and the performance of ideal(ized) masculine virtues. Appearing with these animals, termed "riding the great horse," was expressly about show, reputation, and nobility.[43] With the emergence of the English Thoroughbred, however, long-limbed horses with sloping shoulders increasingly came to dominate fashionable equestrian circles. Designed for covering distances at speed and suited to foxhunting, an increasingly popular pastime, Thoroughbreds and horses with similar physiologies began to supplant the older equine conformation favored by earlier noblemen.[44]

This new equine conformation demanded a change in riding style. Instead of the deep manège seat favored by seventeenth-century horsemen and contemporary practitioners of the art, the new "English hunting seat"—offering light contact and (ideally) lighter control—began to dominate.[45] A horseman could now get up off his horse's back thanks to the widespread introduction of the common saddle with its shallow seat and shorter stirrups, allowing the horse increased freedom of movement and autonomy when traveling at speed and over obstacles.[46] This new technology not only initiated changes in riding style, it also reflected wider changes in philosophies of liberty and tyranny, with profound implications for theories about how horses and humans communicated.

Ideally, and as Donna Landry illustrates in chapter 2 of this volume, communication is not necessarily a process of domination or control. Placing a bit in the mouth of a horse, especially one considered a rider's other, animal half within a centauric relationship, was a process of shared embodiment. Within this more egalitarian, if still hierarchical, framework, animals influence humans and human society, much as humans influence animals and animal society, through the agency of matter—of things such as bits. What we see in the eighteenth century is a gradual move away from the heavy-handed bridling and technological domination common to older forms of horsemanship. The sympathetic appui previously associated with curbs was now thought to belong only to snaffles, and supporters of the snaffle considered that appui attributed unprecedented levels of intelligence, rationality, and agency to the equine participant within the language system. Berenger summarizes this change: "To form a conjecture of the intentions of the ancient horsemen from the bitts they used, they seem to have had little more in view than to awe and command the horses by force and violence, so as to be masters of them at all events."[47]

These ancients, and those horsemen from a slightly earlier generation, "placed all their hopes in the severity of their tools, and the strength of the hand which held them; while all sensibility in the horse, and exactness and delicacy in the man, were either disregarded, or unknown." Indeed, Berenger notes, though horsemen of his own age may believe in the "force, purity, and elegance" of their more "enlightened" bit choices (always curbs), they are "unfortunate and mistaken" in their views. Because of their shape, size, and action, curbs would never enable the "horse to perform his business, be it what it will, with that freedom, brilliancy, and justice, which constitute the perfection of horsemanship; unless, perhaps, in the instances of a few horses, which may be so perfect in mind and body, as to be properly called the Phoenixes of their kind."[48] Rather, as history showed, curbs were useful only for military men who dominated their mounts through what Berenger interpreted as pain and force. By contrast, because a snaffle was a milder bit, especially when used by educated horsemen, it was capable of greater finesse and nuance. It was also essential for maintaining the "freedom" of the equine subject.

Berenger's dislike of curbs and their dominating tendencies springs from period reimaginings of the notion of personal liberty. Previously understood by many merely as freedom from physical restraint, for Berenger and many of his contemporaries liberty now came to represent the unrestrained exercise of individual choice, will, and movement.[49] Taking its impetus from this new idea of liberty, the choice of a snaffle bit allowed for "free forward movement," independence, and the ability to exercise will or reason within the horse-rider relationship.[50] According to Berenger the snaffle was liberating for those who chose it, and for him anyone, regardless of social standing, could chose it: like liberty, the snaffle was an egalitarian and democratic technology. It was available to all regardless of rank or class, and since it "suits all [horses], it accommodates itself to all [mouth conformations], and either finds them good, or very speedily makes them so; and the mouth once *made*, will always be faithful to the hand, let it act with what agent it will." As such, "This bridle can at once subject the horse to great restraint, or indulge it in ease and freedom; it can place the head exactly as the horseman likes to have it, and work and bend the neck and shoulders to what degree he pleases."[51] Snaffles were thus celebrated as the universal bit: suitable for young, old, inexperienced, and master horses and riders, they almost guaranteed discursive appui and the perfected horse-human body.[52]

Once a discursive appui was established, the co-becoming of horsemanship could really take effect. The goal of many horsemen throughout the seventeenth and eighteenth centuries was to become "centaurs." A centaur, Berenger explains, drawing on Shakespeare's *Hamlet*,

> is the symbol of horsemanship, and explains its meaning as soon as it is beheld: for there is such an intelligence and harmony between the rider and the

> horse, that they may, almost in a literal sense, be said to be but one creature; the horse understanding the *Aids* of his rider as if he was a part of himself, and the rider equally consulting the genius, powers, and temper of the horse, justifies the allegory; and may almost be said . . . "incorpsed and deminatured with the brave beast."[53]

To become a centaur was to maintain clear lines of communication and agency between horse and human while also selecting a bit that allowed that communication to flow from each (nerved) being. The snaffle offered a horseman control, but it was a control that allowed individual equine liberty, freedom, and agency within the horse-human relationship. It was a technology that brought horse and human together through the physical mediation of metal. Without the bit, such communication could not occur. As Berenger explains, "this union [of the centaur] being so indispensably necessary, that where it is not, there is no meaning between the man and horse, they talk different languages, and all is confusion."[54] The materiality of the snaffle conjoined horse and man, and where it was missing there could be no kinship.

Technosciences of Companionable Perfection

While Cavendish vehemently disliked Blundeville's bit designs, he also made the point that the improvement and perfection of both horse and human was not necessarily the result of technology. "[You] see it is not a piece of iron can make a horse knowing," Cavendish argued, voicing the usual understanding of matter as inert. Instead, it was "the art of appropriated lessons, fitting every horse according to his nature, disposition, and strength; punishing and with good lessons rectifying his vices; rewarding him, and preserving him in his horse-virtues, which will make him a just and ready horse; and not the trusting to an ignorant piece of iron called a *bitt*."[55] A rider's ability to mold his horse, to obtain true reasoned obedience within the horse-human relationship, was what made a complete horse. Berenger agreed to a certain extent, but he argued that the snaffle, that "ignorant piece of iron," was the material foundation that interspecies communication relied on. For him, and as this chapter has shown, the bit had a direct influence on horse-human relationships.

Riding, according to Berenger, was not understood along the lines of Foucaldian "dressage," or "control for control's sake," but rather as a sensitively discursive interspecies dialogue made possible by technology.[56] Within this framework, to place a bit in a horse's mouth was to initiate co-becoming into one unique and useful, linguistic being. Snaffles were the tools for interspecies harmony and for maintaining the still anthropocentric and hierarchical, but increasingly conversational, relationship between human and horse. Using the snaffle, that piece of metal full of "vital materialism," horse and man could learn to feel each other. Through the controversial technology, they could improve and generate "*One Perfect Whole*," the centaur as cyborg.[57]

TWO

Horses at Waterloo, 1815

DONNA LANDRY

> And one morning, to his great delight, he saw the noble animals form in line, charge, and then retreat, and afterwards gallop about, appearing greatly contented with the lot that had befallen them. These manoeuvres were repeated generally every morning, to his great satisfaction and amusement.
>
> —Sir Astley Cooper watches horses of the Household Cavalry who are recuperating in his park after receiving treatment for the injuries they received at Waterloo.[1]

In British literary culture, warhorse stories came into their own after Waterloo.[2] On Sunday, June 18, 1815, battle-winning performances were accompanied by equine carnage so extreme that ethical questions began to be raised, however implicitly, about horses' participation in war. Especially given developments in artillery, equine suffering and mortality formed a newly painful ground on which equestrian partnerships must be enacted. Chivalric ideals[3] forged in horse-human companionship were being strained to the breaking point. Nevertheless, the officer class continued to fancy that heroic masculinity must be embodied and exhibited on horseback. Why was this so if cavalry warfare was becoming ever more obsolete in an age of intensifying firepower?[4] What was the nature of the attachment of military men to horses and to equine and equestrian "culture"? How might investments in the continual "improvement" of English horses have contributed both to success at Waterloo and to the perpetuation of this attachment?

Nowhere have the species *Homo sapiens* and *Equus caballus* been more intimately and decisively engaged as "companion species" in "co-becoming" than in battle.[5] Yet horses as such have not been of much interest to military historians. Even within the vast industry devoted to Waterloo, little attention has been paid to them.[6] A paucity of archival evidence through the centuries means that in some respects the methodological challenges of attending to horses in history are akin to those for subaltern studies.[7] The incomplete picture offered by the archive, the gaps in our knowledge, and the conditions for knowledge that have produced those gaps mean that the "gossiping" about horses that proves such a distinguishing feature of the sudden "outpouring" of British soldiers' memoirs that began during the Peninsular War and continued after Waterloo represents an important hitherto neglected source.[8] The writing that memorialized Waterloo, reprised with a difference in representing the Crimean War (1854–56), was influential for subsequent writing about horses in Britain, arguably preparing the ground for that apotheosis of the British horse story, Anna Sewell's *Black Beauty* (1877).[9] When the Crimean War veteran captain tells his story, his language echoes accounts of Waterloo.

Writing the Horse at Waterloo

Several reasons have been offered to explain the proliferation of military memoirs within British Romantic literary culture: the cultural freight of a conflict that could be ideologically justified as a defense not so much of imperial ambitions as, in preference to Bonapartist imperium, the self-determination of Britain and the Allies; the increased recruitment of soldiers of all ranks who not only were literate but had literary inclinations; the association of war with the sublime; and the place of sentiment and sensibility as discourses within which to envisage soldiers' self-fashioning and suffering.[10] Ian Haywood has usefully examined the coming together of the sentimental and the sublime in spectatorship of the suffering body of the soldier.[11]

Here I propose to refocus the analytical frame onto the spectacle and suffering of the warhorse, just as Lord Byron did in *Childe Harold*. Walter Scott once claimed that "in the whole range of English poetry there was nothing finer" than Byron's Waterloo stanzas in the third canto of *Childe Harold*, "commencing with the line—'There was a sound of revelry by night'" and "ending with the words—'Rider and horse, friend, foe, in one red burial blent.'"[12] Framing the battle in the context of chivalric ideals, Byron's account of Waterloo begins at the Duchess of Richmond's ball in Brussels on the night of June 15: "There was a sound of revelry by night, / And Belgium's capital had gather'd then / Her Beauty and her Chivalry, and bright / The lamps shone o'er fair women and brave men."[13] Chivalry, like Beauty, comes to grief in the equine and human bodies fallen on the field, the heaps of dead that, in the days following the battle, would cause newly arriving horses to "scream" at "the scent of corruption."[14] Byron renders most memorably the massive carnage that would form one of the most powerful images to emanate from Waterloo.[15]

Problems of Domestication and Attachment

The degree to which horses not only cooperated but actively collaborated with their riders lies at the heart of the mythmaking generated in the aftermath of Waterloo. If we agree with Donna Haraway and Vinciane Despret that questions asked *about* a species should ideally be "good questions" of interest *to that species*, we should be asking what it takes for horse-human partnerships to work and even to flourish. What is necessary, from a horse's point of view, for domestication to be something that cannot be written off simply as oppression or exploitation—something more like collaboration, a working together, grounded in a willingness on both sides?[16] Despret comments: "We should also pay attention to the fact that if domestication refers univocally to situations of control or mastering, it may be so because we still do not have a good theory of attachment."[17] Here Despret challenges those who would reduce human-animal relationships to enactments of "control or mastering"—in other words, domination and exploitation. At one extreme David A. Nibert brands all domestication a violent "domesecration" by which the sacred creatureliness of nonhuman species is desecrated and, following Marija Gimbutas, attributes to the "Kurgans" and other horse-keeping Eurasian peoples the bringing of hierarchy and conflict to previously egalitarian and peaceful Western European societies.[18] Equestrian enthusiasts have offered counterarguments placing these same mounted steppe pastoralists in the vanguard of human history, achieving on horseback previously inconceivable mobility, thus conquering time and disseminating languages and technology.[19] For our purposes, the interspecies "situated histories, situated naturecultures" that Haraway and Despret call for, whereby interspecies collaborations are recognized as such, reveal that human practices are never entirely human, being regularly tested in practice by horses themselves.[20]

"Attachment" in both a literal and a complex metaphorical sense is the foundation of horsemanship. Jacques Derrida asks a pertinent question for real as well as mythological horses when he reflects that "Pegasus, archetypal horse, son of Poseidon and the Gorgon, is . . . the half-brother of Bellerophon, who, descending from the same god as Pegasus, ends up following and taming a sort of brother, an other self" and then concludes:

"I am half (following) my brother, it is as if he says finally, I am (following) my other and I have the better of him, I hold him by the bit. What does one do in holding one's other by the bit? When one holds one's brother or half-brother by the bit?"[21] However cherished may be feelings of attachment and kinship—the horse as second self, as brother—the relationship is always asymmetrical: the (weaker, slower) human seeks to respond to, communicate with, and in some sense "master" the speed and power of the horse but may then subject the horse to an unleashing of technological destruction. Anticipating Haraway and Despret by some decades, the ethologist and horsewoman Lucy Rees decodes horse psychology not as a matter of aggression and hierarchy—the well-known "pecking order" theories still favored by many researchers in the United States—but as a fundamental "responsiveness," the seeking of sociality and friendship.[22] How then might the human and equine combatants at Waterloo have answered Derrida's question—beyond those first-order considerations, water and forage?[23]

What did it signify when Wellington, employing a racing metaphor, called the battle of Waterloo "the nearest run thing you ever saw in your life"?[24] Why did Captain Alexander Cavalié Mercer of the Royal Horse Artillery refer to the retreat from Quatre Bras on June 17, the day before Waterloo, as a "fox chase" and to the French horses he afterward saw being "paraded" by young men in Paris as "managed cats of steeds"?[25] What is the significance of Ensign Rees Howell Gronow, catching his first sight of Wellington on campaign in France on October 15, 1813, remarking that the general "rode a knowing-looking thorough-bred horse"?[26] What can we understand from the fact that, during the occupation of France that followed victory, Captain Mercer crossed unfamiliar open fields in the dark as he rode home to his quarters from Paris and trusted entirely to the "sagacity" of his Waterloo mount, Cossack, who had received eight wounds in the fighting?[27]

Writing British Horses at Waterloo

All day on June 18, 1815, from sunrise until 10:00 p.m., Wellington had ridden that "knowing-looking thorough-bred horse" that Gronow had observed two years before, the former racehorse Copenhagen, who was doubly descended from the undefeated Eclipse, the greatest English racehorse of the eighteenth century, of whom it was said, "Eclipse first—the rest nowhere."[28] Copenhagen's pedigree further reveals that his dam Lady Catherine, by John Bull, was out of a mare by the Rutland Arabian whose dam was "a hunting mare, not thoroughbred."[29] Copenhagen's genetic makeup thus represented the best of that mongrel mixture of imported Eastern strains and native stock, the so-called English Thoroughbred, topped up by a direct infusion of Arabian blood and the sturdier stuff of that possibly handsome but undoubtedly useful "hunting mare." For Wellington and most of the British officers and men who fought that day, war could be most readily imagined as a serious version of sport, and the horses most suitable for the battlefield belonged to the sporting life. The hunting field, not the manège and "high school" airs above the ground (what we today would call dressage), bred proper horsemanship across the British Isles—hence Mercer's amusement at the "managed cats of steeds" the French favored.

Obtaining and breeding the best possible horseflesh was one among the many forms of national rivalry during the Napoleonic Wars. By the time of Waterloo, it was well understood that success or failure in cavalry actions, and in particular getting away safely after a cavalry charge, was most often a matter of "whose horses were best or least blown."[30] "Best" here means showing evidence of "blood," which enables not only speed but staying power. No amount of hard training could compensate for genetic superiority in the fitness stakes. As De Lacy Evans comments, had certain English officers been better mounted at Waterloo, they might have survived to fight another day:

> Poor Sir William Ponsonby might perhaps have been spared to his country had he been better mounted. He rode a small bay hack. He had a handsome chestnut charger, which he meant to mount when real business began, but the groom or Orderly who had charge of the chestnut was not forthcoming or within call at the moment the General wanted his horse. As to myself, I was well mounted on a powerful, nearly thoroughbred bay gelding.[31]

We are in the realm of coded knowledge here in which "powerful, nearly thoroughbred gelding" is shorthand for the product of British agricultural improvement grounded in Eastern imports, principally Ottoman bloodlines.

Connected Histories: Code Thoroughbred

The history of equestrianism in the West is inseparable from commercial connections with "the East" and eventual imperial ambitions regarding it. What I call here "Code Thoroughbred" stemmed from a set of Anglo-Ottoman relationships: the Levant Company trade from the 1580s onward, imports of more than two hundred horses from 1650 to 1750 and import substitution subsequently—the naturalizing of these horses within a generation.[32] "Connected histories" is Sanjay Subrahmanyam's preferred term for identifying such entanglements by means of a comparative yet integrated approach. Subrahmanyam rightly insists that an "openness to other histories and other societal trajectories [is] essential to make sense even of one's own backyard."[33] The Ottoman Empire no less than British India needs to be restored to the frame when we configure the Napoleonic campaigns, beginning with Bonaparte's invasion of Egypt in 1798. Recent scholarship has begun to address what has often been neglected, as when Henry Laurens, in *Europe and the Islamic World: A History* (2013), observes that "the fate of the Ottoman Empire was the great geopolitical question of the late eighteenth century. Not surprisingly, it remained an underlying issue in the Napoleonic Wars."[34] Control of Ottoman territory was certainly one of the ambitions of the rival European powers, but traces of Ottoman influence were already present at Waterloo, most spectacularly embodied in equestrian culture, both in the genetic composition of the best horses on both sides of the field and in the theory and practice of cavalry.[35]

By the time of Waterloo, the ideal remounts on the market for the British army were all to be classified on a sliding scale according to "Code Thoroughbred," as suitable for gentlemen sportsmen and therefore the military: "the hunter type, light, medium, and heavy, suitable for the different types of cavalry, and the so-called coaching type, which set a standard for gun teams," according to the military historian Major Geoffrey Tylden.[36] Even officers' chargers were of the hunter type, though "presumably" "better looking and possibly bigger" (Copenhagen stood only fifteen hands [four inches to the hand]).[37] By the time of the Napoleonic Wars, "The heavy weight hunter was the beau ideal of those responsible for mounting our cavalry," though such "big, compact well-bred" horses were expensive to produce, buy, and feed, immediately raising the logistical question of forage and the relative cheapness and hardiness of the various breeds versus size and power.[38] "With bottoms like barmaids" was how one remount officer described this beau ideal, combining Eastern quality or signs of blood with Northern European size and substance.[39] As Ensign Gronow reported from Hyde Park in 1815 in the lead-up to the Waterloo campaign, men paraded "mounted on such horses as England alone could then produce."[40] According to Tylden, not only English but Irish breeders "were not backward in breeding hunters of all the three types wanted, Heavy, Middle and Light Weight."[41] After Waterloo, Gronow reported hearing from Marshal Excellmann, one of Napoleon's generals, that "your horses are the finest in the world."[42] Although with the Egyptian invasion of 1798 the French had invested in importing horses from Egypt and elsewhere in the Ottoman Empire and Napoleon had established state studs,[43] war and especially the Russian campaign had taken an enormous toll. Napoleon's general recognized that the British had enormous strategic advantage in the highly easternized bloodlines of the Thoroughbred and the hunters and coach horses upgraded from heavier draft stock by such crossings. Whether the British as horsemen were quite up to the job of getting the best out of these horses, however, remains a moot point. Excellmann thought not, and there is evidence to support his view.[44]

Not only speed, endurance, and beauty but human-attuned intelligence, known as "rationality" or "sagacity," was a distinguishing feature of the so-called "hot-blooded" horses of the East and their descendants.[45] This "knowingness" and almost human quality was derived from a different regime of horsemanship and horse-keeping from the one most Europeans were accustomed to. That is to say, the imported horses themselves brought with them certain expectations and ideas about treatment and training.[46] As Lucy Rees puts it, "Horses do think about responsiveness. They read each other's signals constantly, and they are very good at it."[47] Treated with kindness and leniency, the horse "is likely to become more sensitive, more intelligent, and more interested in life if we adopt her attitude rather than forcing her against the grain to adopt an alien one."[48] The English seem to have had a hard time adapting to the devoted attentiveness required:

> The English cavalry soldier looks upon his horse as a machine, as an incubus, which is the cause of all his exertions and punishments. He ill-treats it. And even when forage lies within his reach, he will not, of his own accord, lift a finger to get it. The commissary must procure everything, and actually hold the food to his own and his horse's mouth. . . . How different things are in the German cavalry regiments of the legion! Every officer and man tries to help. . . . Whereas all the English cavalry regiments were going to pot, the German were distinguished from the first to the last moment of the campaign by their fine efficient horses and men. Nevertheless, I must do justice to the 14th and 16th English Dragoons, by admitting that they were an exception to the rule.[49]

So recorded August Schaumann, himself a German and a commissary under Wellington in the Peninsular War. Before we jump to conclusions of nationalist partisanship, we should consider the evidence of the French divisional general Comte Foy, who also criticized the English for not being of quite the same standard as other nationalities in their devotion to their horses. It was a matter, above all, of feeling, of a capacity for attachment: "The men make excellent grooms, but do not expect to see from them the same tender feelings that, in Turkey, Poland, or Germany, unite the soldier and his horse as companions, in life and death."[50] The Ottoman Empire and its more proximate neighbors, then, could be perceived as the epitome of "tender feelings" in horse-keeping, as if proximity spread equestrian philosophy from East to West, with the insular English being at a distance. Might a class difference be imputed here as well, in the targeting of "grooms" rather than officers?[51] Who was at fault in this alleged failure of feeling, given that officers were considered to be responsible for troops' "imbibing" the proper feeling for their mounts, as Thomas Simes had advocated? When the uniting of the "soldier and his horse as companions, in life and death" was present, astonishing feats could be performed—not only acts of conspicuous bravery, but also the successful exercise of control to spare the horse and conserve its energy. When such unity was absent, not only a lack of proper feeding and caring, but also breaches of military discipline might result, as occurred at Waterloo.[52]

The image of combined human and equine carnage at Waterloo, the heaps of dead of both species immortalized by Byron but also present in so many eyewitness accounts, would forever unite horse and horseman, regardless of nationality or rank. To meet death together is to be in the closest possible partnership. This image thereby finesses the question whether ideals of honorable equestrianism were being upheld during the battle itself, but also whether future military prospects augured well or ill for the continuance of these ideals. Because improvements in artillery brought about the greatest equine suffering at Waterloo, the testimony of artillerymen appears particularly valuable. To be a horseman of feeling and an artilleryman presented an intensified version of what all mounted fighters were beginning to experience in modern warfare. If the "chivalry" signaled by horse-human companionship memorialized by Byron was being strained by the increasing effectiveness of infantry firepower (those standing-firm infantry squares Wellington was so proud of), it was surely brought to crisis by artillery devastation.

"'Fire!' The Effect Was Terrible"

We are fortunate to have the testimony of Captain Alexander Cavalié Mercer, a Woolwich-trained writer and artist, who commanded an artillery unit from the back of a horse. The whole point of the gun teams such as Captain Mercer's G Troop was to achieve as much deadly accuracy as possible, however ambivalent about bloodshed its commander may have been. During the retreat from Quatre Bras, Mercer reported coming upon the bodies of a young soldier and his horse so stripped of every "particle of clothing" that their nationality was a mystery, and he felt for the first time about a casualty of war "such despondency—such heart-sinking" that he wondered at it and added, "His horse, stripped like himself, lay by—they had met their fate at once."[53] There is a certain honor in their deaths having coincided, however dishonorable the stripping of bodies by unseen hands. Horse and rider meeting death "at once" here foreshadows the scene of mass carnage to come.

Facing Marshal Michel Ney's charges, led soon after 3:00 p.m. in response to the shockingly effective, if costly, charge made by the Anglo-Allied heavy brigades, Mercer encouraged his men to hold their fire until precisely the right moment: He leapt Cossack up a bank and rode up and down in front of the guns, "a promenade (by no means agreeable)," without even drawing his sword, taunting the enemy and attracting carbine fire at such close range that they missed him.[54] Onward the French cavalry column came, an "imposing spectacle," and "if ever the word sublime was appropriately applied, it might surely be to it": "Their pace was a slow but steady trot. None of your furious galloping charges was this, but a deliberate advance, at a deliberate pace, as of men resolved to carry their point."[55]

> On our part was equal deliberation. . . . "Fire!" The effect was terrible. Nearly the whole leading rank fell at once, and the round-shot, penetrating the column carried confusion throughout its extent. The ground, already encumbered with victims of the first struggle, became now almost impassable. Still, however, these devoted warriors struggled on, intent only on reaching us. The thing was impossible. Our guns were served with astonishing activity, whilst the running fire of the two [infantry] squares was maintained with spirit. Those who pushed forward over the heaps of carcasses of men and horses gained but a few paces in advance, there to fall in their turn and add to the difficulties of those succeeding them. The discharge of every gun was followed by a fall of men and horses like that of grass before the mower's scythe.[56]

On the day following his intense "despondency" at viewing the fallen cavalryman and his horse, Mercer cannot help but be jubilant at G Troop's lethal effectiveness. "Intoxicated with success," Mercer describes himself sitting on Cossack, "singing out, 'Beautiful!—beautiful!'"[57] The morning after Waterloo, he is "forcibly struck by the immense heap of bodies of men and horses which distinguished" G Troop's position on the field, and he reports being gratified that Sir Augustus Frazer, Wellington's artillery commander, later told him he too had noticed how this same "dark mass" "formed a remarkable feature of the field."[58] Yet Mercer's *Journal* also comes closest to expressing the unspeakable horror of what horses now had to suffer in battle.

At Waterloo, artillery horses were themselves subjected to heavy fire while aiding in this wholesale destruction. Earlier in the day, a wounded horse sought comfort among Mercer's gun teams:

> A sickening sensation came over me, mixed with a deep feeling of pity, when within a few paces of me stood the poor horse in question, side by side with the leaders of one of our own ammunition waggons, against which he pressed his panting sides, as though eager to identify himself as of their society—the driver, with horror depicted on every feature, endeavouring by words and gestures (for the kind-hearted lad could not strike) to drive from him so hideous a spectacle. A cannon-shot had completely carried away the lower part of the animal's head, immediately below the eyes. Still he lived, and seemed fully conscious of all around, whilst his full, clear eye seemed to implore us not to chase him from his companions. I ordered the farrier (Price) to put him out of misery, which, in a few minutes, he reported having accomplished, by running his sabre into the animal's heart. Even *he* evinced feeling on this occasion.[59]

The "full, clear eye" of the wounded horse, "fully conscious," issued an ethical demand.

More tender in his feelings than the farrier, Mercer at nightfall expatiates at length on the spectacle of the fallen, "the actors prostrate upon the bloody soil": "Horses, too, there were to claim our pity—mild, patient, enduring," "looking about, as if in expectation of coming aid":[60]

> Some lay on the ground with their entrails hanging out, and yet they lived. These would occasionally attempt to rise, but, like their human bedfellows, quickly falling back again, would lift their poor heads, and, turning a wistful gaze at their side, lie quietly down again, to repeat the same until strength no longer remained, and then, their eyes gently closing, one short convulsive struggle closed their sufferings. One poor animal excited painful interest—he had lost, I believe, both his hind legs; and there he sat the long night through on his tail, looking about, as if in expectation of coming aid, sending forth, from time to time, long and protracted melancholy neighing. Although I

> knew that killing him at once would be mercy, I could not muster courage even to give the order. Blood enough I had seen shed during the last six-and-thirty hours, and sickened at the thought of shedding more. There, then, he still sat when we left the ground, neighing after us, as if reproaching our desertion of him in the hour of need.[61]

Although a quick bullet would be the kindest thing, or even a saber to the heart, Mercer finds the thought of further bloodshed beyond him. It is a failure of nerve, and a failure of sympathy. This is one of many moments when Mercer admits his mistakes, subjects himself to unforgiving scrutiny. Chivalry in horse-human partnerships? How could it possibly be sustained?

This passage has clear resonances with Captain's story embedded within the autobiography of *Black Beauty*. Anna Sewell embarked on writing her equine novel or slave narrative in 1871, the year after Mercer's *Journal* was first published.[62] So although a decade and a half earlier the Crimean War had intervened—including the infamous charge of the light brigade against the Russian guns at Balaclava immortalized by Tennyson's 1854 poem[63]—there is reason to think that the revisiting of Waterloo through the posthumous publishing of accounts such as Mercer's also had an impact, never previously noticed, on Sewell's portrait of a British warhorse.

The intertextual relationship is clearest at the moment when, his rider having been killed in a charge, a bereft Captain (or Bayard, as he was then called), observes the battlefield:

> I wanted to keep my place by his side, and not leave him under that rush of horses' feet, but it was in vain; and now, without a master or a friend, I was alone on that great slaughter ground. . . . Some of the horses had been so badly wounded that they could scarcely move from the loss of blood; other noble creatures were trying on three legs to drag themselves along, and others were struggling to rise on their fore feet, when their hind legs had been shattered by shot. Their groans were piteous to hear, and the beseeching look in their eyes as those who escaped passed by, and left them to their fate, I shall never forget. After the battle the wounded men were brought in, and the dead were buried.

"And what about the wounded horses?" I said, "were they left to die?'

> No, the army farriers went over the field with their pistols, and shot all that were ruined. Some that had only slight wounds were brought back and at-

> tended to, but the greater part of the noble willing creatures that went out that morning, never came back! In our stables there was only about one in four that returned.[64]

The description of the dead and dying parallels Mercer's battlefield descriptions closely. Yet there is a significant difference. As if he himself had read Mercer, Black Beauty asks what might, for a horse, be the crucial question: Were the wounded horses left to die? By the time of the Crimean War, we are assured by Captain, certain lessons had been learned; farriers were equipped with pistols to end the suffering of the irreparably injured. The "noble willing creatures" who met a bloody fate on "that great slaughter ground" could at least expect a quicker end to their misery than some of their predecessors at Waterloo.

Captain's story also embeds the continuing preoccupation with foreign wars characteristic of nineteenth-century British domestic politics. The contrast between the horrors of the "great slaughter ground" and the "fine thing" that horses may enjoy—"exercise and parade, and sham-fight"—cannot be satisfactorily resolved.[65] The final question posed in Captain's narrative is a geopolitical one, none other than the Eastern Question as it has evolved by the middle decades of the century:

"Do you know what they fought about?" said I.

"No," he said, "that is more than a horse can understand, but the enemy must have been awfully wicked people, if it was right to go all that way over the sea on purpose to kill them."[66]

Defending Ottoman territory from Russian incursions while securing trade routes to India, this time in alliance with former enemy France: the Crimean conflict reconfigures but also repeats the strategic objectives as well as ethical dilemmas presented by Waterloo.

In writing "'Fire!' The effect was terrible," Mercer captures far more than the deadly accuracy of G Troop. The effects of Waterloo would long be felt. Byron's memorializing of Waterloo notably spectacularizes the heaps of dead of *both species* and *both sides*, forever joined. The very soil of the field conspires to unite the fallen: "The earth is cover'd thick with other clay, / Which her own clay shall cover, heap'd and pent, / Rider and horse,—friend, foe,—in one red burial blent!"[67] Byron's lines echo contemporary published accounts such as that by the Spanish general Miguel de Alava, the only member of Wellington's staff to remain, along with the duke himself and Copenhagen, "untouched in our persons and horses": "The rest were all either killed, wounded, or lost one or more horses. The

Duke was unable to refrain from tears on witnessing the death of so many brave and honourable men, and the loss of so many friends and faithful companions."[68]

The syntax bleeds together human and equine. There is no question that the "so many friends and faithful companions" belong as much to horse kind as to humankind. This structure of feeling, if we employ Raymond Williams's term, goes a long way toward explaining the asymmetrical but powerfully reciprocal attachments between military men and their warhorses that exceed mere exhibitionism or instrumentalism.

Warhorses are a walking contradiction: companion species in co-becoming—comrades in arms with humans, but also pieces of technology, both fellow sentient sufferers and implements of destruction. Far from an unfeeling instrumentality, the killing of horses, like the decimation of human troops, aroused deep feelings at Waterloo and after. The very attachment that made heroic actions by man and horse in battle possible was also its ethical burden, its unanswerable demand. Can horses consent to war? That they took sufficient pride in their training to perform military maneuvers on their own gladdened the heart of those like Sir Astley Cooper, the surgeon who purchased and attended to wounded horses of the Household Cavalry, removing bullets and shrapnel they had received at Waterloo, as described in the epigraph to this chapter. Here was consent personified—as enjoyment. Here was a vindication of British horsemanship: the willing attending to duty by cavalry mounts (notice, however, that it was followed by their free-form galloping).

After Waterloo, racing and hunting returned to the fore among horse breeders, consolidating the image of the English Thoroughbred or nearly clean-bred cross as the ideal, displacing questions of resupplying the army until the next major conflict. The perfection of horseflesh for which military men strove kept them as keenly engaged in improvement, including new infusions of blood from the East, from Ottoman territory, as subsequent generations of inventors and engineers would be in designing tanks and airplanes, but with a living difference.

THREE

The Agency and the *Matter* of the Dead Horse in the Victorian Novel

SINAN AKILLI

> Matter and meaning are not separate elements. They are inextricably fused together, and no event, no matter how energetic, can tear them asunder.
>
> —Karen Barad[1]

The English Victorian novel introduced many unforgettable human characters whose experiences have informed our understanding of humanity, nature, and human nature. Character is so central in these novels that names are often chosen as titles: Thomas Hardy's *Tess of the d'Urbervilles* and George Eliot's *Silas Marner* are among the many examples. However, Victorian novels also represent nonhuman characters, such as Prince, the cart horse in *Tess of the d'Urbervilles*, or the "valuable" hunter Wildfire in *Silas Marner*. Unlike the human characters in these novels, we remember Prince and Wildfire not for their actions, but for their deaths—perhaps two of the most powerful depictions of equine mortality in a historical period when human dependence on, and exploitation of, the horse was at its historical peak.

Conventional literary criticism has focused primarily on the human characters in these works, and until very recently nonhuman animals in works of fiction have been understood almost exclusively as allegorical devices, symbols, metaphors, and tropes, or as "stand-ins for humans."[2] With posthumanist thought, however, this focus is changing. As Erica Fudge points out, "in different ways, and using a variety of materials, the place of animals and humans is being re-addressed."[3] This new critical approach may be understood with reference to Mario Ortiz-Robles's recent claim that "literature serves to separate humans from animals, but also to confuse and conflate them."[4] But exactly how do we "confuse and conflate" literature, humans, and animals? How can critical inquiry be sustained when the literary animals in question are dead? This chapter addresses these questions with reference to the "narrative agency"[5] of Wildfire and Prince. My specific focus will be on the scenes where, in death, these horses gain agential power by creating ruptures both in the lives of human characters and in the narrative progression of the novels. I undertake this discussion of the agency of two dead horses by examining their *effects* on human orders of signification, production, consumption, and exchange as represented in these works of fiction. This view is a departure from the critical approach that has understood literary horses based on the cultural work they perform for humans, associated with feelings like "nobility" and "service" that we want to attribute to ourselves. Similarly, it differs from approaches that explore how, after death, horses are rendered into "things" to realize every bit of their economic and object value. To move away from these anthropocentric approaches, I draw on Karen Barad's work on "agential realism," focusing specifically on her notions of "intra-action" and "ethico-onto-epistem-ology." Within the larger theoretical framework informed by these terms, I argue that from the mid-nineteenth century onward novelists like Eliot and Hardy were preoccupied with equine death not only because the horse occupied a central place in the social and economic organization of contemporary human society, but also as a result of their awareness of the ontological and Darwinian affinity between human and nonhuman animals. In the same historical period, I suggest, the *effect*s of this realization shaped an ethical ground where the implications of this paradigm shift could be "performed" in the Victorian novel. Accordingly, this chapter explores how the semantic and material body of the dead horse depicted in the physical *matter* of the pages of a Victorian novel "became" the body onto which the ethico-onto-epistem-ological intra-action of the novelist was "inked." In making this argument I maintain that both Eliot and Hardy understood the centrality of the nonhuman, in this case the horse, in the workings of human society and conflated their concerns about the concept of (human) death with equine mortality. In other words, in "confusing and conflating" literature, humans, and animals, Eliot and Hardy intra-acted with, but also responded to, felt responsibility for, wrote about, gave central roles to, and thus accorded narrative agency to animals represented by the characters Wildfire and Prince.

Agency and Animal Agency

Karen Barad's formulation of "agential realism" suggests a fundamental inseparability of epistemological, ontological, and ethical considerations. This inseparability offers an understanding of the role of human *and* non-human, material *and* discursive, natural *and* cultural factors in scientific and other social-material practices.[6] To see "agential realism" in these terms is to move beyond debates that pit constructivism against realism, agency against structure, and idealism against materialism. Indeed, the philosophical framework I propose entails rethinking fundamental concepts that support such binary thinking, including the notions of *matter*, discourse, causality, agency, power, identity, embodiment, objectivity, space, and time.[7]

For Barad, the concept of "entanglement" rejects any static and individual existence or preexistence, causality, or agency. "We" do not, and cannot, forge or create fixed and complete "connections" and "respond" to distinct "others" as a result of these connections because "we" do not exist outside of these others and these connections. In her rejection of the essential separateness of "word and thing," "human and non-human," and "discourse and *matter*," Barad proposes that we are "intra-actively (re)constituted as part of the world's becoming."[8] In other words, we are only "a part of that nature we seek to understand."[9] However, this position does not stop her from also proposing that as humans we "need to meet the universe halfway, to take responsibility for the role that we play in the world's differential becoming."[10] To address the cumulative effect of these ideas Barad has coined the term "ethico-onto-epistem-ology,"[11] which suggests the dissolution of borders between ethics, ontology, and epistemology. Because "ethico-onto-epistem-ology" is the result of "intra-action," or the "mutual constitution *of* entangled *agencies*,"[12] Barad argues, it is also performative.

To capture the complex nuances of Barad's concept of agential realism in relation to *Silas Marner* and *Tess*, I suggest we consider both representations of horses and the work of the novelist as related performances of "intra-action." To understand Eliot and Hardy in these terms is to see them as "semantic humanimals."[13] In writing about horses, in effect, Eliot and Hardy represented and reflected on their daily experience of horses in their everyday environments, giving visibility and agency to equine bodies that many Victorians had learned not to see. This understanding of a human being's writing about horses differs from approaches such as Paul Shepard's, which claims that "the human mind is the result of a long series of interactions with other animals"[14] and thus concludes that animals are "at the heart of human symbolism."[15] As far as literary animals are concerned, I suggest, we need to go beyond discussions of "human symbolism" and instead consider the ways animals become agents in the novel.

My position regarding the agency of the dead horse is informed by Derrida's engagement with a question Jeremy Bentham posed in 1823 about the nature of animal subjectivity: "The question is not, Can they *reason*? nor, Can they *talk*? but, Can they *suffer*?"[16] For Derrida, this question disturbs the logocentric "position, or presupposition maintained from Aristotle to Heidegger, from Descartes to Kant, Levinas, and Lacan."[17] Like humans, in effect, animals have the capability to suffer and to die, thereby exerting primary agency in the "network," to borrow Bruno Latour's term, that brings together the animal and the human.[18] As Derrida suggests:

> Being able to suffer is no longer a power; it is a possibility without power, a possibility of the impossible. Mortality resides there, as the most radical means of thinking the finitude that we share with animals, the mortality that belongs to the very finitude of life, to the experience of compassion, to the possibility of sharing the possibility of this nonpower, the possibility of this impossibility, the anguish of this vulnerability, and the vulnerability of this anguish.[19]

I would argue that Derrida's focus on suffering and death suggests how a reformulation of the logocentric "Cogito ergo sum" as "Morior ergo sum" (I die, therefore I am) is more to the point philosophically. At this point we seem to be in need of developing a notion of (animal) *mortality* rather than being tied to the evidently limited notion of (human) *morality* to understand and acknowledge the agency of animals, both human and nonhuman.

In relation to such shifting of perspective, Derrida scrutinizes Martin Heidegger's claim that in accounting for the difference between humans and animals based on a perception of the "as such" of reality, an understanding of death is central. Derrida doubts that humans have such an understanding and urges that "there is no pure and simple 'as such.' Rather, there are pluriform understandings of the world, always connected to the (animal) need to remain alive; there are, in other words, differences among animals of all sorts, including human animals, and these differences exist in an 'animal' relation."[20] Cary Wolfe interprets Derrida's last point about the "differences among animals of all sorts" and his rejection of ontological continuity thus:

> For Derrida, . . . "no relation to death can appear as such," and "if there is no 'as' to death," then the "relation to death is always mediated through an other. The 'as' of death always appears *through* an other's death, *for* another." . . . And since the same is true *of* the other in relation to its *own* death, what this means is that "death *im*possibilizes existence," and does so both for me *and* for the other—since death is no more "for" the other than it is for me. But it is, paradoxically in this impossibility that the possibility of justice resides, the permanent call of the other in the face of which the subject always arrives "too late."[21]

In other words, it is in understanding death through the death of another that the ethico-onto-epistem-ological sensibility begins. Therefore, the deaths of the horses in fictional worlds set in motion a major disruption of our understanding of the world "as such." They thus represent a nonhuman animal *effect* on human orders, both fictional and factual.

In Eliot's and Hardy's novels the disruptions or the ruptures in the narrative that result from the loss of equine use value occur at the moment of death, when the horse becomes a *thing*. Bill Brown suggests that "we begin to confront the thingness of objects when they stop working for us: when the drill breaks, when the car stalls, when the windows get filthy, when their flow within the circuits of production and distribution, consumption and exhibition, has been arrested, however momentarily."[22] In other words, when a horse dies, its dead body becomes a "useless" *object*, and that object "stops working for us":[23] it disappears from the systems of material production-consumption and exchange, thereby losing its use value. However, in Victorian novels the dead body of a horse also becomes a *thing* with further agential potential in the system of anthropocentric power relations. As Brown notes,

> the very semantic *reducibility* of *things* to *objects*, coupled with the semantic *irreducibility* of *things* to *objects*, would seem to mark one way of recognizing how, although objects typically arrest a poet's attention, and although the object was what was asked to join the dance in philosophy, things may still lurk in the shadows of the ballroom and continue to lurk there after the subject and object have done their thing, long after the party is over.[24]

It is, in fact, "after the party is over" that the dead horse becomes a *thing* and creates major agential *effect*s on human orders. Brown argues that "as they circulate through our lives, we look *through* objects (to see what they disclose about history, society, nature, or culture-above all, what they disclose about *us*), but we only catch a glimpse of things."[25] My immediate intention here is to "catch a glimpse of things" in order to examine what factual and fictional man-horse entanglements in the Victorian novel disclose about nineteenth-century British society and culture.

Horses and Dead Horses

The literary horse is a useful focus for considering animal agency because the horse has occupied a central place in the human imagination since primordial times. Horses have been understood as "the most elusive and intelligent, the . . . deepest in human dreams and imagination, [the] most challenging to our imagination" since the Pleistocene epoch.[26] Not only were horses represented in "the finest sculpted and painted works of the Pleistocene," they were also materially embedded in human life: equine bones have been found in "every archaeological stratum," and "our ancestors had 'horse' in their stomachs and in their heads in every sense: nutritional, metaphysical, esthetic, and metaphorical."[27] Horses also constitute the "heart of the whole thrust of the modern world."[28] As "the idiom of Progress, the genesis, vehicle, and symbol of the civilized world," Shepard suggests, they are "deeply embedded in the human psyche."[29] In other words, horses had a place in human society and human history that is unmatched by any other nonhuman animal. It is therefore not surprising to observe that the horse is the only nonhuman we meet in literature whose agential power is second only to that of the human animal.

To understand the significance of the dead horse in the novels considered here, we must remember the value encoded in living horses in Victorian society. Despite the increased mechanization of production in industrial towns and the spread of railway transport connecting large settlements in Victorian Britain, the use value of horses remained relevant. The increase in the uses of horses in cities was prompted by industrialization.[30] In urban centers where goods and people were transported locally by horse-drawn vehicles, Gina Dorré points out, horses constituted a part of the urban working classes, "undernourished, overworked, and kept in dank, cramped, and squalid quarters."[31] In the rural countryside, horses continued both to perform agricultural labor and to be necessary for short-distance travel. Across Victorian society, then, horses maintained significant use value despite the increased use of machines. As Hannah Velten notes, the prospects of cab horses in London were dismal: It took only three years for cab horses to become exhausted—if they hadn't already dropped dead in the streets.[32]

Velten's suggestion that cab horses routinely "dropped dead" shows that equine mortality was an event one was very likely to witness in everyday life. Even then, the dead body of a horse had value. In *Tess*, for instance, we learn that "the knacker and tanner" are interested in buying "Prince's carcase."[33] Nonetheless, John Durbeyfield rejects the proposition, noting that "'When we d'Urbervilles was knights in the land, we didn't sell our chargers for cat's meat. Let 'em keep their shillings!'"[34]

In the aftermath of industrialization, the horse also remained a signifier of social status and prestige among the landed gentry, aspiring middling ranks, tenant farmers, yeomen, and tradespeople.[35] Of course, the ascription of sign value and exchange value applied almost exclusively to "fine horseflesh," as we see with the death of Wildfire in *Silas Marner*. Even in the age of the "iron horse," then, the death of a "flesh and blood" horse meant a great loss, whether the horse in question was valued for its flesh, its muscle power, or its bloodlines. Clearly, George Eliot and Thomas Hardy had a deep understanding of the value of horses not only through their observations of everyday life, but also given their awareness of the scientific and philosophical debates about the origin and evolution of organic beings, both human and animal. With a new understanding of their own animality, and perhaps also of their entanglement with all *matter*, they wrote about horses intra-actively, using their own bodies and *matter* to encode the semiotic agency and the *matter* of horses in the novels they wrote.

George Eliot's Semantic Humanimality in *Silas Marner*

D. B. D. Asker argues that in the work of George Eliot "we see obvious instances of a novelist's attempts to include the larger rural landscape but this rarely implies the world of animal nature."[36] To refute this argument one only need consider the influence of evolutionary theory and Darwinian thought on Eliot's work as a novelist. Eliot was familiar with the works of earlier evolutionary theorists like Jean-Baptiste Lamarck, Robert Chambers (*The Vestiges of Creation*), Charles Lyell, and Herbert Spencer, all of whom espoused what was then known as "development theory."[37] Her initial reception of Darwin's work was apparently affected by this familiarity. As Gillian Beer explains,

> When George Eliot first began reading Darwin's *The Origin of Species* immediately after it appeared in November 1859 she wrote in her Journal: "We began Darwin's work on *The Origin of Species* tonight. It seems not to be well written: though full of interesting matter, it is not impressive, from want of

luminous and orderly presentation," and in a letter two days later she says that it is "an elaborate exposition of the evidence in favour of the Development Theory, and so, makes an epoch."[38]

Eliot's realization does not necessarily mean she consciously and deliberately transposed early evolutionist and, later, Darwinian ideas to her novel writing. Yet, as Beer influentially points out, from her early years as a novelist "the future is suggested through progeny."[39] Based on this observation, and on Eliot's familiarity with Darwin's work even as early as the 1859 publication of her first novel, *Adam Bede*, it is clear that she was aware of the possibility of humanity's descent from a common origin with animals.

Eliot's 1861 novel *Silas Marner* brings together questions about human-animal intra-action and inheritance in suggestive ways. The novel's overt focus is on the reconciliation of Silas, a reclusive weaver obsessed with hoarding and counting the gold he earns from his trade, with the countryside community of Raveloe to which he migrated fifteen years earlier to escape past disappointments as the member of "a narrow religious sect."[40] Silas's appeasement with life and society begins when he adopts a baby girl, Eppie, who mysteriously "toddled on to the open door of Silas Marner's cottage"[41] on New Year's Eve after the death of her mother. Silas's initial motivation for adopting Eppie is the expectation that he will be compensated for the loss of gold stolen from him a few weeks earlier.[42] Soon, however, Silas's affection for Eppie helps him make peace with life because "there was love between him and the child that blent them into one, and there was love between the child and the world."[43] The mysterious loss of Silas's gold thus gives way to the most visible climax in the plot: the golden-haired infant Eppie miraculously replaces the lost gold with human connection. Of course, so far there is nothing "horsey" in this discussion of human relationship supplanting a focus on economics. When we look carefully at the plot to see what comes of Silas's loss of his gold, however, we encounter the death of a fine horse: Wildfire.

Wildfire, a valuable hunter owned by Godfrey Cass, turns out to be the only means by which Godfrey can regain the hundred pounds of rent money he has collected from a tenant for his father, Squire Cass, but that his younger brother Dunstan has spent on drinking and gambling. When Dunstan suggests he sell his horse, Godfrey's first reaction is to "burst out, in a bitter tone,"[44] though he eventually agrees, recognizing that a fine hunter can be exchanged for a high sum in a world that the narrator characterizes as dominated by "men whose only work was to ride round their land, getting heavier and heavier in their saddles."[45]

Even though Wildfire is "the last thing [he has] got to call [his] own, and the best bit of horse flesh [he] ever had in [his] life,"[46] Godfrey allows his brother to take the horse to the hunting field to be sold. Since "there'll be Bryce and Keating there, for sure," Dunstan points out, "[the horse will] get more bids than one."[47] The next day Bryce and Keating do show up, to the satisfaction of Dunstan, who "enjoyed the self-important consciousness of having a horse to sell, and the opportunity of driving a bargain."[48] Of course, Dunstan's enjoyment comes from appearing to be the owner of a commodity with considerable prestige and exchange value. Accordingly, the bargaining between Dunstan and Bryce develops through a focus on the horse's bloodlines. To keep the price high, Dunstan confesses that "[he'd] got an itch for a mare o' Jortin's—as rare a bit o' blood as ever you threw your leg across" but then asserts his determination to "keep Wildfire."[49] Dunstan's "horse-dealing . . . one of many human transactions carried on in this ingenious manner,"[50] thus ends with Bryce's purchasing the horse for "a hundred and twenty, to be paid on the delivery of Wildfire, safe and sound, at the Batherley stables."[51] At this point Dunstan feels confident he has realized the utmost benefit from the systems of exchange dominant among the gentry. Instead of taking the horse to Batherley at once, however, he is overcome by "the inclination for a run . . . especially with a horse under him that would take the fences to the admiration of the field."[52] Such careless vanity is of course bound to have consequences, which come in perhaps the most climactic moment in the novel: "Dunstan . . . took one fence too many, and 'staked' his horse. His own ill-favoured person, which was quite unmarketable, escaped without injury, but poor Wildfire, unconscious of his price, turned on his flank, and painfully panted his last."[53] Following this loss of the only opportunity to find the hundred pounds he owes his elder brother, Dunstan goes to Silas's cottage and steals the weaver's gold, thereby connecting the novel's subplots.

The entanglement of the two subplots as an *effect* of the death of Wildfire is the very point at which Eliot's ethico-onto-epistem-ological intra-action really takes off: when a dead horse becomes powerfully agential both in the narrative and in an entangled world of human and nonhuman being. The stake that pierces Wildfire's body in fact also pierces the narrative of a novel that initially seems to be exclusively focused on the experiences of human characters. Indeed, the death of Wildfire metaphorically ignites a "fire" in the lives of the human characters that they have limited power or agency to control. In like manner, the stake also pierces Eliot's conception of such entanglement insofar as she grapples with questions about the value and agency of a horse in the human systems of nineteenth-century Britain.

At the core of this concern with value is the narrator's comparison between the "unmarketable" but unharmed Dunstan and the dead Wildfire, who is "unconscious of his price." Clearly, both the narrator's empathy and the value assignment in this scene are invested in the animal rather than in the human. From Dunstan's perspective, the immediate value in question is primarily Wildfire's exchange value. Therefore, the real agential *effect* of Wildfire on human orders, on the plot progression, and on the narrative of a human text can be claimed to appear at the moment of his death when he becomes a *thing*. Of course, in Bryce's view it is Wildfire's sign value that is intended for consumption through this bargain. In death, then, Wildfire arrests the construction of the English countryside as a place associated with "consumption and pleasure, recreation and retreat" rather than "production."[54] He exerts an *effect* on the human systems of exchange and consumption as well as of significance, or signification. However, this "arrest"–to borrow a phrase from Bill Brown–is momentary. In fact, Wildfire's agency as a dead horse, or *thing*, has more *effect* than his agency as a live horse in the world of the landed gentry of the Victorian period. From a perspective of ethico-onto-epistem-ological intra-action, what Wildfire's *thing*ness suggests is thus not really a loss of value. On the contrary, the moment of Wildfire's death represents the point at which Eliot not only problematizes human preoccupations with value but also ascribes a different kind of value to the animal by according him narrative agency. Eliot also uses Wildfire's narrative agency in the novel's larger resolution, ending in a way that acknowledges the essentiality of blood ties as Godfrey asserts his "natural claim"[55] on Eppie as her father. In doing so, the narrative knits, or conflates, the hereditary blood ties between Godfrey and Eppie, which become visible as a result of the spilled blood of Wildfire. This suggests Darwin's influence on Eliot. As Beer suggests, "What Darwin emphasizes is relationship—the ordinary chain of generation—the sense of progeny and diversification, of a world in which profusely various forms co-exist, unseen and yet dependent on each other and related to each other by blood or need."[56] For Beer, then, Darwin's scientific "plots" "sought the restoration of familial ties, the discovery of a lost inheritance" by "restor[ing] man to his kinship with all other forms of life."[57] When Eliot remarks that Darwin's work "makes an epoch," she recognizes that relationality and progeny are of vital importance for life. At the end of *Silas Marner*, Eppie accepts her natural father's claim on her but chooses to stay with Silas, the person who has always met her emotional and material needs. In this instance, in fact, Darwin's emphasis on relations is not very different from Barad's emphasis on relationality.

Thomas Hardy's Semantic Humanimality in *Tess of the d'Urbervilles*

For Asker the novels of Thomas Hardy represent "a wholly different stylistic and philosophical approach to animals and their relationship to mankind."[58] He describes this approach as "an organicist and integrative perspective"[59] in which "describing an animal becomes the same technical problem as drawing a human being."[60] Implying what I would describe as a sense of intraspecies entanglement, this new approach is informed, as Elisha Cohn suggests, by "a radically new conception of ontological continuity"[61] enabled by Darwin's work. Hardy was familiar with Darwin's ideas, and this familiarity influenced his "private formulation . . . of what the relationship between man and animal was."[62] In his novels, this awareness takes shape in representations of death and suffering.

Hardy's personal sensitivity to suffering and death was the result of both a traumatic childhood experience—when he witnessed his father killing a field hare—and the influence of Darwin on his adult worldview.[63] In suffering Hardy saw "an obvious truth" and "a direct link between [animals] and humans."[64] In representing human and animal suffering, however, I would argue that what Hardy achieved went beyond the simple representation of a biological link through the use of animals as "symbolic agents that make more manifest the terms and problems facing humanity."[65]

The plot of Hardy's 1891 novel *Tess of the D'Urbervilles* relies heavily on the use value of a horse and the loss of this value when it dies. To put it very simply, Tess's tragedy, which includes rape, the loss of her infant child, abandonment by her husband, and eventually execution by hanging, begins with the death of Prince, a weak cart horse "only a degree less rickety than the vehicle."[66] Although he has little actual exchange value and no sign value, Prince's labor is necessary to the subsistence of this large peasant family. Having stayed up late getting drunk celebrating the discovery of his noble ancestry, Tess's father John Durbeyfield oversleeps. Dependent on income from the delivery of some beehives (the bees representing another example of the Durbeyfield family's dependence on animals for subsistence and Hardy's perception of the entangled state of the human and the nonhuman world), Tess resolves to undertake the task. At about half-past one in the morning she goes out to the stable to harness Prince, who "looked wonderingly around . . . as if he could not believe that at that hour . . . he was called upon to go out and labour."[67] Growing drowsy during the ride, Tess falls asleep, only to be awakened by a "hollow groan, unlike anything she had ever heard in her life" that "proceeded from her father's poor horse

Prince."[68] She immediately discovers that the horse has been badly injured by "the pointed shaft" of the speeding morning mail-cart that pierces him "like a sword."[69] Prince staggers, "his life's blood . . . spouting in a stream."[70] The inevitable end comes quickly:

> In her despair Tess sprang forward and put her hand upon the hole, with the only result that she became splashed from face to skirt with the crimson drops. Then she stood helplessly looking on. Prince also stood firm and motionless as long as he could; till he suddenly sank down in a heap.[71]

The entire tragedy of Tess is symbolically manifest both in "the blood-pool [that] was still visible in the middle of the road" and in the dead body of Prince, whom John Durbeyfield later buries in the garden of their house after he refuses to sell the body.[72]

In her cultural analysis of the horse in Victorian fiction, Dorré interprets this scene as a foretelling of "what will happen to Tess."[73] In a similar vein, Cohn argues that as "the first animal of the novel, Prince blurs the line between the human family and a broader form of consanguinity reconceived as suffering under exploitative labor."[74] The scene is powerful, therefore, in acknowledging Hardy's perception of relationality and the common sufferings of human and of nonhuman beings that "modulate into each other, one nature & law operating throughout."[75] Extending Cohn's argument, I suggest we need to read the scene as a powerful expression of Hardy's ethico-onto-epistem-ological intra-action with the nonhuman world, which in this case is embodied in Prince. Such entanglement with the horse, especially when it is lost and becomes a *thing*, marks the beginning of Tess's suffering in the narrative and makes visible questions the novel raises about blood and blood ties.

Although no one in the family blames Tess, Prince's death represents a major hardship for the Durbeyfields: "The bread-winner had been taken away from them; what would they do?"[76] Tess's mother suggests applying to the D'Urbervilles for assistance. Such an application to "strange kin"[77] is not easily accepted either by John or by Tess. Yet Tess eventually takes the initiative and journeys to the residence of Mrs. Stoke-d'Urberville, setting off a chain of events that eventually results in her destruction.

The account of how Prince's death precipitates the tragic chain of events in Hardy's novel focuses on the use value of a horse and the consequences of its loss for its human owners. By falling out of the systems of material production and consumption, Prince creates a major *effect* on the lives of the fictional human characters whose subsistence depends on his labor. In relation to my second line of argument, however, Prince's agential power also radically impacts a narrative written by a novelist whose Darwinian sensibility informed the shift from sentimental and idealized representations of English country life to the harsh naturalism of his final novels, *Tess* and *Jude the Obscure* (1895). This shift entailed greater engagement with Darwin's ideas and with the view that animals can be more "loving kind" to each other (as in the opening of *The Mayor of Casterbridge*) than people are in a world that focuses on economic competition at the expense of everything else. Hardy the naturalist was well aware of the necessity of this engagement.

Interpreted by many as simply a twist the realist novel took briefly under the influence of new scientific findings in the late Victorian period rather than as a separate literary movement, the naturalist novel depicts social reality in a way that includes environmental and biological forces that have *effect*s within the larger network of agential entities. As I mentioned earlier, this approach was the result of the emergence of "a radically new conception of ontological continuity"[78] in the Victorian period, prompted in large part by the work of Darwin. Hardy believed that "biological determination negated autonomous human agency."[79] As such, heredity becomes a central issue in his works, and entities in nature, especially those that are deeply embedded in the systems of the human society—like a cart horse—gain agency as new *effect*ive entities.

In *Tess of the d'Urbervilles*, the theme of heredity, or bloodlines, is an essential part of the plot, so much so that it is possible to describe it as a novel about blood. Yet in contrast to *Silas Marner*, and because of the blurring of boundaries between the human and the nonhuman in Hardy's novel, in *Tess* the significance of bloodlines is associated with the human rather than with the animal. After all, as Parson Tringham points out in the narrative, "if knighthood were hereditary . . . as it practically was in old times, when men were knighted from father to son, [Tess's father] would be Sir John now."[80] In more sinister terms, when Tess Durbeyfield is raped by Alec Stoke-d'Urberville, the narrator's sense of the unjustness of the act is set against his reflection on her heredity.

Ironically in the case of Tess's family, the name "d'Urberville" has been corrupted over time to Durbeyfield. It now connotes a lower social order centered on the use value of things, while a morally corrupt Alec "Stoke-d'Urberville"–whose wealthy but untitled family have assumed the name to bolster their claims to prestige–abuses the social power that comes from the sign value of the name. The narrator gives a clear explanation of how Mr. Simon Stoke, Alec's father, has simply chosen (and probably purchased) this name for the family from British Museum records of "extinct, half-extinct, obscured, and ruined families."[81] Even though Hardy's central concern seems to be the moral question of assuming a false family name, his real interest is to reflect on what comes with the blood. It seems that from his reading of Darwin, Hardy also knew that the question of blood ties was complicated. Beer illustrates this complication by quoting at length from Darwin's *Origin of Species*:

> As it is difficult to show the blood-relationship between the numerous kindred of any ancient and noble family, even by the aid of a genealogical tree, and almost impossible to do this without this aid, we can understand the extraordinary difficulty which naturalists have experienced in describing, without the aid of a diagram, the various affinities which they perceive between the many living and extinct members of the same great natural class.[82]

In imagining Tess's tragedy, Hardy seems to have expanded Darwin's understanding of "the same great natural class" and written from the larger Darwinian idea of the interconnectedness of all species in "confusing and conflating" the tragedies of human and horse. That is why in the novel the economic or use value of animals (first and foremost the horse, Prince) gets refracted back onto the human characters, particularly Tess. In writing *Tess*, Hardy, who had a deep understanding of Darwinian interconnectedness, was thus reflecting on a network of *effect*ive agents within the matrix of heredity. This particular reflection was projected on a fictional universe in which the lives of the animals were "subordinated to the . . . needs and desires of humans and where the material and ecological conditions for their survival [we]re frequently disregarded by the pursuit of human . . . advantage."[83] Hardy's expression of this critique, which disturbed Victorian audiences and offered a counterpoint to the ways Darwin's thought was popularized to support economic competition and individualism, was carried out in his representation of the entanglement of the lives and deaths of Prince and Tess.

Conclusion

Both *Silas Marner* and *Tess of the D'Urbervilles* draw attention to the suffering and mortality that we, as human animals, share with nonhuman animals. Eliot and Hardy understood the centrality of suffering and mortality to the Darwinian idea of interconnectedness between the human and the nonhuman. At decisive moments in the plots of both novels, therefore, we encounter dead horses whose narrative agency makes visible the conflicted human experiences of alienation and interconnection. Moreover, Eliot and Hardy understood that nonhuman animals become even more agential in human society when they die and fall out of human systems of production, consumption, exchange, and value: when they become *things*. From daily experience and observation of life in Victorian Britain, they knew that the primary nonhuman animal that had agential power as a figure simultaneously alienated as object and yet entangled with human experience was the horse. In the novels analyzed here, characters who cause the death of a horse also die sooner or later and thus become dead matter, a *thing* rather than a person. Dunstan Cass dies in the stone pit near Silas Marner's cottage, and Tess is executed. The existence, life, and death of these human characters are portrayed in relation to the existence, life, and death of horses, because both authors grappled with notions of the multispecies entanglement of existence (or nonexistence). Both Eliot and Hardy also understood from their exposure to Darwin's ideas that while blood ties were of essential importance in such entanglement, they were not always determinable. Accordingly, they recognized that if there was to be a "confusion and conflation" of the human animal with the nonhuman animal, it would have been, and must have been, primarily with the horse. For horses were literally everywhere in Victorian Britain, not only in the streets or the fields, but also in the names of the machinery that was ultimately to replace them.

Eliot and Hardy lived in an age when beliefs about the human's place and role in nature were beginning to be replaced with a new understanding based on interconnectedness. They also lived when nature itself was beginning to suffer and die as a result of industrialization, and they therefore worried about damage inflicted on the nonhuman world. Having an understanding of their own animality (and maybe also of their own materiality), both Eliot and Hardy responded to the horse through ethico-onto-epistem-ological intra-action and grafted their performance onto *matter* by writing novels.

FOUR

The Aura of Dignity

On Connection and Trust in the Photographs of Charlotte Dumas

RUNE GADE

Whereas in art history the horse has often been employed to associate its rider and master with power, dignity, and prestige, Dutch photographer Charlotte Dumas (b. 1977) represents horses in a very different manner. Although traces of more traditional modes of representation inevitably find their way into Dumas's photographs as part of a visual heritage that still exerts a strong influence, horses no longer evoke strength, discipline, mobility, and wealth but rather enter into a more ambiguous, symbolic register as both abject feral animals and sublime ceremonial creatures. While marked change in the real and symbolic cultural location of horses is indirectly the subject of Dumas's work, however, her primary interest is portraying singular animals outside their functional working contexts. In this regard she concentrates on individual animals and shows them not as emblems of power, but as living creatures communicating with other living creatures. Dumas's photographs thus seek to empower horses in their destiny as domesticated animals, showing them as unique creatures with sensibilities and the ability to communicate. Perhaps most notably, she draws attention to aspects of equine being that have been overlooked in traditional representations of horses: their raw, unsentimental animal quality and their presence as fellow beings we can connect with in nonexploitive ways.

In the foreword to her 2013 publication *Anima*, Dumas explains that she is interested in the affectionate relationship between man and animal in situations where existence is threatened: "This matter of our connection to other living creatures is still of crucial importance for our existence, as they are our witnesses."[1] Although she operates within a paradigm of representation, Dumas cultivates feelings of presence and empathy that let us sense much more than abstract notions such as power or dignity within her subjects. Her photographs thus look toward an almost lost past where the interdependence of humans and animals was experienced much more directly in everyday life, while at the same time they look to a future when understanding such interdependence will be more urgent than ever. As Karen Raber notes, "Modern medicine is rediscovering the interdependence and benefits for humans of everything from parasites to pets," thus providing us with scientific arguments both for the sense of shared embodiment between species and for the lack of an ontological distinction between humans and animals that is intuitively present in Dumas's work.[2]

At many levels simultaneously we are thus asked to question and revise the dominant understanding of animals as species subordinate to human beings. Charlotte Dumas's ongoing focus on horses offers both a strong investigative and thought-provoking contribution to the understanding of interdependence between species and an important plea for a sustainable future when we rethink and reinvent our connections to animals. Dumas's photographs contribute to this rethinking by insisting on the importance of animal gazes and the haptic qualities inherent in the images, through which we are drawn into the domain of accountability described by Donna Haraway. For Haraway, "Accountability, caring for, being affected, and entering into responsibility are not ethical abstractions; these mundane, prosaic things are the result of having truck with each other."[3] Perhaps it is such accountability that Dumas is implicitly locating in her photographs when she speaks of the animals she portrays as our witnesses. Her animal subjects not only witness our subjection and dominion, however; often they also return our gaze. The effect—to borrow Nicholas Ridout's phrase—instills in us "a form of shame . . . at being discovered in our own acts of domination, over animals and over ourselves."[4]

The act of photography is part of a long history of "making the invisible visible."[5] Rooted both in the Renaissance fascination with dissection and in a deep history of "traceology," the photographic medium produces insight while tracing process and recording it for posterity.[6] The photographic medium thus does more than simply record the visible for human beings, although this is probably its most recognized quality. As Marta Braun has noted, photography, especially high-speed photography, has provided us with "a world that is unavailable to our vision—a world beyond the reach of our senses."[7] Almost from the outset, photography has taken the horse as an object of study in this quest to understand process.

Indeed, the convergence between hippology and the investigative, even dissecting, quality of photography as a medium first appeared in the 1870s and 1880s when systematic experiments were undertaken to reveal visual facts about the movements of horses that are invisible to the human eye. Among the most famous instantaneous photographs are British photographer Eadweard Muybridge's studies of horses in motion from the album *Animal Locomotion*. Commissioned by horse lover Leland Stanford in Palo Alto, California, these images were produced in 1878 and published in the French journal *La Nature* in December of that year. Muybridge's photographs appear to have immediately changed artists' renderings of horses in motion. As Aaron Scharf notes in his classic study *Art and Photography*, after seeing Muybridge's photographs Edgar Degas changed his way of representing horses: "After this date [about 1880], for the first time in his work, running horses appear in the accurate positions of instantaneous photographs."[8] Muybridge's photographs revolutionized pictorial representations of horses in motion. As Robert Taft notes, "After the Muybridge photographs became known, artists were forced to change their ideas and methods of representing a moving animal."[9] Technological visuality here conquers human perception and significantly changes our understanding of animal movements.

The historical coincidence of stop-motion photography of horses at the trot or gallop and new renderings of horses' movements in nonphotographic visual mediums was followed by the even more remarkable general decline in artists' representations of horses. This shift suggests that the mechanics of the photographic medium were part of an overarching industrial and technological development that, among many other things, made the horse superfluous in Western societies and in the world at large, delegating it mainly to symbolic and ceremonial tasks and pastimes. In the twentieth century working horses were increasingly replaced by automobiles and engines much more powerful and efficient than any one horse, although the strength of these machines was still measured in "horsepower." Not surprisingly, the disappearance of working horses from everyday life is evident in the history of the visual arts as well. Whereas in the eighteenth and nineteenth centuries the horse was a prominent subject in painting and sculpture, the twentieth century witnessed significant changes, particularly in public representations of horses. Equestrian statues that for many centuries had been a preferred means of representing might and power became almost anachronistic, and artistic representations of horses in general became rarer and more exotic, associated almost exclusively with aristocratic culture or sentimental, romanticizing popular culture. From having been the norm in art, Douglas Fordham notes, the horse became an exception and a subject to be dealt with mainly within a critical framework.[10] British artist Mark Wallinger's conceptual work on horses as markers of class, race, and sexual identity testifies to this shift. His Turner Prize–nominated *A Real Work of Art* from 1994, for example, involves an actual racehorse named A Real Work of Art. The irony is clear enough: the photographic medium that succeeded so well in making the invisible visible is allied with the very technological developments and productive forces that inevitably made the horse superfluous and thus invisible in second degree.

In light of this trend it might seem strange for a young color photographer in the twenty-first century to devote herself almost entirely to photographing horses. This is nonetheless what Charlotte Dumas has done, although she also photographs other animal subjects such as dogs, wolves, and tigers. In what follows I discuss Dumas's work in light of these developments, paying particular attention to her use of the photographic medium as she explores the complex psychological and social relationships between humans and horses in compelling images patiently produced under difficult conditions, using large-format and medium-format cameras. Dumas's photographic works extend the dissecting impulse of photography that Muybridge's systemic stop-motion photography introduced while simultaneously contesting the very notion of slicing up time that is inherent in this tradition. Although Dumas's interest might be as analytic as Muybridge's, and though to a large extent she may even share his interest in temporality and vision, her approach is less about *stopping* time by quantifying it than about raising questions of *timing* and temporality by examining both duration and the way moments fold into each other. As contradictory as these strategies may seem, both depend on the photographic medium and its particular potential for rendering time.

Charlotte Dumas received her formal education as an artist at Gerrit Rietveld Academie (1996–2000) and Rijksakademie van beeldende kunsten (2001–2) in Amsterdam. Since her graduation she has produced a steady flow of projects on an international scale, including both exhibitions and books. The complexity of her projects explains the low output: according to Dumas, it usually takes a year and a half of work to produce only six to nine images.[11] Throughout her career Dumas has focused on animals and their conditions within human environments. Her first project, *Four Horses* (2002), was about working police horses in Rotterdam, and *Day Is Done* (2005) showed the working horses from the Carabinieri a Cavallo in Rome. Many of her projects have been published in limited edition artist's books such as *Anima* (2012), *The Widest Prairies* (2013), and *Work Horse* (2015). Dumas travels the world to document and represent the rare working horses remaining in modernized and modernizing societies, work that has taken her to Japan, Italy, Sweden, and the United States, among other places. Her interest lies not so much in the representation of animals as in the investigative portrayal of the interrelation between humans and animals—what Michel Frizot has termed "'animal communities' with a past through which something of a human history is conveyed"—even if this is often manifested only indirectly as the outcome of the photographic act and the psychological tension between the photographer and the animal subject.[12] This has been the case also in Dumas's projects involving wild animals kept in zoos, such as wolves and tigers, working dogs in the United States, and stray dogs in Palermo, Italy, all of which reflect on the interrelation between human beings and animals. This focus sets Dumas's project apart from seemingly similar projects such as Hans Silvester's 1979 *Horses of the Camargue* or the more recent Roberto Dutesco project *The Wild Horses of Sable Island*, which is occupied with representing "true wilderness in its primal state."[13]

In her 2012 project *Anima*, Dumas photographed the caisson horses of Arlington National Cemetery in Virginia. These horses are among the diminishing number to actually perform a function within the military, being used daily to accompany the soldiers laid to rest at the cemetery. As funerary horses, they perform a solemn function that has deep historical roots. Paul Roth notes that "horse-drawn caissons date to the advent of field artillery in the 18th century; though originally used to carry re-supply armaments into battle, they often returned from the front bearing the bodies of soldiers killed in action."[14] This concise history reiterates the observation that horses have changed their role and function in culture over the past centuries, transforming from creatures fully integrated in war zones, among other places, to noble symbolic relicts of this history in contemporary ceremonies. As Charlotte Dumas remarks in the preface to her book that contains thirteen images from the *Anima* series, these horses "now have the sole and exclusive privilege of accompanying soldiers to their final resting place."[15] In her work on funerary horses, however, she is not primarily interested in the ceremonial function they perform or in their history as warhorses; indeed, she reduces this aspect to a paratextual element. Context is not explicitly shown in any of the images of the burial horses from the Arlington National Cemetery, and Dumas's photographs do not document the horses' ceremonial funerary processions at all. Rather, the information about their location and function is provided only in the book's preface, and one may conclude from this choice that to the artist the specific function of these horses is somehow secondary, although it is obviously not without importance.

Instead of showing the funerary horses performing their duties, Dumas depicts them in moments of rest at the end of the day. The horses are in their stables, lying directly on the floor or on a modest bed of straw or shavings, on the verge of sleep, and are thus photographed in situations remote from their ceremonial functions (figs 4.1 and 4.2). Although both all-black and all-white horses are used at Arlington National Cemetery, Dumas concentrates on the white, or more accurately grayish, Lipizzan horses whose well-groomed coats contrast with the dark walls and floors in the stables. The horses are portrayed in full figure or half figure horizontal cropping with little or no background detail, allowing us to focus fully on the horse's body. The images are recorded in color, but the photographs appear almost monochrome or *brunaille* because of the limited natural light available. The

Figure 4.1. Dumas, *Ringo Arlington VA 2012.*

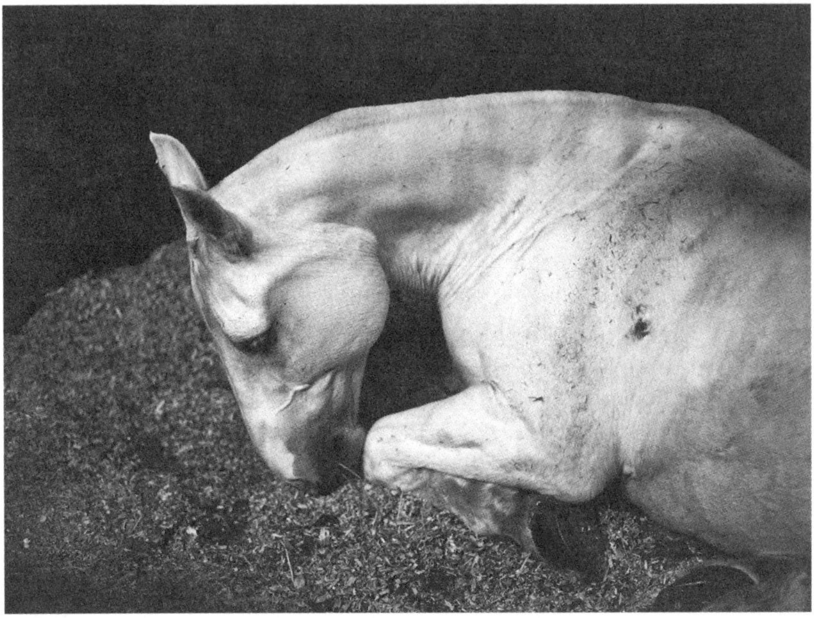

Figure 4.2. Dumas, *Peter Arlington VA 2012*.

stunningly beautiful lighting, which has a soft and diffused quality while still concentrated directly on the horses, highlights details of the animals' bodies and coats and allows the remaining space to fade into an almost completely closed darkness. Were these images portraits of humans, they would probably be categorized as semiformal portraits in intimate settings. This association is pertinent insofar as the horses are in fact portrayed in their intimate spaces: their bedrooms, as it were. They are also portrayed at moments when they appear both vulnerable and at peace, inhabiting the fragile liminal space between waking and sleeping at a time of day when light returns.

The passage between waking and sleep thus depicted can at its most obvious be read as a symbolic rendering of the funerary horses' function, suggesting an analogy between the transition from waking to sleep and the passage from life to death. As Paul Roth notes, "These spectral horses appear as tutelary spirits, succoring the soldiers they carry over, guiding the transmigration of their souls."[16] The somber quality of the images certainly affirms and underlines this reading, which is enhanced by the decontextualized spaces of blurry darkness against which the animals are depicted. There is something profoundly melancholic about these beautiful grayish creatures on the verge of drifting out of consciousness and entering sleep, and this graceful melancholy easily offers itself as a metaphor for death. However, I believe something quite different is also at play in these images, something less symbolic or allegorical, less connected to death than to life—indeed, more affiliated with *eros* than with *thanatos*. If we look plainly at the images without considering the paratextual knowledge provided, we are confronted simply with horses' bodies. In a very literal sense we are asked to witness their coats, muscles, and veins. We are also offered the opportunity to study in detail their individual features—the patterns of their coats, the shapes of their muzzles and ears, eyes and eyelids. Everything is minutely presented in Dumas's large-format photographs, which accurately record every detail.

The lighting and the horses' postures invite not so much an allegorical reading as reflections about the bodies and the psyches of specific horses. Furthermore, the sensitive interrelation between the body and mind of the photographer and the individual horses becomes evident. The title of the series, *Anima*, hints at this, since in Latin *anima* means "soul" or "mind." What we are looking at, then, are portraits of individual animals that clearly demonstrate—although in subtle gestures—individual tempers, personalities, and psychological traits. In a sense this is the opposite of seeing the horse as a metaphoric or allegorical figure, which has for so long been one of its primary roles in art. In Dumas's photographs we are not presented with an analysis of the horse's movement either, as we saw in Muybridge's works. Even the most superficial survey of her oeuvre will confirm that she has very little interest in moving animals, preferring to portray them at rest or dormant. The static animals Dumas represents are nonetheless often *moving* in the sense that they reach out and touch the viewer in an affective capacity. Yet there is really nothing sentimental about Dumas's photographs. On the contrary, they carefully avoid all the girlish stereotypes of fascination and adoration of horses that abound in popular culture, while nonetheless exploring the eroticism of the horse that might also be covertly at work in such stereotypes. Instead, the moving qualities of Dumas's photographs are of a more analytic and haptic nature, allowing us to sense these animals as psychological or even soulful presences.

The soulful presence of the animals depicted in Charlotte Dumas's *Anima* is indeed suggestive of psychological traits that we usually associate with human beings. Thus we can recognize in these horses elements of longing, melancholy, and reverie, postures of grace and dignity, a touching abandonment to fatigue, or an alert curiosity. In this they appeal to something we might call a premodern sensibility of the animal as a creature with capacities equivalent to those human beings are endowed with. This is not simply a question of anthropomorphically projecting human emotions onto images or onto animals incapable of speaking for themselves. As Karen Raber has convincingly argued, the modern distinction between rational living creatures (human beings) and nonrational living creatures (beasts), which can be traced back to René Descartes, introduces a logic "responsible for banishing animals from their prior, problematic, intimate equivalence with humans."[17] In Dumas's photographs we get a glimpse of this premodern sensibility based on a sense of "shared embodiment" in which, to borrow Raber's phrasing, we experience "the body as a site of shared (but not identical) experience, a site of shared consciousness, a kind of zone of exchange where we can come together with animals and comprehend them as ourselves."[18] The photographs in Dumas's *Anima* are exceptional because they do not depict these horses as the noble creatures depicted standing or imposingly rearing in equine statuary but instead show them lying down, at rest, dormant. I believe this choice promotes a sense of shared embodiment, since it positions the animal in a gestural situation that is intimately known by human beings, and thus bodily and intuitively recognizable to them.

Most of the photographs in *Anima* focus on heads, except for the small groups that either depict the entire bodies of specific horses or focus on their coats. All the photographs in the series highlight specific bodily features of the Lipizzan horses, particularly the well-defined muscles underneath their grayish coats and their heavy heads, which they struggle to hold up by the end of the day. The haptic qualities of the images are underlined by the lighting that makes every fold in the animals' coats visible and almost *reachable*, while their body mass stands out against the dark background. The soft, natural quality of the growing daylight hides parts of the bodies in shadowy areas while highlighting other parts, bathing the scenes in serenity. For anyone who has ever touched a horse, not to say groomed one, these images invoke a rich reservoir of sensory memories, reminders of the sensual interactions between humans and animals. In short, these images are full of an eroticism imbued with gloom, as if they depict both the shared intimacy of man and animal and the insurmountable distance between them. Dumas would not be able to create such evocative images without a finely tuned and respectful connection with her subjects that produces an elemental bond of trust. In this sense her images are the very opposite of Muybridge's dissecting photographs of horses in motion: Dumas's images are not penetrating or partitioning but rather evoke closeness and intimacy through a respectful distance, through vision, and—

most important—through a trust literally earned *over time*. As Dumas has explained, before beginning to photograph, she would stay with the horses for hours at night to get them accustomed to her presence:

> I often went at midnight, but they're very restless animals. They lie down, they get up. . . . So, after a while, I would go between midnight and 4 a.m. I would see them lying down and, most of the time, I would just sit there and watch, taking pictures occasionally. Then I noticed, after a number of visits, that they began to get used to my presence and they would really, literally fall asleep.[19]

Although the indexical traces are certainly manifest and strong, the resulting images not only establish a reference to something outside the image, they also produce something. I believe these images perform reciprocal trust at the level of production and through this performativity produce it at the level of reception as well, making the photographs in *Anima* images of trust as a matter of engagement and duration. Trust being an interrelational quality that can only be earned over time, it is this durational aspect that fills Dumas's images, paradoxically in spite of their short exposure times.

The images in *Anima* use photography to represent and recreate moments of such durational quality that encode the hard-earned trust between humans and animals. Although evidently drowsy, many of the horses depicted seem to look straight into the camera, an effect that in reality is more likely produced by their looking straight at Dumas while she is behind or beside her camera. In other words, the horses visibly acknowledge the presence of someone else, *an other*, demonstrating awareness of a nearby human being even at times of sleepy watchfulness. However, this relaxed watchfulness never appears intimidated or anxious; instead it has an air of quiet curiosity about a slight anomaly in an otherwise habitual situation where a different but recognizable being shares the space they inhabit. Within this awareness, be it watchful or introversive, I locate the element of mute acceptance from which trust grows and is performed in Dumas's photographs. In visually explicating this element of trust, Dumas describes the diminishing interrelational dependence that exists between humans and horses, taking in the working horse as a sociological phenomenon but adding to it the psychological relationship that has historically enabled and conditioned humans' use and exploitation of animals as tools and as companions. Lurking within the images in *Anima* is the question of domestication, be it by "gentling," "taming," or "breaking," which impregnates the images with a strong sense of melancholy or even unease. There is, so to speak, a double loss at play in *Anima* insofar as, having long ago left their wild natures behind, these Lipizzan warhorses are now about to lose the very condition for which this nature was sacrificed: their present function as working horses.

Photographing objects, sites, and work conditions on the verge of disappearing is hardly novel. Indeed, photography not only dissects moments in time, it also conserves them, and thus the medium has always appealed to preservationist sensibilities. As a consequence the camera has often been turned toward sites, people, or functions at risk of disappearing in order to preserve them with a visual record. This strategy is particularly true of Charlotte Dumas's photographs, which intentionally set out to document the increasingly rare cultures of working horses. Her 2015 book *Work Horses* documents eight native horse breeds of Japan, explicitly stating in the supplementary introduction that "once necessary for farming and transportation, most of these breeds have lost their practical purpose and have declined in number. Primarily confined to small islands, the horses have never been able to migrate, and their future existence is now uncertain."[20] As was the case with *Anima*, the *Work Horses* project documents a phenomenon that will probably be extinct within a few generations. This interest in recording disappearing moments and situations—and its accompanying impulse to sense a *presence* within the historical realities of photographic images—was what led Walter Benjamin to develop the notion of an aura when speaking about the photographic medium. When looking at a photograph, Benjamin notes, we "search such a picture for the tiny spark of contingency, of the here and now, with which reality has (so to speak) seared the subject."[21] For Benjamin, photography captures "another nature that speaks to camera rather than to the eye: 'other' above all in the sense that a space informed by human consciousness gives way to a space informed by the unconscious."[22] Such unconscious spaces are very much part of Dumas's photographs, which depict spaces that evoke a deep history of human-animal interrelations while pointing to the weakening of such relations today. Not all of Dumas's projects, however, focus as explicitly as *Anima* on temporality and the psychological interrelation between man and animal.

In *The Widest Prairies* (2013), Dumas documents a quite different and less intentional kind of interaction between humans and horses.[23] The 2013 project was completed in Nevada, where herds of feral horses roam the desert and the hills surrounding the northwestern town of Dayton. This area is closely associated with the idea of the Wild West, for in the nineteenth century it was on the westward route for thousands of immigrants. The horses living wild there are descendants of Spanish mustangs (from Spanish *mesteña*, meaning "wild or straying beast") brought to America by the Spanish conquistadors in the sixteenth century. A shared deep origin can thus be traced with the Lipizzan horses at Arlington National Cemetery, although the destinies of the feral horses and the funerary horses—and their significance in contemporary American culture—are as far apart as can be imagined. Dumas visited Nevada several times in 2013 to photograph the horses during different seasons of the year. Instead of documenting a romantic or picturesque notion of the wildlife of Nevada, however, the resulting book depicts the zones where wildlife and civilization make contact and often cause tension and conflict. The existence of the feral horses being a contested issue in Nevada—as indeed it is in many other parts of North America—in her photographs Dumas confronts the clash between animals and civilization directly, although in a discrete and subtle manner. The book contains fifty photographs from the project, most portraying the feral horses in nature or roaming the fringes of civilization. These images thus differ significantly from the interior photographs in the *Anima* project, with their intimate focus on individual animals at rest. In *The Widest Prairies* the horses are depicted not only outdoors, but as active animals that often move in large herds. The feral horses roam the land and are often photographed close to houses, roads, and vehicles—the very sites where their presence gives rise to tensions (figs. 4.3 and 4.4). Although no human beings are seen in Dumas's photographs, there are many indications of their regular presence. Any inclination to perceive the photographs as nostalgic depictions of some primordial state of wildness is thus obstructed by the blunt and often harsh reality of contemporary feral horses' experience. As Dumas writes in the afterword, these horses might be roaming freely, but they are "surrounded by human boundaries since their habitat overlaps and infringes upon those who live nearby them."[24] In effect, the photographs document conflicts growing out of an anthropocentric colonialism where owning land occurs exclusively on the conditions set by human beings, without regard for territorial or nonterritorial animals living on the same land.

In contrast to the well-kept Lipizzan horses in *Anima*, the feral horses in *The Widest Prairies* are rugged, scarred, and coarse. They are photographed at a distance because it is difficult to get close to these wild animals, so the resulting images depict the topography and landscape as much as the horses. The animals are clearly situated in surroundings that connote the vastness of the prairies and evoke the Wild West, although such signs of

Figure 4.3. Dumas, *Wagon Wheel Way Stagecoach NV 2013.*

modern civilization as electric wires, dirt tracks or asphalt roads, barns, small houses, mobile homes, and pickup trucks appear in most of the photographs. There is no story line or chronological ordering of the images in the book, but nonetheless a trajectory can be observed from depictions of horses in the wilderness to depictions of horses in close encounters with civilization. The last third of the book, shot at the Northern Nevada Correctional Center in Carson City, depicts horses in captivity, thus dramatically undercutting the associations of freedom and wildness that the opening images suggest. Here, Dumas explains, horses are part of a program "that teams them up with inmates of the low security section of the prison, training them both."[25] Each year the inmates, who often have little or no experience riding, domesticate sixty to seventy horses, which are then auctioned off to families or ranchers. In a sense *The Widest Prairies* thus concludes its cycle of images with photographs of working horses once again: horses that serve a provisional function within a prison system, where the domestication of wild horses corresponds to the "correction" of the inmates who train them. These photographs visually emphasize the animals' captivity, although not in a simplistic or condemnatory fashion. The horses are portrayed in small pens with high metal fencing, often in bright daylight; as a result, the grid-shaped shadows from the fencing fall on their bodies, visually highlighting confinement and restraint. The few close-ups of horses' heads are also found in this final section of the book, attesting to the different conditions of these animals that may be approached more easily than the free-roaming horses. A few of the photographs also bear witness to domestication in that they show horses wearing halters and with numbers written on their coats.

What might at first sight look like a celebration of the wild horses in Nevada thus turns out to be a much more complex and even somber portrait of the contemporary relations between humans and horses in the area

Figure 4.4. Dumas, *Sam Clemens Avenue Stagecoach NV 2013.*

around Dayton and Carson City. In this way *The Widest Prairies* is not unlike Dumas's earlier project focusing on ownerless dogs in Palermo, Sicily, which resulted in the 2008 book *Heart Shaped Hole*. The stunningly beautiful photographs of roving dogs in the middle of a large Italian city could appear sentimental at first glance, but on closer inspection the images' evocative emotional appeal to pity and compassion prompts reflection on the dogs' connections to the urban environments they inhabit. *The Widest Prairies* also evokes mixed feelings that force viewers to contemplate the rigid dichotomy between nature and culture that impacts horse and human experience. Dumas eventually asks for a revision of such simplified binary notions, pointing toward an understanding of the interrelation between humans and animals more akin to the "species interdependence" that Donna Haraway describes as a game of "response and respect."[26] What soon becomes clear when looking at Dumas's photographs is the impossibility of maintaining strict categories such as nature and culture as separate entities when what is so evidently at play is a "natureculture" situation where species cohabit in shared spaces and thereby deeply affect each other. Dumas's photographs bear witness to a process of development in which human beings seem to have become less and less aware of the interdependence between species, even when it comes to animals with whom humans have historically enjoyed very close and intimate connections.

As I noted at the outset, Charlotte Dumas works within a photographic tradition that prioritizes documentation and verification. The photographic medium has always been viewed as particularly well suited for producing images that give evidence and substantiate events, situations, and identities, because photographs most often correspond to reality with a penetrating and exact veracity not found in other visual mediums. Owing to their undiscriminating recording of what is in front of the camera, photographs can even contain a wealth of the unintended "tiny sparks of contingency" that Benjamin speaks of, inviting us to look for "the here and now" in pictures from the remote past. This element of optical unconscious is allied with the dissecting quality of photography. As Benjamin notes,

> Whereas it is a commonplace that, for example, we have some idea what is involved in the act of walking (if only in general terms), we have no idea at all what happens during the fraction of a second when a person actually takes a step. Photography, with its devices of slow motion and enlargement, reveals the secret.[27]

Dumas's photographs are certainly made within a documentary mode and comply with the implicit *doxa* of the documentary tradition, such as prohibition against artificial lighting and other forms of "manipulation" of what is considered the pure photographic recording of observed and objective reality. However, her photographs capture something that goes beyond the dissecting character of documentary form, or at least supplements it. The almost anthropological interest in "natureculture" and complex interrelations between human beings and animals evident in her photographs does belong within the documentary tradition, but there is also an element of performativity or agency in Dumas's photographs that invokes an uneasy sense of presence attesting to the deep connection between humans and animals. The photographs not only document horses in contemporary culture, they evoke a certain collective memory about horses as close companions to human beings and even bring forth a sense of shared embodiment. As Maurice Halbwachs notes of collective memory, "It does not preserve the past but reconstructs it with the aid of material traces, rites, texts, and traditions left behind by that past."[28] The horses in Dumas's photographs share the condition that they are made to perform various rites that recall and even reenact lost pasts, thus in a sense doubling the performative aspect of the production of presence in photography.

Dumas chooses to a large extent to let the images speak for themselves. In her books the images do not bear titles or captions, and textual information—often only a factual introduction to the specific project written by the photographer herself—is relegated to the margins in a foreword or an afterword. In my view this choice reflects the way Dumas intentionally downplays the documentary dimension, trusting the images to speak for themselves *as images*. As I mentioned earlier, the *Anima* project mentions only in a paratextual aside that the horses portrayed in the book are actually funerary horses. Obviously this is not because she considers it an irrelevant detail that these are working horses performing a ceremonial ritual. Rather, as with all her projects on working animals, Dumas prefers to show animals outside their work environments in order to focus on something that is not directly connected to their highly specialized working capacities: the interdependence and interrelation manifest as the bonds between human and animal that are the prerequisites for the work. Dumas thus chooses her subjects with great care in order to show how animals are not only conditioned and controlled by human beings, but also inevitably related to them in complex ways. Her subjects include working animals resting, implicitly attesting to their fates as exploited creatures within a modern capitalist logic, but they also feature feral animals whose disturbing presence on the margins of human society challenges capitalist concepts such as right of ownership and privacy. A constant in Dumas's oeuvre, however, is the direct gaze of the animals photographed. It is an intimate gaze that fundamentally evinces recognition between species and thus attests to a deep history of communication between humans and other animal species.

It may also be an uneasy gaze that prompts responses not unlike the ones experienced in the theatrical presence of live animals. As Nicholas Ridout has argued, animals within representational regimes such as the theater confuse the levels of "real" and "symbolic" because the animal lacks the intention of a human actor and so "means nothing by what it does."[29] Although images do not possess the live presence of theater, they still operate within a performative and representational register in which the gaze of the animal appears disquieting because it makes us recognize, if only unconsciously, "a phantom of an earlier animal presence which humanity had not yet violently compelled to succumb to its own rational purposes, nor stripped of its power to mediate."[30] One component of the unease engendered by the returned gaze of Dumas's horses could be attributed to the experience of *shame* in recognizing our own dominion over animals. This shame, however, merely attests to the deeper and perhaps only semiconscious experience of connection with the animal, which is—after all—more like us than otherwise. The horses Dumas portrays mediate elements of the real and the symbolic animal, enabling us to move beyond the manifest historical and symbolic layers of meaning and into recognition of a deeper latency of interdependence. The contemporary realities of horses documented in her photographs appear on the surface to be split between the abject and the sublime, but underlying this divided conception is the gaze of the animal that expresses both "the here and now" of the aura and the interrelational acknowledgment of a bond between man and animal.

PART TWO

Commodification and Consumption

FIVE

Stabilizing Politics

The Stables of Weißenstein Castle in Pommersfelden (1717–21)

MAGDALENA BAYREUTHER
AND CHRISTINE RÜPPELL

If stables have historically aided in domesticating horses, they have also played a central role in representing elite human identity. From the elaborate historical buildings at Bolsolver Castle in Derbyshire to the expensive structures associated with the modern thoroughbred industry, stable design has traditionally been used by the wealthy to signify power and positon. This is apparent in the baroque stables of Weißenstein castle in Pommersfelden, Germany, the private residence of a noble family in the Franconian countryside.[1] Located directly opposite the castle, the stable was erected in 1717–21 according to plans drawn up by the architect Maximilian von Welsch.[2] The buildings exhibit not only beautiful interior fittings but also a unique decorative scheme: a stable hall covered with frescoes depicting scenes of horsemanship.

From a modern point of view this stable seems to have been built by a passionate horseman. But its original owner, Lothar Franz von Schönborn (1655–1729), was not a nobleman schooled in the art of dressage, but rather an avid collector of paintings by Dürer, Rubens, and Titian.[3] Indeed, during the design phase of the stable, when his nephew suggested that the area between the two stable wings was the best place to erect a covered riding school, Lothar Franz—already in his early sixties and corpulent—rejected the idea, not intending that much riding be done at Pommersfelden.[4] Moreover, since he held a religious office, his education probably did not include lessons in dressage,[5] though at the riding school of his official residence in Bamberg he bought several horses trained in the haute école movements.[6]

So why did Lothar Franz von Schönborn build such a magnificent stable? In part, the answer is that noble circles during the seventeenth and eighteenth centuries focused on the horse as a symbol of the aristocracy's claim to rule. Images of rulers performing difficult dressage movements such as passage, piaffe, or the "airs above the ground"[7] were central to their claims to power. As Pia Cuneo points out, riding correctly "demands a tremendous amount of theoretical knowledge, physical skill . . . , emotional equilibrium and even moral rectitude."[8] Training in equitation thus traditionally was part of the construction of noble identity through the performative act of riding at the high school level.

Riding lessons were obligatory for young nobles, and high school equitation—like dancing and fencing—was central to education as a courtier.[9] Equitation manuals circulated at European courts from the sixteenth century onward, including Grisone's *Gli ordini di cavalcare* (Naples, 1550), Pluvinel's *Maneige royale* (Paris, 1623), and de la Guérinière's *École de cavalerie* (Paris, 1733).[10] Pictorial sources were also important. One of the most popular books on the subject in Germany was Georg Engelhard von Loehneysen's *Della cavalleria* (Remlingen, 1609), a source that included large copperplate illustrations depicting dressage and saddlery. More than a century later this work was republished by Valentin Trichter (*Neu eröffnete Hof- Kriegs- und Reit-Schul* [Nuremberg, 1729]) with copperplate illustrations updated to reflect the latest fashion.[11] Taken together, literary and pictorial representation played a key role in creating the ideal of the nobleman entitled to rule by virtue of his skill at controlling highbred horses.[12]

While representation played an important role in articulating identity, however, the material culture and arrangement of the stable were also critical components of equine discourse, from equine portraits,[13] to richly embroidered saddles and bridles, and even to riding arenas and stables such as Pommersfelden. As with human society, horses were arranged within a hierarchy. Stable inventories always listed the riding horses—above all those of the prince—first (including their names), while the carriage horses were recorded after the breeding stallions and the young riding horses in training. This order was preserved inside the stable as well, where the riding horses occupied the most lavishly decorated areas in the stable.[14] As part of noble rituals, moreover, horses were frequently sold or exchanged between courts, and equine vogues such as Ottoman riding equipment, French names, and other fashions proliferated throughout Europe. Even knowledge about training a horse in the airs above the ground circulated in books written by *écuyers* (professional riders) and stable masters at noble courts, during visits of princes to foreign courts, and at festive court events such as carousels (equestrian games).[15]

Collectively such practices created an equine culture with one main goal: to constitute and reinforce elite identity.[16] Over the past several years scholarly interest in the representative use and symbolic meaning of the horse for the upper classes has resulted in a number of studies.[17] In what follows we contribute to this line of research, taking up the largely neglected topic of baroque princely stables. Giles Worsley notes that although "stables were places of display for princes" and were "favoured by architects," "the stable seems to have passed the architectural historian by."[18] Very little research has been done in Germany on historical stables. Today the stable of Weißenstein castle is one of the very few baroque stables in Germany that is almost intact in both architectural structure and unique decoration. We argue that the stable and frescoes in the stable hall form a visual program that reflects how horses were used as objects and symbols for communicating a prince's political power and reputation—even though the prince himself was not a passionate horseman.

Lothar Franz von Schönborn and Weißenstein Castle in Pommersfelden

Lothar Franz von Schönborn descended from an old German family of counts and held several influential ecclesiastical and worldly offices: he was prince-bishop of Bamberg, archbishop and elector of Mainz, and imperial electoral chancellor. In the early modern period the Holy Roman Empire was a political union of comparatively independent territories of various sizes with multiple spheres of power. Although Mainz and Bamberg, Lothar Franz's territories, were middle-sized with limited resources and political power, in cultural matters they, like many smaller European courts, tried to equal the large and important courts of Paris and Vienna. As elector, Lothar Franz was one of seven bishops and princes who elected the Holy Roman emperor, and as imperial archchancellor he had an office at the Vienna Imperial court with high political influence. Although he was an influential personality, as a churchman he had no children who could inherit his offices. Instead, he used his influence to advance the careers of close family members, as he did for his nephew Friedrich Karl von Schönborn (1674–1746), or to negotiate advantageous marriages.[19]

The impressive three-winged Weißenstein castle in Pommersfelden was built as Lothar Franz's private residence. Construction took place from 1711

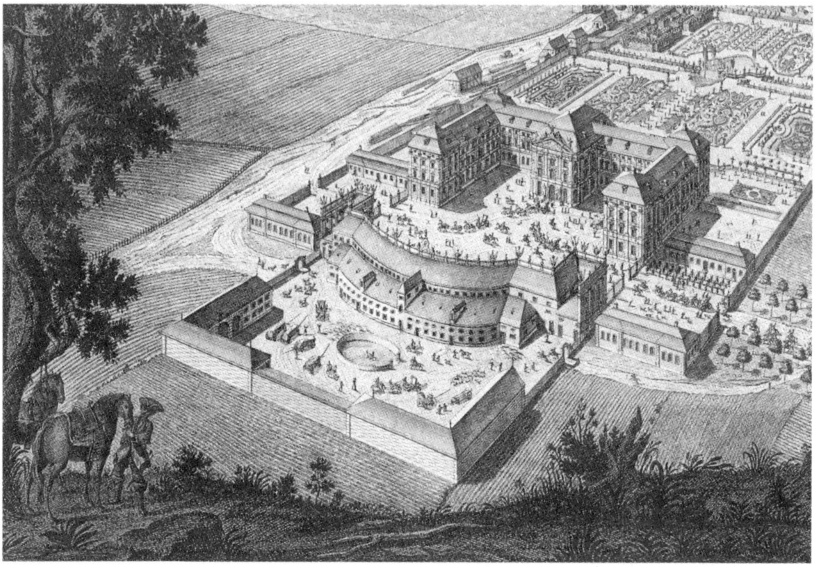

Figure 5.1. Weißenstein castle and the stable from bird's-eye view, copperplate engraving. From Salomon Kleiner, *Wahrhaffte Vorstellung beyder Hoch-Gräffl: Schlösser Weissenstein ob Pommersfeld und Geibach, sambt denen darzu gehörigen Gärten, Stallungen, und Menagerien* (Augsburg: Wolf, 1728).

to 1718 and was planned by the best designers of the time, including local architects Johann Dientzenhofer and Maximilian von Welsch, and Vienna court architect Lucas von Hildebrandt.[20] Its construction was made possible by a special payment from the Vienna court, the result of Lothar Franz's involvement in the election of Emperor Karl VI. When Emperor Joseph I died unexpectedly in April 1711, his brother Karl, then king of Spain, wanted to succeed him. Lothar Franz supported Karl, both in his capacity as leader of the Hapsburg loyalist party and in his office as imperial archchancellor—head of the council of electors charged with overseeing the election of the emperor. In return for securing Karl's election, Lothar Franz demanded concessions regarding the balance of power between the new emperor Karl VI (1711–40) and the imperial estates. One day before the election, Lothar Franz received a payment of 100,000 Taler from the imperial court in Vienna to ensure Karl's election, which he used to build Weißenstein castle.[21] Intended to equal or outshine other contemporary castle complexes, the castle was equipped with an extraordinary staircase, a marvelous *sala terrena,* and symmetrical baroque gardens in addition to a lavish stable complex (fig. 5.1).

Princely Stables for Princely Horses: The Pommersfelden Stable

In 2017 the Pommersfelden stable was three hundred years old. The trend toward integrating stables within the residential building complex originated in France some decades before its construction. One of the earliest examples is the stable in Vaux-le-Vicomte, built in 1655, followed by the famous ones in Versailles, planned in 1685 by Jules Hardouin-Mansart.[22]

The Pommersfelden stable is composed of a central pavilion between two curved stable wings shaped like segmental arches, each terminating in an outer pavilion (fig. 5.2). Behind the stable lies an access yard with a pond for bathing the horses.[23] The stables are close to the castle, and the *cour d'honneur* in front of the castle is enclosed by the stable, creating a boundary between the courtyard and the outside world. The stable's curves enhance the dynamic appearance of the dominant central pavilion of the castle. Visually, it is subordinate to the castle while balancing its proportions and concealing the access yard.

Mirroring the design of the castle, the central pavilion is the most striking part of the otherwise modest facade. It consists of three parts, with round-arched French doors and mezzanine windows flanked by Tuscan

Figure 5.2. Weißenstein castle, Pommersfelden: stable building (1717/18), front view. Photo by the authors.

columns and pilasters, and by two statues showing an unidentified Roman emperor and Alexander the Great with the Gordian knot lying at his feet. A corniced entablature above the middle door is topped by a gable from which a sculpted Pegasus appears to emerge. Above Pegasus, a clock with bell chimes is crowned by two putti planting a flag while the allegories for day and night enclose it on both sides. The gable is flanked by two Greek heroes. On the left Perseus, holding Medusa's head, is next to an animal representing the sea monster he slaughtered to free Andromeda. The warrior on the right is Bellerophon, and the animal beside him is a lion with a tail in the shape of a snake, representing the chimera he killed with the help of Pegasus.

The installation of luxurious interior fittings and decorative elements began in November 1718 and ended in 1721.[24] The stable wings were decorated with stucco strapwork and rocaille.[25] Each stable wing accommodates tie stalls for the horses; those in the two inner wings are equipped with a niche in the wall for the hayrack and decorated with rocaille cartouches along the top edge. The conchiform troughs are made of oak. The splendid interiors of these stalls suggest that the prince-bishop's personal riding and carriage horses were housed here, whereas the horses for the court and guests' animals were quartered in the outer wings where only the ceilings are stucco decorated. All together, the stable provided space for fifty horses,[26] about two dozen of them in the finer part.

Horses, Humans, and Heroes: The Frescoes of the Stable Hall

An extremely fine feature of the stable is the oval hall between the two stable wings. The term "stable hall" comes from a letter written by Lothar Franz on September 24, 1718, in which he refers to the hall as *ovales stallsalet* ("oval stable hall").[27] This designation seems appropriate considering the hall's purpose. The designation "tack room" in the older literature, which seems to originate from the saddlery depicted in the frescos, is not accurate because the room was not used to store riding equipment.[28]

The domed hall is entirely decorated with frescoes painted in 1718–19 by the Swiss artist Johann Rudolf Bys, who completed the figures, and the Italian painter Giovanni Francesco Marchini, who executed the architectural representations—a typical feature in the baroque era.[29] The frescoes reinterpret the room, with architectural paintings in a pavilion with eight arcades and lunette caps under a cupola. Six real doors and two illusionist views of architectonic landscapes are set between the pillars. Three French doors open to the *cour d'honneur*, two others open onto the stable wings, and the sixth door, flanked by the two illusionist views, leads into the access yard. On its gable, an inscription in a cartouche reads AD IUCUNDAM POSTERITATIS MEMORIAM ("To be remembered pleasantly by posterity"). People, horses, saddles, bridles, and putti playing with weapons, making music, and creating flower garlands are represented in the illusionist architectural paintings. Four supporting figures hold a trompe l'oeil painting in the cupola representing the rescue of Andromeda.

The figural paintings of the stable hall can be divided into three parts: the wall, the attic, and the cupola (fig. 5.3). The wall section is covered with depictions of horses, grooms, and court members and also adorned with paintings of precious saddles, saddle cloths, and bridles. Entering visitors stand on the same level as the mural of life-size horses and people, and their first glance falls on the illusionist scenes, each showing two horses of different breeds and coat colors held by grooms. The scene to the left of the door represents a bay horse and a gray of European breed, with compact

Figure 5.3. Weißenstein castle, Pommersfelden: stable hall, interior view. Photo by the authors.

Figure 5.4. Weißenstein castle, Pommersfelden: stable hall, fresco with horses, grooms, and saddles. Photo by the authors.

builds, rounded forms, and convex faces, led by Europeans; the other scene depicts a black horse and a chestnut horse of Oriental breed, both with more graceful frames. The black horse is held by an Ottoman, the chestnut by a Moor. The arrangement of both pairs seems to have been inspired by the example of antique horse tamers (fig. 5.4).[30]

The paintings of tack suggest the different origins of the horses pictured. Precious European saddlery is depicted alongside the European horses, including saddle cloths, holsters and holster covers, breast collars and cruppers, and bridles with curb bits. These objects are sumptuously decorated with embroidery, tassels, bows, and ribbons. In its form and presentation, this equipment corresponds to tack at the French royal court, though similar saddlery can be found in the collections of German courts.[31] As a counterpoint, exotic Turkish saddles and bridles are pictured with the two Oriental horses. The saddle on the left has begemmed stirrups, while the matching bridle, breastplate, and crupper are adorned with decorative rivets, rosettes, and tassels. Associating the saddle with military endeavors, the handles of a saber and a mace are visible behind the saddle cloth. On the right side, a very special saddle is depicted, covered entirely by the skin of a large cat—a lioness or a young lion.[32] The matching bridle, embellished with a half-moon pendant and a feather plume, is equipped with a bit *à la Genette*, a typical Turkish and Oriental item.[33] Lothar Franz himself owned both European and Ottoman riding equipment: a Bamberg stable inventory of 1714 lists Turkish equipment with gilded brass fittings.[34]

In addition to horses and saddlery, life-size figures are depicted on the walls of the *cour d'honneur*. Two servants bring food and serve wine. Two men are shown in animated conversation, while another is portrayed with a periwig and riding crop and accompanied by a dog. We can suppose the gentleman is a stable master while the two other men are riders employed at Lothar Franz's court.

The attic section claims the visitor's attention with a crowd of putti making music and playing with tack and tournament equipment used for equestrian games, including carousels.[35] One group of putti suggests "running at the quintain" by handling the saddle, breast straps, boots, and two delicate lances. Such lances came into use in France about 1700 and appear to have been the inspiration for those depicted at Pommersfelden.[36] Another group of putti shoot pistols, and the standing putto, who has pulled a pistol out of the holster, aims it outward at the room. Pistols had become a common component of carousels at the time, occasionally substituted for traditional weapons such as swords or lances.[37] The third group of putti imitate "running at the head" with a papier-mâché head as their target. One putto is sitting on a saddle, playfully aiming a sword at the head, while another is beginning to draw a sword, with an outward look toward visitors. In the final game represented, a group of putti play "carisell," a group game of Ottoman or Asian origin played only rarely at German courts.[38] Other putti play musical instruments associated with carousels.[39] Above the scene, additional putti fix a flower garland between the lunette caps, creating a transition to the cupola section.

Here Andromeda, daughter of King Cepheus, is shown chained to the rocks as a sacrifice for the sea monster Cetos. Her family is depicted in the background, while in the center Perseus, mounted on the bridled Pegasus, attacks Cetos with a sword. While putti try to free Andromeda from her chains, the goddess Athena comes to the warrior's aid from the left, holding Medusa's head. The head references the myth of Perseus killing Medusa, with Athena's help, and Pegasus, the equine child of Poseidon, arising from her bleeding body.[40]

Piaffing to Divine Status: The Symbolism of Pommersfelden Stable

Describing this magnificent baroque stable provides a sense of its unique appearance, but the ornamentation is also symbolic. To understand that purpose, we have to know that the structure of early modern noble society was strictly hierarchical. The most important thing for a nobleman was his rank as divinely appointed ruler of his people. If he gained his rank by birth, he had to preserve and possibly augment it through an intelligent use of his resources, both real (money, possessions) and symbolic (education, knowledge, behavior).[41] The social and symbolic capital related to social position was often communicated through a system of symbols that for us today are almost invisible. In modern scholarly terms, these practices and forms of behavior are called symbolic communication.[42]

The Vienna Connection

The Pommersfelden stable is a perfect example of symbolic communication in that it asserts Lothar Franz's cultural and political superiority by demonstrating his familiarity both with equine pictorial programs traditionally used to display status and with the design of contemporary elite stables. The interior fittings of the stable wings are similar to the stable of Prince Eugene of Savoy (1663–1736) in Vienna.[43] This is no coincidence, since Lothar Franz was in close contact with his nephew, Friedrich Karl von Schönborn (then imperial vice chancellor in Vienna) about them.[44] Friedrich Karl arranged for the architect Lucas von Hildebrandt to advise on the matter because Hildebrandt had already drawn the plans for the stables in the Lower Belvedere, Prince Eugene's Vienna residence, that were finished about 1716–17, just earlier than the Pommersfelden stable.[45]

Furthermore, in and around Vienna representative noble buildings repeatedly exhibited the motif of Andromeda's rescue by Perseus. Such representation often conflated mythical subjects with actual political and military events such as the liberation of the Netherlands from Spanish rule or the numerous Turkish wars with the Ottoman Empire.[46] The Perseus scene at Pommersfelden can be interpreted as a symbolic expression of the successful defense of the Christian Occident against the Ottoman Empire. Several Christian victories between 1697 and 1718 were associated specifically with Prince Eugene of Savoy, who won important battles against the Turks as general of the imperial army.[47] Indeed, one fresco at the Belvedere shows Andromeda's rescue by Perseus. In this depiction the prince is equated with

Perseus, who represents the Christian knight, while the rescue of Andromeda suggests the liberation of Austria from the Turks.[48] The Pommersfelden stable hall fresco can be understood in a similar way. As a bishop, Lothar Franz could not participate in military campaigns; however, he could connect himself with the reputation of the successful warrior Prince Eugene, a close family friend.[49] The Ottoman theme also connects the glorification of the emperor with the political activity of Lothar Franz, who, by using his influence to affect the outcome of the election, gave the empire a successful defender. This connection between mythological symbolism and princely virtues in the design of Pommersfelden announced the loyalty of the Schönborn family to the emperor and affirmed their interconnection. The emperor was literally the noblest knight, whose duty it was to defend the Christian faith. As a religious leader, Lothar Franz showed his support for this mission in the pictorial programs of the stable hall and castle, both of which used mythical images to connect his political and religious activities to military power.

Continuities between the visual designs of the stable and the castle offer significant insight into the political role of decorative elements in expressing status. The interior paintings in both structures were executed by Bys and Marchini. Given this connection, the stable continues the iconographic and symbolic themes of the castle. This connection has gone unnoticed in preceding scholarly work;[50] we therefore turn briefly to the castle's iconography to develop a more complete understanding of the symbolic meaning of the stable's features.

Although Weißenstein castle was the private residence of a noble family, it invites comparison with higher-ranking princely residences in that it too used symbolic representation to legitimize claims to power and social status. To recognize the iconography, it is essential to bear in mind the circumstances of the castle's erection, particularly the relation between its construction and the election of Emperor Karl VI, which is reflected in the iconography of the exterior and in the most representative rooms of the castle: the great staircase, the *sala terrena* on the ground floor, and the ceremonial hall on the *belle étage*. According to Walter Jürgen Hofmann, the castle's decoration alludes to the imperial couple and the role that Lothar Franz played in the election of the emperor[51] via images praising royal virtues, which refer both to the imperial couple and to Lothar Franz.

Representations of Mercury and Hercules on the facade and in the interior fittings are direct references to Lothar Franz. Mercury appears as a personification of Sapientia, representing wisdom. As the intermediary between heaven and earth, he suggests Lothar Franz's clerical office. Mercury is also the planet closest to the sun, an association that hints at the importance of Lothar Franz's position as both the primary elector in the empire and the esteemed adviser to the emperor. Hercules similarly symbolizes the virtues and bravery of Lothar Franz and his worldly actions, translating statesmanship into a form of military leadership.[52]

In several of the main rooms this iconography is complemented by representations of the four seasons, corresponding signs of the zodiac, and the four continents, represented in the concave molding of the ceiling as large groups of figures in front of architectural staffage. In the *sala terrena*, the cosmological theme is continued with references to the quadripartite universe, part of a common repertoire demonstrating the ruler's integration into the world's divine order.[53]

Both inside and outside the stable, elements corresponding to the castle's iconography are evident. Personifications of day and night on the stable's facade continue the cosmological theme. The inscription above the courtyard door, expressing the wish that the stable hall be remembered by posterity, picks up the theme of time evident in the castle, where a bound Chronos appears in the vestibule of the staircase. Both castle and stable are designated for eternity, as, presumably, is the reputation of its owner.[54]Inside the stable hall, the four horses of different colors and temperaments symbolize the four elements, repeating the emphasis on groups of four in the visual scheme of the castle. Similarly, the four groups of putti with weapons represented in the stable repeat the cosmological number often associated with carousels and masquerades.[55] During a carousel, participants were divided into four groups, or "quadrilles," that competed against each other in four armed exercises on horseback. Dividing the participants into four groups expressed the totality of creation, invoking the four parts of the world, the four monarchies, or the four elements.[56] Closely related to the military purpose of carousels, the topic of war is revisited in the stable, where trophies of combat appear both on the attic of the stable front and on the front facade, as do antique warriors such as Perseus and Alexander the Great.

The Stable Hall Personnel

The iconography inside the stable hall not only matches that of the castle and connects both buildings but also has its own special, highly symbolic pictorial program focusing on horses and the art of riding. Building on the mythic, cosmological focus of the castle's ornamentation, the stable's decorations merge symbolic representation with reminders of Lothar Franz's status as the owner of fine possessions and his associated claims to rule.

The illusionistic scenes with the two pairs of horse trainers immediately capture the visitor's attention. In most antique or contemporaneous depictions of horse training pairs, each man is occupied with handling and training one horse. In the Pommersfelden stable hall, by contrast, one horse has already been calmed. Normally the depiction of this human-animal interaction shows the person with a wild, untamed animal—for example, two early eighteenth-century statues of horse trainers in front of the Upper Belvedere in Vienna.

The next step for the successful trainers would be to saddle their horses. This connects them with other painted images of riding equipment in the stable hall. There are several matching sets of European and Ottoman riding equipment (see figs. 5.3 and 5.4). It is possible to select among them because there are more saddles, bridles, and saddle pads available than horses; moreover, the quality and value of the riding equipment is significant. The person who owns such valuable tack can be identified as a noble of high rank and great means. We can read the scene in an emblematic way by associating each part of the painted equipment with a special quality of the ruler. Bridle, bit, and above all reins symbolize the early modern ruler's claim to absolute power. The saddle represents a throne: on the horse it elevates the rider above other people, suggesting the ruler's position at the top of social hierarchy. The elaborate design of the riding equipment underscores the economic capital that was a necessary and legitimating element of rule. In the case of Lothar Franz, this connection between horse, tack, and human identity is more symbolic and has coalesced in the act of ownership rather than a demonstration of mastery by skilled horsemanship.

Depictions of elaborate riding equipment offer the only visual link to a higher social rank, since neither the grooms nor the life-size servants and riders painted on the ceilings are of noble origin. Heinrich Kreisel describes this group as the "real and fantastic residents of this stable."[57] Yet their purpose is more than purely decorative. Although the servants, riders, stable master, and horse trainers/grooms occupy different social ranks, they are all subordinates of the stable's princely owner.

Horse-Related Discourse

Just as representations of servants depict a human hierarchy with Lothar Franz at the top, the four horses also confirm his symbolic and actual power. Each is a different color—bay, gray, black, and chestnut. These representations invoke equine literature of the sixteenth to the eighteenth century, which associated temperament with color.[58] According to this doctrine, chestnut horses are choleric and attributed to fire, while bay horses are sanguine and correspond to air. Black horses have a melancholic temperament and are associated with earth, while gray horses are phlegmatic and associated with water.[59] The men who lead these horses also appear to reflect these temperaments. The sanguine bay horse rears and is held with difficulty by a man with eyes and mouth wide open. The phlegmatic gray, by contrast, stands calm and relaxed with a handler who likewise appears calm. The melancholic black horse and the Ottoman walk sedately while the choleric chestnut resists the Moor. The doctrine of color was a common contemporary topos and fits perfectly in the lowest section of the stable hall fresco, where "natural" tendencies of temperament suggest a similarly "natural" social hierarchy of servants.

Besides their different colors, these horses also exhibit different levels of training. The bay horse is on the long line, wearing a bitless bridle, and thus seems young. The gray horse is highly trained, bridled with a curb. The Oriental horses wear visibly different tack, corresponding to their temper and training: the "melancholic" black horse's bridle is adorned with a precious noseband and is bitless, signifying its good behavior, while the wild chestnut horse is undecorated. Arabian, Syrian, and Turkish horses were admired in Europe, but few reached European courts except as spoils of war or direct acquisitions.[60] The extraordinary quality and rarity of Turkish horses and tack prompted a fashion at European courts,[61] which Lothar Franz invokes here in scenes that conflate the political ability of the empire to quiet its Oriental foes and Lothar Franz's understanding—and possession of—fine horseflesh. The painted horses may in fact be representations from Lothar Franz's stable, which included a black stallion from Denmark, a Neapolitan stallion named Stella, and a Moorish-type gray called Berber.[62] The different training levels also suggest activities that took place, if not at Pommersfelden, then at Lothar Franz's official residence in Bamberg—where, for example, a five-year-old black stallion named Weißfuß (White Foot) was intended ultimately to perform the airs above the ground.[63] Actual and represented horses, in these instances, confirmed the elite identity of their owner, for even if Lothar Franz never sat in Weißfuß's saddle to perform a levade, he elevated his social rank by investing economic, social, and cultural capital in training and owning such horses.

Another aspect of equine symbolism depicted at Pommersfelden was the medieval tradition of tournaments. Beginning in the sixteenth century, court tournaments evolved into sophisticated competitions adapted to changing military requirements.[64] A flexible cavalry able to handle various weapons became increasingly important, and carousels became popular training regimes among the nobility.[65] This connection between the art of riding and military purposes also identified the horse as the characteristic animal of Europe, representing, along with the weapons, Europeans' superior military capability.[66] Although it is unlikely that Lothar Franz ever participated in such games during his rule—if not because he lacked ability, then because he was a man of the church—he clearly understood the perceived relation between accomplished riding and the ability to rule.

In the Pommersfelden stable hall, real military endeavors are replaced by the four groups of putti playing equestrian games that were part of a carousel. The group of putti on the left of the door to the access yard engage in a *Ringrennen* (running at the ring) and a *Quintanrennen* (running at the quintain) (fig. 5.5), both introduced in the middle of the sixteenth century. In the first, the rider tried to drive his lance through a ring suspended between two pillars. In the second, the rider attacked a wooden figure with his lance. Both exercises required riders to engage with effigies that could strike back if they were not hit perfectly. Figures of Ottomans were particularly popular at the German courts, making it possible to beat the enemy symbolically in the course of court festivities.[67] On the left of the *cour d'honneur*, the second group of putti engage in a *Kopfrennen* (running at the head). This discipline evolved from running at the quintain in the early seven-

Figure 5.5. Weißenstein castle, Pommersfelden: stable hall, fresco with putti playing with riding equipment. Photo by the authors.

teenth century. The target was a papier-mâché head that was to be impaled with a sword or lance or shot with a pistol. As with the quintain, heads of Turks, Moors, and Gorgons were popular.[68] The third group of putti use pistols, a new weapon that increasingly replaced swords and lances in battle and equestrian games. The final group of putti on the right of the *cour d'honneur* represent a very rare discipline in which two groups fought with clay balls, lances, and shields. Characterized by Helen Watanabe-O'Kelly as "carisell," this was probably a game of Ottoman or Asian origin.[69] This group of putti seem to have darker skin than the other groups, suggesting that they are dressed up as Africans, a typical aspect of carisell because the game came to Spain by way of North African Saracens.[70]

In all probability no such tournaments were held at Pommersfelden during Lothar Franz's reign. Indeed, one would be more inclined to expect allusions to activities such as hunting, and existing analysis of Pommersfelden tends to interpret the putti in this sense.[71] Nonetheless, equestrian games remained important occasions in the eighteenth century, even though the rulers of this time increasingly did not fight wars directly as riders. The symbolic meaning was still important for the early modern prince, however, because his legitimacy as a ruler was based on traditions, especially military ones.

Representations of the carousel putti contribute to Lothar Franz's effort to legitimate himself as ruler, although as a churchman he would not have taken part in military campaigns. The putti in the attic section are the link between his worldly and clerical positions. They occupy a higher place than humans, suggesting they are intermediaries between earth and heaven and thus between the people and the prince. They hint instead at a divine sphere. Although worldly princes generally used mythic imagery to link their power with divine dispensation, the Pommersfelden putti double this effect and unite worldly and religious leadership.

The Flying Horse

The final level of the pictorial program is the cupola, which depicts the most famous equine in ancient mythology, the flying horse Pegasus, carrying Perseus. Pegasus has already welcomed visitors to Pommersfelden stable in a sculpture above the main entrance. In the ceiling painting this relationship is represented again with added symbolic meaning. First, the connection between the mythological scene and the riding equipment depicted below is suggested by a small detail: in mythology, Pegasus could be tamed by Perseus only with the help of a golden bridle. In the ceiling illustration, the flying horse is bridled not with an antique bit but with a baroque one, a contemporaneous golden curb. This shift associates Lothar Franz's possessions (his worldly riding equipment) with the power of the divine sphere. In this upper section of the building, moreover, all the human figures are either noble persons or gods: Perseus and Andromeda are royal children, while Pallas Athena is a goddess. Material details in these depictions further suggest how possessions may confer power and consolidate identity. Thus, for instance, the flying sandals Perseus wears, a gift from the god Mercury, represent a hero literally lifted above human limitations by owning special objects. The fight against the sea monster Cetos and the rescue similarly represent heroic characteristics such as courage, strength, and wisdom, but in a way that distributes their symbolic power to a man who neither rides high school dressage nor engages in military combat.

Within this scene the central figure, and ultimately the most transformative possession, is Pegasus himself. Pegasus appears occasionally in connection with elite stables and stable halls. The stable of Troja Castle in Prague, for example, has a ceiling painted by Abraham Godyn[72] featuring the liberation of Andromeda by Perseus and Pegasus. Rudolf Bys, one of the painters of the Pommersfelden stable hall, lived in Prague for an extended period, and it is likely that he knew Godyn's painting.[73] The alliance between the mythological figure of Pegasus and the stable is also confirmed by Lothar Franz's remark that the Pegasus represented on the facade of the stable expressed the purpose of the building.[74] In the stable hall fresco, moreover, Pegasus knits together several layers of symbolic meaning central to Lothar Franz's self-representation. As son of the sea god Poseidon, Pegasus is of divine origin, while his taming by Perseus, the son of a king, hints at a ruler's claim to power by divine dispensation. In this representation, Pegasus's connection to the divine emphasizes that rulers derive the right to rule directly from God, a quintessential expression of early modern absolutism.

Pegasus and the differentiated riding equipment thus bring together two important early modern expressions of elite identity: the art of riding and classical mythology. Both were rediscovered in the Renaissance and were often connected. In one of the copperplates in "La méthode nouvelle et invention extraordinaire de dresser les chevaux" (1657-58), the Duke of Newcastle is depicted executing a capriole on a horse with wings. This visual representation underscores the author's belief that horse and rider "aspire towards heaven but, through the combined wildness yet groundedness of horses, [retain] the physical presence of the earthly."[75] In the ceiling fresco in Pommersfelden we find both rediscoveries united and interpreted in a similar heaven-earth connection by a baroque ruler who wants to claim both "divine" and worldly power.

Conclusion: Real, Symbolic, and Political Horses

The stable hall frescoes at Pommersfelden replicate an earlier tradition of arranging emblematic topics in a strictly hierarchical structure, placing ruled persons at the lowest level along the wall while the ruler occupies the highest section to suggest his nearly divine status. In the visual program at Pommersfelden, moreover, Lothar Franz is represented as both a religious and a worldly ruler. The mythological figures depicted in and around the stable announce the importance of his religious office as archbishop, while the connection to the Viennese court underlines his worldly position as prince and elector by emphasizing his association with Prince Eugene of Savoy and Emperor Karl VI.[76]

In this respect Lothar Franz was not unique. Many nobles communicated their social position by building huge residences complete with elaborate gardens, galleries, and stables. Other German princely stables were richly decorated and had pictorial programs.[77] Yet in no other remaining stable of this epoch—not even those of rulers who loved horses—do we find such detailed and elaborate representation as in the stable and stable hall frescoes of Pommersfelden. So what do we learn from this paradox of a religious ruler who was not a keen rider but nonetheless built one of Germany's most splendid baroque stables? We suggest that horses and the art of riding continued to play fundamental roles in communicating claims to noble or princely status through the early eighteenth century. With the support of the horse, the prince symbolically stood, seemingly in his natural place, at the top of the social hierarchy. At the same time, the example of Lothar Franz and Pommersfelden offers another insight into horse-human relationships. Although the elite horses housed at Pommersfelden and the Bamberg residence were connected with precious riding equipment and were well and competently trained, they were not subjects their owner interacted with. Lothar Franz did not ride them for show and, as a clergyman, was not obliged to do so, given that there was no established tradition of performative horsemanship associated with the clergy. Indeed, Lothar Franz's incorporating aristocratic equine motifs in the decorative scheme of Pommersfelden represents a significant departure from Renaissance depictions of clergymen riding mules, sterile animals that emphasized chastity.[78] In imitating the equestrian culture of secular courts, using the horse as a symbolically charged object in the highly political decoration of his private residence, Lothar Franz thus suggests a subtle shift in equine discourse. To determine his political and social attitude and rank, it was not necessary to look at the "real" horses in his stables and to judge his riding skills; one had only to interpret and understand the meaning of the decoration of his stable. Although such political imagery was common in palaces and town halls, it appeared in very few princely stables. The Pommersfelden stable can thus be seen as part of a contemporary phenomenon in which equestrian culture was used to perform ideological work that supported not only elite identity but also a specific political agenda. More research on eighteenth-century German equestrian culture is needed to further refine these interpretations.

SIX

Trading Horses in the Eighteenth Century

Rhode Island and the Atlantic World

CHARLOTTE CARRINGTON-FARMER

In July 1732 Captain Crow loaded his sloop and set sail out of Rhode Island heading for St. Christopher Island in the West Indies. Crow's cargo was primarily livestock, with sixteen horses, all traveling on deck. Crow and his horses never made it to St. Christopher: after a month at sea, off Bermuda they were hit with a gale that capsized the sloop and quickly cleared the deck of its equine cargo. Although the horses put up a valiant struggle, they were quickly carried out to sea and drowned. Crow and his crew clung to the sloop and were "almost up to their middle in Water, for 36 Hours" before cutting away the mast, righting the vessel. They continued for nineteen days and were again hit by hard gales. In the "Hazard of perishing," they met with "divine Providence" when fellow Rhode Islander Captain Jonathan Remington picked them up and delivered them to safety.[1]

Crow's sloop was one of many ships that braved the dangerous aquatic highway of the Atlantic delivering horses to the sugar colonies. Planters needed horses, and from the late seventeenth century to the American Revolution, Rhode Island dominated this trade, even developing its own (much sought-after) breed, the Narragansett Pacer. The breed is often recognized as the first "American" horse breed, and this chapter examines why they were so highly prized, building on the growing literature on the connections between New England, the Caribbean, and South America in the early modern period. I argue that horses were one of the many products New England produced that were central to upholding and sustaining the vast, sprawling machine of sugar production, which at first glance might seem isolated from New England.

Breeding Horses in Rhode Island

Rhode Island's horse industry was centered in Narragansett, an area stretching approximately twenty miles from Wickford to Point Judith and westward to Charlestown. The area, on the west side of Narragansett Bay, was under agricultural development in the seventeenth century owing to its fertile, level, well-watered pastureland. The swamp grasses made excellent hay, and the numerous saltwater ponds provided not only water access but also natural fencing. By the turn of the eighteenth century, large "plantations" had been established in the area. Because of the soil and the climate, the Narragansett planters were stock and dairy farmers and did not grow cash crops such as sugar, tobacco, indigo, rice, or cotton.[2] Although some raised oxen and made cheese, the planter's most lucrative commercial effort was breeding horses.[3] Importing horses to New England began a decade after the initial settlement at Plymouth, but when they were first received in Rhode Island, especially in Narragansett, is unclear.[4] The first recorded mention of any type of horses in Narragansett was made in 1666 in a letter from Peleg Sanford to his uncle Samuel Hutchinson: "in Respect of the Extremity of the winter I could not gett your horses from Narragansett." Sanford lived in Barbados from 1663 to 1664, and on his return to Newport he pioneered trade between his new home and Barbados.[5]

A 1672 letter from John Hull reveals that he was probably the first to consider developing a pure strain and to fully realize the lucrative prospect of shipping the horses to the sugar colonies:

> if we . . . procure a verry good breed of large & fair mares & stallions & that noe mungrell breed might come amonge them . . . wee might have a verry choice breed for coach horses. . . . saddle . . . [and] draught others & in a few years might draw of Considerable numbers & shipp them for Barbados Nevis or such parts of the Indies.[6]

Hull's desire to have a "verry good breed" of mares and stallions and to ensure that "noe mungrell breed" come among them raises the question of what "breed" meant in early modern parlance. Rhode Island planters clearly sought to raise specific types of horses with defining characteristics of height, gait, and strength, but how they defined the breed and policed the boundaries is unclear. The origin of the Narragansett Pacer has been widely debated. Its ancestors were probably among the English and Dutch horses that arrived in Massachusetts between 1629 and 1635.[7] Some believe the

Narragansett Pacer was produced from the Irish Hobby, the Suffolk Punch, and the Scottish Galloway pony; others believe it came from the Spanish Jennet or the Andalusian.[8] Thomas Hazard, who went on to become one of the leading breeders in Rhode Island, introduced "Old Snip" to the breeding pool. It is not certain how Hazard acquired the stallion, and rumors range from his finding Old Snip wandering wild near Point Judith to his importing him from Tripoli.[9] Regardless, proving lineage to Old Snip was used as a hallmark of a true Narragansett Pacer.

A natural pacer, the breed moved in an unusual fashion; its "backbone moved through the air in a straight line without inclining the rider from side to side."[10] Narragansett Pacers were typically chestnut, with liberal white markings. Several contemporary writers described the Pacer as "no beauty" or even as "villainously ugly."[11] Others were more complimentary, noting that a Pacer could travel one hundred miles a day over rough roads without tiring itself or the rider. Pacers also adapted to hot climates, which made them highly sought-after in the sugar colonies.[12] If the breed's exact origins are a mystery, however, by the mid-eighteenth century Narragansett Pacers were "steeds most prized for the saddle." People sent for them "at much trouble and expense," and the "breed was propagated with much care."[13]

Uncovering how Narragansett's horse breeding program progressed is difficult, since there are no studbooks. Estate inventories tell us part of the story but rarely mention specific breeds. Ichabod Potter's estate inventory from 1739 specifically mentions "one small white pacing horse £6."[14] George Hazard's inventory from 1746 offers a few more details, such as the age and sex of the horses: "1 Stallion, 4 young horses; 1 mare & colt, 7 mares & 5 colts, 2 two year old mares, 10 yearling horse kind." William Gardiner had thirty horses and mares and one "young Stone horse" (stallion) in 1732. In 1759 Jeffrey Hazard's estate listed a "riding beast" valued at £300, a "Sorrel stone horse" valued at £400, "13 old breeding mares," 3 geldings, 5 three-year-old mares and 8 two-year-old mares, all valued at £2,010.[15] More typical are estate inventories that simply list the number and genders of the horses. When Rowland Robinson Sr. died in 1716, his estate in Narragansett simply listed "64 horses, mares and colts."[16]

Although the lack of stud records and vague estate inventories are a problem, newspaper advertisements provide a rich resource on how breeders valued pedigree and constructed the parameters of the breed. Newspaper advertisements for Pacers, both for shipping and for breeding services, reveal that natural pacing ability, height, agility, pedigree, and color were central to classification.[17] Breeders from around New England regularly advertised their stallions and stud facilities in local newspapers. "Brown Bay, Whose Name is derived from his Colour" was offered for stud services in the summer of 1768 in Newport and North Kingstown. The advertisement in the *Newport Mercury* emphasized that he was "an excellent Saddle Horse, remarkable for fast pacing . . . is fine carriag'd and good natur'd; has extraordinary Courage, is of a delicate Make, about fourteen Hands and three Inches high, neatly ornamented with natural Marks of White." Moreover, Brown Bay was "a true genuine Extract of the old Narragansett Snip Breed."[18] Other breeders also stressed that their stallions were of the Old Snip breed; for example, when George Irish advertised his "fine pacing" stallion in the *Newport Mercury* in 1774, he noted he was "of the Snip breed."[19] When Charles Eldridge's "famous sorrel pacing Horse" stood at stud in 1775, his advertisement noted that the stallion was "of the old Narragansett snip Breed, and for Size, Resolution, Beauty and Behaviour equal to perhaps any Horse in America."[20] Selah Norton's stallion Smiling Ball, which covered mares in 1785 and 1786, was a "Narragansett Horse, of the old Snip breed . . . Chestnut Sorrel, fifteen hands high, paces exceedingly fast & easy . . . will travel 80 miles a day, without tiring himself or rider; his colts make excellent saddle Horses." Norton noted, "I cannot learn that he was ever beat in pacing."[21] Pacing ability, suitability for riding, and claiming linage to Old Snip were central to how the features of the breed were constructed.

During the summer of 1792, William Hyde ran a series of advertisements in the *Connecticut Gazette* proffering the stud services of the "famous Naraganset pacing HORSE . . . THE PEACOCK." By the end of the eighteenth century, breeding Pacers had expanded to Connecticut, but Hyde emphasized that the stallion "was formerly owned and raised by Governor POTTER of Rhode Island." Customers could pay "the moderate price of Two Dollars the season, and One Dollar the single Leap," and Hyde offered "Good pasturing for Mares." The advertisement offers an insightful description of the breed's desirable characteristics: "His size is good, his colour is a bright chesnut, his courage and carriage none will exceed." The five-year-old Peacock also was "as good a saddle horse of that breed as ever was in America."[22]

Several pivotal planting families pioneered the horse breeding industry in Rhode Island, including the Hazards, Robinsons, and Gardners. The Robinson family spanned three generations of horse breeding in Narragansett. Rowland Robinson Sr. emigrated from England and initially settled in Newport, but in 1700 he bought from Andrew Willett three hundred acres of land "east by the salt water, west by the petticomcott pond" (present-day Saunderstown). When Rowland Sr. died in 1716 he left a sizable estate, valued at £2,166. William Robinson added to the family fortunes and landholdings. When William died in 1751 his estate was inventoried at £21,573/5/5.[23] The third generation of Robinsons, headed by Rowland Jr., continued the tradition of raising horses to supply key merchants such as the Browns from Providence. At various times during the eighteenth century, the Robinson family held from nineteen to twenty-eight slaves and also raised sheep and cattle. Other families, such as the Hazards and the Gardners, were equally influential Narraganset breeders: the Hazard plantation on Boston Neck reputedly shipped over one hundred horses.

The success of Rhode Island's equine industry was directly linked to slave labor and the slave trade. On the plantations on Narragansett Bay, chattel slaves toiled alongside Native Americans, mixed-race servants, and wage laborers. Of 1,523 total residents in South Kingstown, the 1730 census listed 965 as "white," 333 as "negro," and 225 as "Indian."[24] North Kingstown had an additional 165 "negros." By the time the American Revolution swept through, Narragansett, which contained one-third of the population of Rhode Island, was home to more than a thousand slaves.[25] Slaves lived and labored on "plantations" in Narragansett, helping to breed, raise, and train horses. Newspaper advertisements regularly listed for sale slaves who were skilled animal husbandmen. For example, when Thomas Brown advertised his slave in the *Newport Mercury* in 1764, he described him as a "valuable Negro Man, who understands all sorts of husbandry Business."[26]

The language used to describe slaves and horses was often the same, and merchants sought the same qualities in the humans and the horses. The advertisements are peppered with descriptions of slaves and horses that have excellent breeding and are strong, sound, and of good temperament. Slaves, like horses, could be traded at will. Slaves often used horses in efforts to escape: for example, when Richard Dodge's slave ran away from his master in Wenham, Massachusetts, in 1751 he escaped on "a fine large Bay Horse, Fourteen Hands high . . . a natural Pacer."[27] The plight of Samson Seedux, a fourteen-year-old "Indian boy" who belonged to Thomas Ninegrett, reveals the dangers of working with horses. When Seedux ran away in 1766, his master placed an advertisement in the *Newport Mercury* to recover him. The ad described how a horse had kicked him in the face and "broke his upper Jaw and knocked out three of His Teeth."[28] The lives of slaves and horses were further intertwined as merchants paid for horses using slaves as currency, and vice versa. On arriving in the sugar colonies, the horses toiled alongside the slaves in the sugar mills.

Rhode Island Merchants and the Atlantic Market

In seventeenth-century New England, horses were used primarily for riding, with oxen performing most of the heavy draft work. In the sugar colonies, however, horses were in high demand for riding, for turning the mills to crush the sugarcane, and for the militia. One record of the secretary of customs in London shows that in a single year the New England colonies shipped 7,310 horses to the British West Indies alone.[29] The New England colonies were perfectly situated, literally and figuratively, to serve this purpose, since they (unlike Virginia) had a surplus of horses at a time when the sugar colonies were expanding.[30] In Rhode Island, most of the horses were shipped as deck cargo from Newport, which emerged as an epicenter of trade. However, some horses were shipped from Providence, and some directly from the docks in Narragansett.[31] As the seventeenth century progressed, the increasingly lucrative export trade in horses led to a corresponding increase in commercial horse breeding in Rhode Island, especially in Narragansett. Because of export trade with the West Indies, horses of any sort would have been a valuable revenue source for the Narragansett planters, and it is probable that many of ordinary New England stock were bred for this purpose. Thomas Hazard, one of the wealthiest Narragansett planters, reveals in his account book the prices that horses fetched. In 1753 he sold a three-year-old for £153, and the next year a thirteen-year-old bay "with a white nose" brought £70. In 1755 a "black trotting mare" brought only £55, but in 1763 a black mare sold for £244. In 1766 a "dark colour natural pacing horse with some white on his face" fetched the high price of fifty-five "Spanish milled dollars."[32] The breeders in Narragansett raised both Pacers and other mixed stock. The mixed breeds were mostly likely the least expensive horses, sent to power the sugar mills. The purebred Pacers were more expensive, used under saddle by the planters and their staff to cover ground quickly and smoothly.[33] In addition, a host of other people who lived in the sugar colonies also needed horses, including "Divines, Lawyers, Physicians, Gentlemen, Merchants, Factors and Tradesmen."[34]

Rhode Island's equine breeding and shipping business was directly linked to the rapid rise of the sugar industry from the latter half of the seventeenth century through the eighteenth. Rhode Island and the other northern colonies sent fish, foods, building supplies (such as timber, boards, and staves), cattle, and horses. In return they obtained sugar, molasses, rum, dyes, Spanish dollars, and bills of exchange from London.[35] By 1680 Rhode Island's governor John Sanford acknowledged to the lord of trade and plantations that "the principal matters which are exported among us is horses and provisions."[36] By 1700, after the Dutch and French colonies entered the sugar market, the demand for horses had increased still more.[37] Over the next twenty years the shipping of horses grew "sixfold," and horses were sent to Jamaica, Barbados, Nevis, Antigua, St. Christopher, Montserrat, and Suriname, among other places.[38] Writing in 1731, Governor Joseph Jencks noted that horses were of chief importance in Rhode Island's export market; he estimated there were at least ten vessels engaged in this trade with the West Indies alone.[39] Ten years later the number of vessels had grown to 102.[40] Narragansett's Reverend James MacSparren noted that "fine horses . . . are exported to all parts of English America."[41]

Until the mid-eighteenth century, it appears that Rhode Islanders could not keep up with the demand for their horses. As early as 1661, Felix Spoeri observed that Barbadian planters "have no livestock other than what is brought onto the island."[42] In the seventeenth century, English parliamentary leaders often heard from planters and merchants who had invested in sugar production in Barbados about their "great need of drawing horses . . . for the mills, without which a great quantity of sugar is likely to perish and bee lost, and for wante of grinding."[43] By the mid-1650s the never-ending struggle to secure an adequate supply of horses led planters to investigate windmills as an alternative technology for crushing their sugarcane.[44] But even after the number of windmills on the island increased by the 1730s, plantations kept teams of at least eight horses.[45] To compound the supply problem, the sugar colonies also needed horses for the militia. The anonymously published *The British Empire in America* (1732) described how for every one hundred acres of land a plantation had to supply the militia with one horse. The pamphlet averred that Barbados's equine power "was the principal Reason why the French durst not attack Barbadoes." However, if Rhode Islanders continued to supply horses to the French, this advantage would be lost, and the "Island will be lost along with it in the Case of a War."[46]

As the French and Dutch built up their sugar colonies, Rhode Island sought to meet their need for horses. The Brown family of Providence was involved in a wide range of commercial endeavors throughout the Atlantic world. Most notably, James Brown and his son Nicholas Brown were key players in shipping horses to the Dutch colony of Suriname. In the two years from 1764 to 1766, Nicholas Brown assembled a total of 255 horses from dealers and breeders around the area to ship to Suriname.[47] The Browns' letters to their business partners around the colony emphasize how keen they were to acquire horses to export. As James Brown wrote to Sall Cutler in 1739, "I beg . . . you would get me teen or a dusin Surnam horses . . . I hope that you will not fail me for I shall depend on you."[48] The Brown family had specific expectations. In 1737 James requested "some Horses that are in Case fitt for Shiping, that are worth between Seven & fourteen pounds, Mares will do if they are in good Case, they must be between three & . . . Eight years of Age."[49] The accounts contain repeated references to the need for "a score a small horsis" that are "fit to Go to sea" or "in good trim for shipping." The letters also contain many references to height, as the horses had to be small enough to turn the sugar mill: "PS. none of the horses to be more then fourteen hands high" and "not exceeding thirteen & a half hands high, or fourteen hands at the most." There are endless requests for horses that are "in good care," "free from lameness," "have two good eyes," and "have good teeth."[50] The weight of the horses was important too; in 1738 James requested "some Good fatt horsis," presumably because several months at sea would leave them lean.[51] The Browns were the only merchants who specifically referred to the horses as "Suriname horses" in their letters, account books, and newspaper advertisements. Other merchants typically referred to "shipping horses," "horses for a particular market," or occasionally "horses to be shipped to" the West Indies. As late as the 1780s, Griffin Green sought "shipping horses" for "a particular Market." Green's requirements that they be "young, active, of good Courage" were typical. However, it seems that Green wanted to send riding horses rather than cane-crushing horses, since the advertisement noted that the horses had to be "natural Pacers" with "little or no White in their Faces," most likely to avoid sunburn.[52]

The Browns repeatedly specified how much they were willing to pay. In 1765 Nicholas allowed "twelve dollars a piece" for "good Surinam horses."[53] In 1766 he declared "the price to be forty eight gallons New England rum for each horse."[54] In March 1765, Nicholas contracted with Isaac Tripp to purchase "Forty Horses . . . fitt for the Suranam Markkett." With hard money in short supply, he proposed to pay for the purchase in goods, including rum, sugar, molasses, and "one Negrow Garl."[55] To Nicholas the horses, humans, and commodities were all simply part of his trading empire. There was a clear sense of urgency and competition in the equine export business. For example, Nicholas explained to Tripp that he wanted the horses as soon as possible, "our vesel being ready much sooner than we expected & there being many other vesels who will get away before."[56] To meet the high demand for horses in Suriname, Nicholas Brown and Company advertised extensively in the *Providence Gazette* for "Surrinam Horses" to ship.[57]

Shipping Horses wanted.

Nicholas Brown,
and Company,
Want to buy immediately, a few likely Surinam HORSES.

Figure 6.1. Nicholas Brown's advertisement "Shipping Horses Wanted" in the *Providence Gazette*, January 29, 1763. By permission of America's Historical Newspapers, published by Readex (Readex.com), a division of NewsBank, Inc.

The Browns clearly saw no value in keeping the horses or selling them in Rhode Island. Nicholas Brown wrote to Frank and Evan Malbone in November 1765 that "our Brigg George" has already sailed and "we have . . . thirty Surinam horses . . . we have no particular use for them at present and you . . . proposd sending a sloop for Surinam about the last of this month." Nicholas then offered Frank and Evan the horses for the price he had paid, twelve dollars a head. He assured them that the horses were "very good horses for that market" and that several "indifferent persons" reckoned they would fetch double the price of a rival group that had just sailed to Suriname on a competitor's vessel.[58]

Even though the Browns and their colleagues were experienced at sourcing horses to ship to the sugar colonies, they were not immune to rogue dealers. James wrote warily in 1736, "I have been informed that you did not tell me the truth about that little horse and I depended upon your word about the Age of him, you told me he was but Six years old. . . . but [if] that Horse is above Eight years old I will not have him."[59] The Browns did not like to ship horses out of Rhode Island during the cold and treacherous winter months, and, like many other merchants, they kept the horses in Rhode Island during the winter and shipped them in the spring. Nicholas kept horses in Narragansett during the winter of 1765–66 with a view to shipping them to Suriname in March or April. During that winter, he loaned out several horses to work on farms in Narragansett on condition that if they died they would be paid for.[60] The horses that were not loaned out were sent to South Kingstown to stay on the Robinson plantation, with explicit instructions: "We expect them well kept so that they will get fat by spring."[61] On December 20, however, Rowland Robinson Jr. informed Brown that many his horses had died.[62] Robinson estimated that the horses were at least thirty-five years old. He promised to "take all the pains I can to keep them alive but it is my opinion they will all die" unless housed and fed grain, which would greatly increase the livery cost. Robinson concluded that even if the horses survived, he would not give Nicholas "a dollar a head . . . I shall expect to be paid for each horse till he dyths."[63] Nicholas replied, requesting that Robinson do his "utmost in every respect . . . to preserve there lives" so he could still ship them, though he acknowledged he had been "most shockingly deceav'd" as their grinders were worn out.[64] Early modern horsemanship manuals, such as *The Smithfield Jockey*, document the ways horse dealers duped potential customers.[65] Philip Astley's *The Modern Riding Master*, published in 1776, discusses at length how "the Country Dealers, by pulling out two Teeth, and cutting the Gums, make [horses] appear older [or younger] than they really are."[66] Another pamphlet, the *Gentlemans Complete Jockey* (1700), shows how to "fatten a lean horse in a short time" but acknowledged that if "he is very old it will not work."[67]

While the Browns concentrated on the Suriname market, Newport merchant Godfrey Malbone shipped horses to all corners of the Atlantic world including the West Indies, St. Lucia, Antigua, Jamaica, the Leeward Islands, St. Christopher, Nevis, and Suriname. Over the nine years from 1729 to 1738, Malbone sent eighty-four ships throughout the Atlantic carrying 1,601 horses. Most went to Jamaica (17 in total), followed closely by 15 to Barbados. The price paid for each horse varied widely, from as little as £5 to as much as £65, with most fetching from £12 to £20. The first entry in Malbone's account book meticulously recorded the color of each horse, but almost every subsequent entry simply lists the number of horses shipped and their price.[68]

Malbone's account books also record the expenses he incurred for horses over a nine-year period, including how much he paid his agents in Rhode Island for sourcing horses. In 1733 he paid Nathaniel Sheffield £20 for buying twenty horses to ship to the Leeward Islands.[69] In addition, Malbone's accounting offers a rare glimpse into what the horses were fed on voyages, listing the exact amount of hay and bushels of Indian corn, oats, and bran allocated on board the ships. He even recorded the price of new and used water tanks for the journey and how much livery he paid to keep the horses while waiting to ship them. In March 1729, for example, he paid a total of £496.10 for twenty-one horses to ship to Antigua, then spent £20 more to keep them before their voyage.[70] Most entries also list how much he paid to mark or brand the horses and the cost of transporting them to the ship.

Although Malbone also shipped plantation supplies to the sugar colonies, horses were at the heart of his trade. By contrast, Newport merchant John Banister was a global trader for whom horses were a much smaller part of his empire. While both Banister and Malbone traded in slaves, Banister's trade catered to the consumer revolution by providing New Englanders with a range of goods from around the globe. Banister's entries regarding horses are scattered. For example, in November 1747 he shipped nine horses costing £638 to Jamaica.[71] The following May he shipped to Jamaica eleven more horses costing £1,150.[72] Most likely these two groups were the "general" horses destined to crush sugarcane in the mills. Banister and the people he did business with distinguished between horses intended for the mills, for saddle, and for coaching. In October 1749 Banister shipped "A pair of Brown Stallions" costing £452, to be used as a coaching pair, and a "Bald face Gelding" for riding for £362.[73]

Horses in the Sugar Colonies

Merchants like Banister took a significant risk when they shipped horses, since not all arrived safely. Newport merchant Aaron Lopez lost three horses en route to Jamaica in 1767 owing to inclement weather, and the eight that did land were "in bad order, poor and much brused."[74] Newspapers from around the Atlantic contain endless reports of entire shipments of horses wiped out by ferocious weather. In addition, pirates interrupted the Atlantic horse trade. A report in the *Boston News-Letter* in 1716 noted that a sloop bound for Suriname had lost its horses, since "There is Pyrate in those parts between Porto Rico and Salteruda, of 130 men."[75]

Many of the horses that made it there toiled crushing sugarcane. In the mills the horses were harnessed to long poles that turned a shaft rotating three upright iron-clad rollers in the center of the platform. Typical is John Oldmixon's description of a "horse mill" from 1741: "Horses . . . being put to the tackle, go about, and turn by sweeps the middle Roller: which being cogged to turn others at the upper end, turn them about." Richard Ligon described how animals supplied the power in Barbados, harnessed to "sweeps" that were connected to the middle roller: "Being Cog'd to the two, at both ends, turne them about; and they are three, turning upon their Centres, which are of Brass and Steel." The horses toiled alongside the slaves, as "Negre puts in the Canes of one side, and the rollers draw them through to the other side, where another Negre stands, and receives them, and returns them back on the other side of the middle roller, which draws the other way."[76]

Other animals such as oxen and mules were sometimes used to turn the sugar mill.[77] Each animal had its pros and cons: oxen were strong, but they were slow, were relatively expensive, and did not thrive in hot climates. Mules were also expensive and hard to come by, but they were stronger and did not succumb as easily to harsh treatment. Horses were cheaper but weaker, and they often died in such numbers that plantations used up several teams a year. Figure 6.2 shows an idealized horse mill in action, and

Figure 6.2. Horses operating the sugarcane crushing mill: *Comble de Moulin* (1724). By permission of Manuscripts and Archives Division, the New York Public Library, Astor, Lenox, and Tilden Foundations.

the horses are depicted as powerful, graceful, and healthy to show the sugar mill as an efficient piece of machinery and entice planters. While the illustrations in promotional tracts did not show the reality of weak and broken horses, other written sources provide a glimpse of the horrors. According to Governor Jan Nepveu, it was not unusual for an estate in Suriname to lose fifty to sixty horses a year.[78] Planters almost always overworked animals, making them vulnerable to disease.[79] When he visited Barbados in 1655, Henry Whistler noted that the sugar mills "destroy so many horses that it begors the planters."[80] In Suriname, John Gabriel Stedman observed that most of the horses died from overwork. On occasion, horses were also killed by wild animals such as the "jaguar of Guiana. . . . [that] frequently kill on plantations; and though they cannot carry [the horse] . . . off into the forest on account of their weight, they tear and mangle them in a dreadful manner, only for the sake of their blood."[81] Other accounts reveal how horses were abused by slaves as a form of sabotage. Indeed, slaves primarily cared for the horses and were perfectly positioned to add to the already high mortality rates.[82] Ligon noted that in Barbados slaves "never got any meat unless cattle or horses died." Therefore, "if any horse [died] then the whole bodies of them were distributed amongst the Negroes, and they thought a high feast, with which never poor souls were more contented."[83]

In the sugar colonies horses were rarely used to transport goods, and by the mid-seventeenth century Barbadian planters used asinegoes (small donkeys from the Azores) because they could carry nearly two hundred pounds through deep gullies and narrow forest passages. Richard Ligon noted that asinegoes were "of great use in the Island in carrying our sugar down to the bridge." Horses did not do well with the gullies, which were deep and full of roots: if they fell they labored to get up again, unlike the asinegoes, which could "pick and choose their way."[84]

Decline of Rhode Island's Horse Trade

In the 1720s and 1730s Britain became increasingly angry that Rhode Islanders did not give preference to the British colonies. The British Parliament felt that Rhode Island's horse trade "greatly enriched" the French sugar colonies, while the British sugar islands were "impoverished."[85] In 1730 the House of Commons heard Sir John Rushout's report, "Colonial Trade [and] His Majesty's Sugar Colonies in America." The report railed against the French colonies for selling molasses to New Englanders at a cheaper rate that disadvantaged the British sugar colonies. To add insult to injury, the French themselves had little use for molasses, viewing it as a waste product to give to "their Horses and Hogs." The report provided evidence of the trade from around the Atlantic. In Martinique, at least sixteen vessels from New England docked "loaded with Horses . . . which were sold," and in return they got "Molasses and Rum . . . but chiefly Molasses." The report concluded that the New England horse trade was critical to French success in the sugar industry, as they "can't be supplied with Horses . . . from any other Place . . . the Navigation of Canada being so difficult and dangerous; nor can they carry on their Sugar Works without them." Consequently, this trade "greatly increased the Price of both at our English Sugar Colonies, where all the Horses . . . they can supply them with, may be disposed of."[86]

Parliament heard both sides, and some felt that the "French colony at Canada" could easily "with a very little encouragement" furnish the French sugar islands with horses.[87] The anonymously published pamphlet *The British Empire in America, Consider'd . . . from a Gentleman of Barbadoes, to His Friend in London* (1732) explored the issue at length.[88] The pamphlet asserted that without Rhode Island horses both the French and the Dutch sugar colonies would suffer. He noted that the Dutch had no spare horses and pointed out that they would not trade with a "Foreigner" unless he imported "a certain Number of Horses in Proportion to the Burthen of his Vessel." The author also felt that Spain would not help, since while Spain had mules on the Continent, it was "hardly more than sufficient for their own Service, and they set a very great Value on them, much more than they do on Horses." Moreover, the planters in Barbados would "gladly prefer" mules to "the Horses of New England" if they could they get them "upon any reasonable Terms." The author added that there had been no more than six mules in Barbados for the past thirty years, while there had always been at least six thousand horses at any one time.[89] The author also averred that horses were important for military reasons, and without this advantage, Barbados would fall to the French.[90]

With this in mind, King George II passed the Molasses Act of 1733, which put prohibitive duties on molasses, rum, and sugar imported into Great Britain's American mainland colonies from non-British colonies. The 1733 act was only laxly enforced, and customs bureaucracy allowed colonial commerce to continue without reprisal. Rhode Islanders even smuggled horses to the French during the Seven Years' War through neutral Dutch and Spanish ports.[91] This all changed when the Seven Years' War ended in 1763. Although Britain and her allies triumphed, victory came at the price of considerable debt. Britain thought her American colonies needed to pay their share, especially since Britain had removed the French from North America. Looking for ways to raise revenue, King George III and George Grenville, his lord of the treasury and chancellor of the exchequer, decided that taxing sugar would help raise the necessary money. Since the laxly enforced Molasses Act of 1733 was just about to expire, Britain debated renewing the act and enforcing it with more vigor.

Rhode Islanders were vehemently opposed to this plan, meeting in South Kingstown on January 24, 1764, to discuss the state of affairs.[92] They tried to play down the importance of their trade in horses with the French, noting that the only articles "furnished by the colony for exportation, are some lumber, cheese, and horses." The horses, they noted, were for "luxury" purposes and were not of any "real use" in the plantations. In contrast to British parliamentary reports, Rhode Islanders stressed that the French could easily be supplied with mules and horses by the Spanish and sought to prove both that Great Britain would easily remain in possession "of the profit and advantage arising from the article of sugar" and that the law would be "highly injurious to the interests both of Great Britain, and these northern colonies."[93] These pleas were ignored, and Britain passed the Sugar Act in April 1764.

This more effective tariff collected more revenue than any other duty over the next decade. By lowering the levy on molasses from sixpence to threepence per gallon, moreover, molasses became less profitable to smuggle. In many ways this was the beginning of the end of Rhode Island's Atlantic horse trade. Acts of Parliament, wars, competition and rivalry between sugar-producing colonies shifted the direction of the larger trade network of which horses were a part. In 1767 Isaac Pereira Mendes informed Newport merchant Aaron Lopez of some bad news from Jamaica. Unable to sell his horses in Kingston at the £15 price Lopez had set because of the quality and quantity of other horses available, he had been forced to send them to the countryside to be sold.[94] In 1769 Benjamin Wright wrote to Lopez with more bad news: describing the sugar market as "very dull," he feared it would "not be better this Crop." Wright advised Lopez to explore the idea of sending horses to Antigua in the future. Things were made worse because Captain Nichols's vessel had arrived from Connecticut with forty horses six days before, which was a "great Determent to the Sale of your Horses."[95]

In the wake of the 1764 act, some Rhode Islanders decided they should carry on their economic enterprises closer to home. In 1767 an anonymous writer to the *Providence Gazette* exhorted Rhode Island to focus on its domestic market and move away from shipping goods out of the colonies, since "we have too much trade. . . . We are rich within ourselves." The writer noted how a considerable part of "Rhode Island's produce perishes between here and Surinam" and discussed at length how the "prodigious number of horses thrown overboard, in hard gales of wind, is so much loss to the country, we having no return for them. The same hay and grazing that would be sufficient for a horse, would rear two horn cattle."[96] Others had different ideas, and by the end of 1763 merchants, farmers, and breeders sought to revive an interest in horse breeding, most notably of Narragansett Pacers. The following advertisement appeared in the *Newport Mercury* on March 28, 1763:

> Whereas the best Horses of this Colony have been sent off from Time to Time to the West Indies and elsewhere by which the Breed is much dwindled, to the great Detriment of both Merchant and Farmer; therefore, a number of public-spirited Gentlemen of Newport, for the Good of the Colony, and to encourage the Farmers to breed better Horses for the future, have collected a Purse of ONE HUNDRED DOLLARDS to be Run on Thursday, the Fifth of May next, on Easton's Beech, free for any Horse Mare or Gelding bred in the Colony.[97]

Sadly, there were only three starters, and the winner belonged to Samuel Gardiner of South Kingstown.[98]

When Cuban planters began to cultivate sugar extensively, they too sought out Narragansett Pacers.[99] In the years 1771 and 1774, according to the record of the Secretary of Customs in London, the British islands imported 7,130 horses from North America.[100] The trade with the French islands, however, fell off considerably because of the new Molasses Act.[101] When the British occupied Newport during the American Revolutionary War, they upset America's trade in a host of commodities. During the Revolution the sugar islands were forced to work with their own resources, and they began to raise their own horses. In many places water power was substituted for horse power. At the same time, there was less pasture available in New England, and with the cultivation of new land, horse breeding there was substantially reduced.[102] As roads improved in New England, travel by saddle horse decreased and carriages became common.[103] Their unique movement, which made them so desirable under saddle, made Narragansett Pacers unsuitable as carriage horses. As early as the 1760s, Rhode Islanders, like others in New England, sought a more versatile horse. One 1763 buyer advertised in the *Providence Gazette* for a "Likely Horse" that "will both trot and pace," that was "easy in the Saddle" but would also "go in a Chair."[104]

Rhode Island's trade in sending horses to the sugar colonies did not die overnight. Through the 1780s the *Providence Gazette* printed advertisements seeking "good shipping horses."[105] As late as 1801 Benjamin and Edward Aborn advertised in he *Providence Journal* for "20 or 30 Horses . . . for Surinam, or the Winward-Islands."[106] By the 1790s, Connecticut had eclipsed Rhode Island as New England's hub of horse breeding and export. By 1820, when Charles Henry Hall, Esq., addressed the Windham County Agricultural Society in Connecticut, he lamented that "there was a time, when New England could boast of a race of Horses equal in most respects to those of any country." The "true Narraganset Horse was a most noble animal" that had been lost by "want of care and circumspection." Hall blamed crossing the pure breed with "the Arabian stallion" in the 1770s and "finally by degrees, one by one, the whole race disappeared, not leaving a solitary cross blood to procure the species."[107] The breed was slowly dying out, and in 1823 one solitary "Naraganset breed Mare" was offered as part of an estate sale in Connecticut.[108] In the same year, the *Common Place Book of a Gentleman* acknowledged that the "Narraganset breed" was "nearly extinguished."[109] As late as 1826 breeders in Hartford sought to revive the breed, and "Sachem A Narragansett Pacer" stood at stud. The breeders, J. Ramsay and H. Kirkham, stated that their purpose was "reviving that most valuable breed of Horse, so esteemed for their extraordinary performance under saddle." To demonstrate that he was true to the breed, they publicized that Sachem was "dark brown, of moderate size, well made, and for strength and speed has few equals."[110]

Ultimately, the way horses were used and traded was shaped by technological developments, politics, trade, and warfare. The Narragansett Pacer emerged in response to a specific set of circumstances, and when those

Figure 6.3. Ernest Hamlin Baker, *The Economic Activities of the Narragansett Planters.* Courtesy of the United States Postal Service and South Country History Center.

circumstances changed in the nineteenth century, the breed faded out and new and more versatile types of horses emerged. Although the Narragansett Pacer may be gone, it is not forgotten. The Pacer has influenced a range of modern breeds, including the Standardbred, the Tennessee Walking Horse, the Canadian Pacer, and the American Saddlebred. The Pacer's story also has a lasting legacy thanks to Franklin Delano Roosevelt's New Deal, through which the Treasury Department's Section of Painting and Sculpture commissioned a mural by Ernest Hamlin Baker. Titled *The Economic Activities of the Narragansett Planters*, the mural hung in the Wakefield, Rhode Island, post office from its completion in 1939 until 1999 (fig. 6.3). It is now on display at the Pettaquamscutt Historical Society, where it was moved in 2003 after the post office closed. As the title suggests, the mural captures the area's slave-dependent economy in the eighteenth century. It also provides a reminder of the Narragansett Pacer's importance to Rhode Island and the wider Atlantic world.

SEVEN

Narratives of Race and Racehorses in the Art of Edward Troye

JESSICA DALLOW

Horses often inhabited privileged places on nineteenth-century farms and plantations because of their stamina, speed, and choice bloodlines. In turn they required specialized handling and care. In the antebellum South, slaves performed those duties. These men did everything including feeding, mucking stables, grooming, breaking, breeding, scouting horseflesh, exercising, jockeying, and determining conditioning programs and racing schedules. In his 1884 memoir, Charles Stewart, a former slave who worked with Thoroughbred racehorses his entire life, describes his surprise in finding two boys to every horse at his first post in Virginia.[1] Stewart's Jim Crow–era story is published in dialect and suffused with deferential language praising his former masters. His narrative nevertheless offers a rare glimpse into an enslaved horseman's life, detailing his rise from lowly exercise boy to jockey to respected trainer and stallion man.[2] Fifty-two years earlier, Edward Troye (1808–74) portrayed Charles Stewart in one of the artist's earliest portraits, *Medley and Groom* (1832, fig. 7.1). Troye met Stewart, a slave owned by eminent Virginia turfman William Ransom Johnson, during the summer of 1832 at Carleton, the Pennsylvania farm of Troye's patron John Charles Craig. Stewart had brought Medley, Johnson's Thoroughbred stallion, to Carleton to stand at stud.[3] Of Swiss birth, Troye came to the United States from England in 1831. He quickly found a niche in the growing market for animal portraiture. His greatest patrons were pre–Civil War southerners active in the Thoroughbred racing and breeding centers that emerged first in Virginia and the Carolinas, then in Kentucky, Tennessee, and the Deep South.[4] Troye had relied on English models, picturing horses alone and with attendants, but he adapted his paintings to suit his context, replacing English servants and professional jockeys with enslaved African American grooms and riders. In *Medley and Groom*, Stewart cuts an

Figure 7.1. Edward Troye, *Medley and Groom*, 1832. Oil on canvas. Private collection. From Genevieve Baird Lacer, *Edward Troye: Painter of Thoroughbred Stories* (Prospect, KY: Harmony House, 2006), 157.

elegant figure, exemplifying how the artist's paintings of black hostlers provide an important visual record of the labor and expertise that built and maintained the sport of American Thoroughbred horseracing. Yet Stewart's presence alongside the horse articulates the industry's schema of power and privilege, where horses and human beings are valuable commodities. Troye's portraits are thus ambivalent, conflicting images that simultaneously distinguish their enslaved subjects and reinforce a deeply entrenched racial order.

Recent scholarship has shed light on the history of African American horsemen in American racing, focusing on how deeply slavery was enmeshed in the development of the industry.[5] Katherine C. Mooney's marvelous *Race Horse Men: How Slavery and Freedom Were Made at the Racetrack* offers a fascinating picture of Thoroughbred racing's racial dimensions,[6] building on earlier histories like Edward Hotaling's *The Great Black Jockeys*.[7] Hotaling sought to recognize and pay homage to these men's existence; Mooney emphasizes how their competence and privilege functioned within the system to preserve, rather than disrupt, slavery's power and resilience. Troye's paintings are often interpreted as transparent illustrations of his patrons' worldview of racial harmony: idylls of fast blooded horses maintained by skilled slave labor.[8] Elsewhere I have made a case for understanding Troye's portraits of both horses and human beings as ambiguous, multivalent images.[9] This chapter examines how Troye's compositions of Thoroughbred racehorses and enslaved attendants enact reciprocal relationships between human and animal so that each is always understood through the other. I focus on three of the paintings Troye created early in his career that feature African American hostlers: *Medley and Groom* (1832), *Trifle* (also 1832), and *Tobbaconist* (1833). I argue that these paintings reveal how the circumstances of the antebellum southern horse industry, with its largely black, slave labor force, express a unique equestrian culture around the American Thoroughbred horse.

Troye's Paintings of African American Hostlers

Troye tackled many compositional types during his career: horses alone, broodmares with foals, attendants holding horses, jockeys astride, and multifigure human and horse combinations.[10] On occasion he supplemented his equine business with portraits of cattle and sheep as well as of humans. His horse portraits hung in his patrons' homes; with the rise of the sporting presses in the 1830s, they also appeared as engravings in periodicals to illustrate racing reports and equine biographies. Troye's experimenting with various human-horse combinations in the 1830s with and without formal commissions reflects his desire to establish his reputation and build a clientele. He may have painted *Medley and Groom* for Medley's owner, Johnson, or to show to prospective clients. The *American Turf Register and Sporting Magazine* featured an engraving of it in its May 1833 issue.[11] Thus, while this painting clearly expresses the system of southern antebellum racing where purebred horses were owned by white slaveholders and trained and ridden by enslaved black men, its audiences included both southern and northern readers of the racing press. These readers would recognize in it a generalized depiction of a racehorse and groom and a specific depiction of the racing industry's regional differences. In the South, African American slaves filled groom and jockey positions; in the North, other ethnic minorities often did.[12]

Troye's portrait of the mare Trifle (1832, fig. 7.2) created at Craig's Carleton farm the same summer as *Medley and Groom*, includes both William Alexander, an enslaved African American trainer, and the red-haired Wil-

Figure 7.2. Edward Troye, *Trifle*, 1832. Oil on canvas. Collection of Kirk and Palmer Ragsdale, Rockwall, Texas. From Genevieve Baird Lacer, *Edward Troye: Painter of Thoroughbred Stories* (Prospect, KY: Harmony House, 2006), 164.

lis, an Irish jockey. *Trifle's* owner remains a mystery, in part because of the convoluted network of people involved with the horse. Craig had recently purchased Trifle from Virginian J. Miles Selden at a Virginia racecourse where Craig's sometime partner, Johnson, kept a training stable. Standing only fourteen hands three inches, Trifle won an astounding twenty races out of twenty-four starts in her four-year career, most at four-mile heats. Willis's blue silks are Johnson's racing colors.[13] Selden often acted as Johnson's deputy when Johnson could not be present at a race. Selden owned the trainer Alexander, who wears the artificial and alienating antebellum trainer's uniform worn at races: beaver top hat, white shirt, bright vest, velveteen trousers, and tailcoat. Alexander would have traveled with Trifle to Carleton, where she had gone to rest after the spring racing season. Reliable slave hostlers like Stewart and Alexander were privileged to cross state lines and, with slave jockeys, frequented farms and tracks throughout the country. Therefore, it is likely that Craig owned the horse but raced her under Johnson's colors and kept her at Selden's stables where Alexander trained.

Troye's portrait of *Trifle* thus portrays a horse owned by a northern patron, ridden by an Irish jockey, and trained by a southern slave, reinforcing both the racial and social organization of an industry comprising elite owners and breeders, profit-seeking turfmen, and paid and slave minority laborers who mingled at tracks and stables throughout the United States.

Tobacconist (1833, fig. 7.3) is a more straightforward picture in that it was one of four equine portraits created in Virginia for southern politician and racing man John Minor Botts. It depicts a horse in top physical form, with well-muscled rump and strong back, standing with neck outstretched, having recently won an important race that fall.[14] Botts's slave jockey Ben, who appears because he was allegedly Botts's favorite, wears dark-colored silks and red stockings.[15] He holds the horse, ready to mount as soon as trainer Manuel saddles him. Manuel wears a trainer's more casual costume of trousers and yellow-backed vest, his shirtsleeves rolled up to reveal muscular forearms. Like Alexander and Willis in *Trifle*, Ben and Manuel both turn and gaze outward to contemplate the viewers looking at them. Troye

Figure 7.3. Edward Troye, *Tobacconist, with Botts' Manuel and Botts' Ben*, 1833. Oil on canvas. Virginia Museum of Fine Arts, Richmond, Virginia. Paul Mellon Collection. Photo: Katherine Welzel.

painted two other notable canvases in 1834 that include black trainers for southern patrons: *Richard Singleton* for Kentuckian Willa Viley and *Bertrand* for South Carolinian John Spann.

In subsequent decades Troye turned away from multifigure groups. When he did include enslaved African Americans it was as jockeys, standing alongside horses or mounted, to mark important races. This was the case in *Wagner* with Cato (1839, National Museum of Racing and Hall of Fame) or *Planet* with Jesse (1858, private collection). Cato became well known throughout the racing world, riding Wagner to win an 1839 match race against Grey Eagle, and his name appears throughout period sporting journals. Less is known about Jesse. He rode for Virginian Thomas W. Doswell at his Bullfield Plantation and is pictured in Bullfield's orange colors atop Planet, a horse out of Nina, Doswell's beloved former racing broodmare. Planet and Jesse won many races, with the exception of a notorious, hotly contested match against Albine in 1861.[16] Troye does not attempt another sophisticated horse-trainer-groom-jockey canvas like those from the 1830s until 1864, near the end of the Civil War. For his Kentucky patron and friend Robert Aitcheson Alexander, Troye pictured Asteroid, son of the great racing stallion Lexington, being prepared for a race by trainer Ansel Williamson, jockey Edward Brown, and an anonymous groom (1864, Virginia Museum of Fine Arts). *Asteroid* is unique in that it shows a group of Confederate soldiers in the background to represent the raid on Alexander's Woodburn farm by Confederate marauders. Though Asteroid was stolen, he was eventually returned to Woodburn to resume his racing and breeding career.[17]

Why did Troye create these multifigure paintings featuring so many African American slave hostlers in the beginning of his career? Creating multifigure compositions was a means of advertising his skills as on a par with the best English sporting artists like George Stubbs and Edwin Landseer who, Alex Potts notes, had transformed animal art from an "off-shoot of still life or portrait painting" into a more dramatic, charged historical genre that was now recognized and respected as a serious form of art.[18] Troye's early pictures reveal an especially strong debt to Stubbs, not only in the handling of his horses' colors and forms, but in his careful portrayals of grooms, jockeys, and trainers who are "studied presences, about whose features, clothing, and posture the artist has taken minute care."[19] His painting of Asteroid in the last decade of his life can be understood as Troye's final gesture to the grand canvases of Stubbs, and Asteroid exemplifies both victorious racehorse and gallant Civil War hero.[20] That he painted mainly African American enslaved hostlers with horses indicates that he catered to a growing market comprising members of the southern slaveholding racing elite who, like Botts, likely asked him to include their slave trainers, grooms, and jockeys. Building his career in the 1830s, Troye was thrown into the world of racing. He often stayed in his southern patrons' homes and assumed a fashionable artist persona in the tradition of his fellow English artists, who became members of the sporting communities they painted or companions to their squire patrons.[21] Before arriving in the United States, Troye first traveled to Jamaica, and if his obituary is true, became acquainted with livestock and blacks under bondage in his brief stint as an estate manager.[22] His ensuing travels in the southern states where his chief patrons lived and raced their horses made him more familiar with the system. While Troye's views of slavery remain unknown,[23] his pictures of enslaved hostlers obliged his patrons with images, Mooney has argued, of an allegedly just, smooth-running system of black labor serving white economic interests.[24]

In this reading, Troye's images also appear to support theories of scientific racism, emphasizing the inherent inferiority and animal nature of a race of people, which circulated as justifications for slavery by pro-slavery apologists in the years before the Civil War. Texts such as John Campbell's odious *Negro-Mania: Being an Examination of the Falsely Assumed Equality of the Various Races of Man* (1851) encapsulate these theories. Using various writers of the period—including statesman Thomas Jefferson, physician Johann Friedrich Blumenbach, naturalist Robert Knox, and rabid pro-slavery politician and planter James Henry Hammond—Campbell validates polygenesis, professes the inferiority of blacks, and justifies the existence of slavery.[25] His choice of writers also highlights how animal models served scientific racism, like Peter Browne's taxonomy, which classified sheep hair to determine that "sheep breeders should never cross" woolly sheep with hairy sheep and which arranged human hair "into three species of mankind based on race."[26] Early modern physiognomy and naturalism had long made correlations between animals and humans, as with artist Charles LeBrun's studies that drew analogies between animal and human facial features. Knox's *Races of Men* (1850) used similar illustrations to show how the facial features of Africans related more closely to apes.[27] *Negro-Mania* resonated with southerners like J. T., who, in his review of the book, deemed "the animal [a word he uses interchangeably with 'negro'] inferior." His only "hope for redemption is under the mastery of the Caucasian. . . . The negro is a slave to the Caucasian for the same reason that the horse, the ox, and the ass are subject to him—because of natural, unalterable, and eternal inferiority."[28]

Such an equation between man and beast is indeed part and parcel of

Troye's paintings. Yet Troye's paintings also create fissures in this equation by portraying enslaved hostlers who possessed a degree of agency in shaping their lives and sometimes even in redefining their status as enslaved versus free. Further, Troye's audiences varied, including those national readers of the sporting presses in which engravings of paintings like *Medley and Groom* and *Wagner* (with jockey Cato) appeared. As debates about slavery simmered on the national stage, Troye may have become increasingly attentive to the reception of his multifigure compositions showing black men with elite Thoroughbred horses in plantationlike landscape settings. Consequently, as his career flourished, he responded to the growing needs of a market for more paintings of horses and jockeys to herald notable races, and of horses alone that served the Thoroughbred industry's new initiative to visually record its pedigreed stock. In doing so, he turned away from subject matter that might prove untenable in an increasingly volatile political landscape.

Nature Culture Human Horse

Troye typically locates his animal and human figures in the foreground of his pictures within a landscape setting, suggesting their relation to nature. In *Tobacconist* he sets the animal against a leafy backdrop and frames him with nearly barren tree trunks. Autumn colors of reddish brown, moss green, and forest green, juxtaposed with the gray bark of a shedding tree, evoke Virginia in late October, when Troye painted the horse. Troye's leafless trees also balance the horse's form, their sharp verticals anchoring a horizontal swath of glimmering deep bay coat. Towering gangly trees align with human figures in *Medley and Groom* and *Trifle*, mirroring the lines of handler Stewart's right leg and jockey Willis's back. *Trifle*, created during summer rather than fall, uses lighter color combinations of sunny yellows, khakis, and pastel blues and greens for its landscape elements. In contrast, *Medley and Groom* portrays a darker summer landscape—perhaps at dusk or dawn—with the horse and Stewart surrounded by a dense, verdant forest.

Throughout these compositions, animals and humans coexist harmoniously in nature. In *Medley and Groom*, Stewart even appears like the animal (an often-used manifestation of nature) he attends. He stands gracefully at the horse's head, the sinuous curve of his left arm balancing his right leg as he steps slightly forward, raising his hand to Medley's bridle. His hair is longish, brushed back from his forehead, and he wears a thin mustache and goatee that emphasize his angular face. His reddish lips complement his skin tone and pick up the red browband of Medley's bridle. His white sleeves and collar match the horse's color as well and balance the bright white expanse of the animal's body that fills so much of the picture. Ian Finseth describes compositions of African Americans in natural settings as "racial landscapes," which invite viewers to analyze racial meanings encoded in natural iconographies.[29] With an industrious slave tending an animal amid a lush setting, Troye's composition resembles a plantation idyll, with those allegedly closest to nature—animals and slaves—existing comfortably within it.

Stewart, however, cultivates Medley into a cultural or social being, a racehorse and breeding stallion, who thus also belongs to the world of the white barn that appears in the right of the canvas. In *Tobacconist* and *Trifle*, human figures do more than stand alongside their horses: they engage in productive activity. As Kirk Savage has argued, to depict slaves performing skilled, meaningful work in visual imagery was problematic to slaveholding audiences because it asserted their creative and intellectual capacities.[30] However, because they train the horses for leisure and gambling—an activity usually off-limits to African Americans—their work involves a "speculative economy whose rewards lie beyond their reach."[31] The fence, which Troye deploys as a compositional tool to draw attention to his main subjects, does more than separate them from the landscape background, Finseth argues; it also isolates the hostlers, containing them within a sociocultural realm apart from the dominant white culture.[32] In becoming cultural agents, they are nevertheless segregated, marginalized, and subjugated. Such precarious positions, neither fully inside culture nor outside nature, propel Troye's human figures literally and metaphorically back toward the horses. Horses occupied a privileged position in the animal kingdom during the eighteenth and nineteenth centuries precisely because of their proximity to man as well as their unique capacity for domestication. This made them especially charged mediators between nature and culture.[33]

Karl Jacoby observes that antebellum Americans, both black and white, drew recurrent parallels between the status of domestic animals and of slaves.[34] It is well known that under chattel slavery in the United States and West Indian colonies, the term stock was used interchangeably for both livestock and slaves. Philip D. Morgan, in his work on Jamaican stockpens and plantations, stresses how white attitudes toward animals were linked to attitudes toward slaves. Whether "harsh or compassionate, distanced or intimate, the implications for slaves seem almost always to have been negative."[35] Whites charged that slaves ate voraciously, were sexually promiscuous, smelled, and wore little clothing.[36] If he wasn't already familiar with them, Troye's time in Jamaica surely acquainted him with such attitudes that he then saw reproduced in the American South. Slave narratives also use animal metaphors to describe lives under bondage. Slaves, Mia Bay argues, knew little of contemporary ethnology or racial theories of polygenesis that whites used to perpetuate racism and subjugate blacks. They cared little about "black intellectuals' anxieties about being mistaken for monkeys and apes," animals unfamiliar to them. Instead, their worries revolved around domestic animals they did know: the pigs, mules, horses, and dogs that whites identified them with in order to dehumanize them.[37] Whites repeatedly describe how children and adults slept on the floor like hogs and ate out of troughs like pigs. Whites worked them, knocked and kicked them around like mules, stripped them naked, and whipped them like horses.[38] They branded them and cut notches into their ears.[39] And, of course, they sold them like stock, driving them to auction like oxen or cattle.[40] Charles Ball, caught cooking a stolen sheep, describes being hung from a post and beaten: "I felt my flesh quiver like that of animals that have been slaughtered by the butcher and are flayed whilst yet half alive."[41] Like animals, they could as easily be reduced to dead flesh.[42] According to Bay, former slaves' extensive use of animal comparisons to express their treatment shows that slaves "looked to the barnyard, rather than to the patriarchal family, to find other living creatures in their plantation world whose subjugation resembled their own."[43]

When slaves and former slaves described being compared to horses, they usually meant workhorses, the lowly livestock they toiled alongside. But because horses appeared everywhere, in agricultural fields, on open roads, in training stables, on racecourses, and in cities, they operated within the landscape of slavery in more varied ways. Slaves became well attuned to the use of horses for policing fields and hunting escaped slaves, the slaveholder on horseback visually commanding the landscape.[44] For the men in Troye's paintings, horses could symbolize the master's control. Yet they too could observe how good horseflesh could make social standing. Riding a handsome horse, owning a winning racehorse, or driving an animated team signaled wealth and power. From the early eighteenth century forward, sporting art put such practices on display and became a powerful material means of uniting horseflesh and (white) human privilege. Troye's paintings operate in this way to glorify his patrons, the owners of special horses, and to validate their participation in an elite pastime known as the "sport of kings." They also, however, picture animals that, for the enslaved men caring for them, functioned as both forces of control and potential tools of mobility that might elevate their standing within a highly circumscribed world or perhaps even take them beyond it.

Thoroughbreds were the most valuable of horses during the first half of the nineteenth century, already selling for thousands of dollars. The *American Turf Register*'s 1833 description of Medley, published alongside the engraving after Troye's painting of Medley and Stewart, noted that although the engravers failed to do justice to Troye's original, they successfully captured the "buoyant bearing and self complacent expression of highly pampered animal."[45] Medley, it seems, was used to being cosseted. His very nature ordained quality care, but so too did the fact that owners made sizable investments in horseflesh, which would "mean nothing if the animals were not well trained and ridden."

While slaves were not "precisely 'bred' for the race course,"[46] owners often selected them because of physique or demonstrable skill to undergo a lengthy apprenticeship with experts, like the one described by the *American Turf Register*:

> Worthy of Regard—William Alexander. A very judicious and worthy man, reared in the stables of Col. W. R. Johnson, and a first rate trainer, who finished off the "Trifle" that won the Jockey Club purse at the Central Course [Baltimore], is now, as then, Mr. Selden's trainer. A few likely boys (from ten to thirteen or fourteen years old) will be taken, and under him, thoroughly instructed in the art of training horses for the turf;—they being bound for seven years to the business. Even those who are not in the way of bringing horses on the turf would do well to embrace the offer; as they would be sure to get first-rate grooms. The knowledge of training the racehorse thoroughly well is at this time a profitable trade, few others adding as much to the value of a slave, or to the productive capacity of a free laboring man.[47]

The anonymous groom in *Trifle* may well have been one of those boys sent to learn the ropes from Alexander, his youthful education resembling the training program of his equine charges. Slaves might even be nicknamed for horses: jockey Edward Brown, pictured in Troye's painting *Asteroid*, earned his nickname, "Brown Dick," after a racehorse of the same name as a result of his ability to run.[48] In his autobiography Jacob Stroyer, a hostler who grew up in the stables of South Carolina planter and turfman Richard Singleton, offers a more telling account of "thorough" instruction in the "art of training horses for the turf." Stroyer yearned to be a hostler after visiting the Singleton plantation barnyard with his father, who took care of the horses and mules. Singleton granted his wish, but Stroyer found that his "new occupation demanded a little more" than he cared for.[49] Instructed by the whip, he learned to ride quickly. The Singleton head trainer, a white man named Boney Young, was especially cruel. Stroyer remembers: "I got many little floggings by the colored groom as the horse threw me a great many times, but the floggings I got from him were very feeble compared with those of the white man."[50] Jockeys also underwent torture to reduce their weight, like being starved and made to run long distances. Mackay-Smith describes a method used on Ben by his owner, John Minor Botts: sweating him by burying him in manure, a troubling practice linking the black body to animal waste.[51] Troye's paintings elide the sweat, dirt, and blood—the ugly underpinnings of slavery and of horseracing—but animal and human bodies in Thoroughbred racing stables were often shaped into submission by violence. Blood from gashes made by the whip and spurs flowed regularly in the stables and on the tracks. Horses were frequently run to exhaustion and injury in brutal races of three to four heats at three to four miles each—twelve to sixteen miles a day. One of Trifle's most famous races was her 1832 battle with Black Maria, a grueling five-heat race of twenty miles, at the end of which she broke down.[52]

Black Mobility and Equestrianism

For the African American men who appear in Troye's equine portraits, working with blooded horses increased their social, economic, and physical mobility in the slaveholding South. White turfmen relied on their expertise and often granted them unusual autonomy. That whites distinguished them from the average field or house slave is evident in the tradition at the Forks of Cypress, a plantation and racing stable near Florence, Alabama, where slave jockeys were buried in the family graveyard.[53] Stewart earned money that he used to purchase his own horses.[54] He managed stables for both Johnson and Porter and traveled across state lines to tracks and breeding farms with his charges.[55] He and Alexander, the trainer in Troye's portrait of Trifle, supervised and trained slave workers as well as horses.[56]

Slaves also ran breeding programs, which required precise knowledge of pedigrees as equine breeding became more complex over the nineteenth century. Ann Norton Greene explains that before the nineteenth century "breed" often meant a type of horse found in a geographical region or country. Thoroughbred breeders, however, looking to English models, had already begun to assert the value of pedigree, understood to mean an identifiable biological group, with horses descended from a common sire and with specific hereditary traits.[57] They tested various practices of crossing (mixing different breeds or stock), inbreeding (breeding related horses), line breeding (breeding horses in the same line of descent), and progeny testing (breeding horses that had been demonstrated to transmit superior qualities such as speed or endurance). But because Thoroughbred breeders "wanted to stop change at the point at which a breed was considered pure," they increasingly rejected progeny testing and "relied on pedigree to choose animal combinations.[58] Medley, Tobacconist, and Trifle, all tested, pedigreed racers, exemplified the contemporary American Thoroughbred. Each descended from Sir Archy, who became known as the Godolphin of America: Medley, through his dam Reality's sire line and Tobacconist and Trifle, through their immediate sire lines. Sir Archy is the celebrated son of Diomed, who descends from Matchem, one of the three foundation English stallions, with Herod and Eclipse, whose roots trace to the Godolphin Arabian, the Byerly Turk, and the Darley Arabian, the three Middle Eastern stallions whose blood crossed with light English stock mares to produce the first Thoroughbreds.[59] In the end, breeding could be made simple if one was well versed in pedigree history via word of mouth or studbooks. It is perhaps ironic that breeding practices in the South rested in the hands of African Americans decried for their lack of intelligence. That these men were trusted to produce and oversee pedigreed animals reveals the incongruities of the Thoroughbred, which while linked to whiteness was literally produced by blacks. Stewart, not William Ransom Johnson, handled the breeding of Medley, collecting money for his owner and doing the work in the breeding shed. In the Singleton stables, where Jacob Stroyer got his start as a hostler, breeding was done by the slave trainer Cornelius. Indeed, pedigree validity depended not only on the work, but also on the word of slaves.[60] Future *Turf Register* editor Allen Davie wrote to the magazine in 1833 to affirm the pedigree of Medley's granddam because the "blood was so stated by Austin Curtis (who purchased the mare for Mr. Johnson) and who, though a [freed] man of color, was one on whom all who knew him relied."[61]

Slave hostlers' knowledge and status increased their worth to slaveholders, which often ensured their continued enslavement. Johnson was offered $550 for his "boy Ben," even without a guarantee of Ben's health, and $3,500 dollars for Stewart.[62] South Carolinian Wade Hampton II wrote to another racing man, Richard Singleton, for whom the horse in Troye's painting is named, attempting to hire his slave trainer Cornelius.[63] It was also common for grooms, jockeys, and trainers to be sold with the animals they tended and rode, and on the rare occasion when a man might purchase his freedom, he often remained where he was. As Mackay-Smith reports, Harry Lewis, a trainer depicted in Troye's portrait *Richard Singleton*, continued to work for his former owner Willa Viley for $500 a year.[64]

Horses offered a form of mobility distinct from other animals. Sometimes equestrian skills carried slave hostlers and jockeys out of bondage. Parson Dick, a slave groom and later butler at the Forks of Cypress, whose portrait Troye painted along with those of several of the Forks' Thoroughbreds, disappeared near the end of the Civil War on a visit to his wife, who lived on a neighboring plantation, riding, as "was his privilege," his favorite mount, a Thoroughbred horse named Rubens.[65] Jockey Cato allegedly attained freedom by piloting Wagner to victory over Grey Eagle in a famous match race held in 1839 at the Oakland racecourse in Louisville, Kentucky, before a crowd of ten thousand.[66] William T. Porter, editor of both the *American Turf Register* and the *Spirit of the Times*, described Cato's ride with admiration, distinguishing his skills from those of the white jockey who rode Grey Eagle.[67] Troye captured Wagner and Cato on canvas soon after the race, with Cato holding the horse, his saddle and blankets on the ground below and the racecourse grandstand in the background. Referring to the engraving after Troye's painting that appeared in the *Turf Register*, Porter extolled Cato's riding, drawing attention to his physical and mental strengths: his "capital seat" and "coolness and presence of mind."[68]

When composing jockeys, Troye typically chose to place them standing alongside the horse because, Alexander Mackay-Smith reasons, he lacked the technical skills to portray them either astride or with horses in motion.[69] In rare cases, such as in *Trifle* and *Planet*, he does depict a jockey mounted, though Irish jockey Willis's slack body atop the mare in Troye's portrait of Trifle looks as if he was "sitting on a horse for the first time."[70] With Jesse, the jockey in orange silks depicted in *Planet*, Troye achieved more success. Jesse sits up straight on the imposing chestnut, with both hands on the reins and a whip in his right hand. In picturing slaves and Irishmen in the roles of skilled equestrians, Troye's paintings record the existence of a racialized, nonwhite, nonindigenous American equestrian subculture.

Resisting Kinship

Viewers of Troye's paintings are often struck by their liveliness, by the artist's rendering of both human and horse as expressive beings. His jockeys and trainers seem aware of us looking at them, as in the portrait of *Tobacconist*, where trainer Manuel and jockey Ben peer intently toward us, Ben waiting for Manuel to finish saddling the horse so he can mount. Stewart stands carefully to present Medley in *Medley and Groom*, conscious of eyes upon them, but his gaze doesn't follow the horse's eye, which is directed at the viewer; instead, he looks toward Medley, whose ears prick forward in curiosity, wearing what the *Turf Register* described as the "self complacent expression of a highly pampered animal."[71] The diminutive chestnut mare Trifle seems to listen for her jockey's voice. Tobacconist crankily flattens his ears, flares his nostrils, and switches his ears in anticipation of the impending tightening of the girth.

In endowing his animals with humanlike behavior, Troye reveals his debt to Stubbs. Stephen Eisenman and Diana Donald have argued that Stubbs ushered in a new mode of equine portraiture through his depictions of animals that had "names, unique comportments and attitudes" and that, like humans, "bear marks of weariness, anxiety, and loss."[72] These expressive portrayals suggestive of an animal's inner life diverged from eighteenth-century naturalists like Georges-Louis Leclerc, Comte de Buffon, who believed animal behavior derived solely from instinct and habit, following Cartesian understandings of animals as soulless machines.[73] Indeed, Horace Walpole chided René Descartes in his 1763 poem about Stubbs's illustrious *Lion Attacking a Horse* (ca. 1762, Yale Center for British Art), asking, "Is that an engine? That a mere machine?"[74] In Stubbs's *Hambletonian, Rubbing Down* (ca. 1800, Mount Stewart, County Down, National Trust) the overwrought horse looks nothing like a mechanical apparatus but palpably conveys his distress after a brutal, exhausting race through his flattened ears, open, foaming mouth, wide eye, and bulging neck muscles.[75] Troye's horses communicate similar feelings: Tobacconist's body carriage and bad temper closely resemble Hambletonian's.

Through his training in animal portraiture, Troye likely knew early modern natural history treatises that depicted animals and theorized their place in the animal kingdom. He studied Stubbs's *Anatomy of the Horse* (1766) and even made a copy of a Stubbs's *Attack by a Lion upon a Horse* that he exhibited in 1832.[76] He may also have known of Stubbs's *Comparative Anatomical Exposition* (ca. 1802–6) investigating animal and human homologies.[77] It is doubtful, however, that he intentionally sought a radically new mode of picturing animals; instead, he tried to impress patrons with skill on a par with the English exemplar of equine artistry. Through his imitation of Stubbs, especially in pictures like *Tobacconist,* where horses react to human actions, it could be said that he recognized the "uniqueness and autonomy" of animals.[78] Troye's canvases thus move the human-animal resemblance beyond an equation between man and beast, where both labor in bondage at the behest of their owners, into contemporary theories of kinship, expressed, Donald suggests, "not by an attempt to assimilate animals to a human frame of reference, but by creating a sense of their own inner life, and of the universality of suffering in nature."[79]

This emerging consciousness of kinship aided activists and writers who recognized similar power relationships at work in animal subjugation and in human slavery. Natural history, Ingrid Tague writes, had long drawn such parallels between animals and humans. In 1772 Oliver Goldsmith wrote that in changing the "very nature of domestic animals by cultivation and care, the domestic animal has become a slave."[80] Buffon too asserted that slavery disfigured nature, leading to the degeneration of animals.[81] Such associations between animals and human slaves suffuse British and American abolitionist and welfare tracts, particularly in children's literature, where children were instructed to recognize suffering in their fellow creatures and to practice kindness toward them. In *Cousin Ann's Stories for Children* (1849), human slavery is introduced through a tale of animal captivity, with little Howard keeping his pet squirrel in a cage. Realizing that "he should not like, A little slave to be," Howard sets the squirrel free. The squirrel's liberation correlates with the inclusion of the condensed story of Henry Box Brown, the Virginia slave who famously mailed himself from slavery to freedom.[82] Another verse in the same book tells of Lucy, an enslaved black girl sold like a calf, "though she was as good as you."[83] Perhaps the best-known text in which cruelty to animals and humans unites is *Uncle Tom's Cabin* (1852), where Master Tom stones and drowns George's dog. The benevolent Mrs. Bird, the opposite of Tom, protects animals, punishing her sons for stoning a kitten and extending sympathy to fugitive slaves, "poor, starving creatures" who have been "abused and oppressed all their lives."[84] The problems inherent in texts that advocate for both the abolition of slavery and more humane practices toward both humans and animals is that animals and enslaved people are often used interchangeably or conflated in ways that "reinforce, rather than destroy racialist hierarchies."[85] Furthermore, the reader-viewer is meant to respond to animal subjects not through sameness or kinship, but despite difference, becoming a steward of the animal.[86] Extending this stewardship back to enslaved humans who are interchangeable with animals invokes the same rhetoric professed by period paternalism.

African American intellectuals apparently recognized this challenge, asserting the humanity of blacks and distinguishing them from animals. Frederick Douglass opens his autobiography with the statement that he knows as little of his age as a horse.[87] But even the horse, barnyard fowl, and dog, he says in his later speech, *The Claims of the Negro, Ethnologically Considered* (1854), know "the Negro is a MAN."[88] His focus on men, Melissa Stein argues, illustrates the gendered nature of period ethnology that was written by men and directed to men and even held that "race was more pronounced in the bodies of men."[89] In his *Appeal to the Colored Citizens of the World* (1829), David Walker, the son of an enslaved father and a free mother, asked of his predominantly black male audience, "Are we MEN!!—I ask you, O my brethren, are we MEN?"[90] For former slave James Pennington, "No man is anything more than a man, and no man is less than a man."[91] It is within these avowals of a black (male) humanity that I would like to read Charles Stewart's narrative.

Stewart acknowledges his affection for the horses he worked with—"How I did love dem horses!" He also bestows anthropomorphic qualities on them—"It 'peard like dey loved me too, an' when dey turned der rainbow neck, all slick an' shinin' aroun' sarchin' fur me to come an' give 'em deir gallops, whew-e-e!"[92] Yet Stewart uses them as a means of distinguishing himself: they recognize him as master, like the horse in Douglass's address, who bears a black man on his back, admitting his mastery and dominion. Animals also helped Stewart advance in the social order above other slaves and lowly white stable workers; he describes how early in his career he became "boss" of four older and nine younger slaves, two "white trash" helpers, and a stable full of nags—including Medley.[93] Traveling with the animals and making his own money made him "jes' as free an' independent as any gen'leman en de land."[94] He even spoke in front of white gentlemen, as when he asked Major Isham Puckett if he could purchase Puckett's slave Betsey for his wife in front of the Richmond courthouse. That Stewart claims the right to speak publicly for himself about his wife's purchase reveals the extent of slavery's dehumanizing customs, even as it shows how Stewart's conception of manhood circulated around his control both of enslaved black and free white hostlers and horses in his stables and of enslaved women. Stewart thus conforms to black ethnology that focused on championing manhood, but he also diverges from it in the way his own actions echo those qualities of aggression and domination associated with white men. Bay explains that white avowers of black inferiority often denounced blacks for being cowardly, weak, and overemotional, and even white abolitionists celebrated blacks' virtues by lauding their affectionate natures, moral instinct, and insight—qualities associated with women.[95] Black theorists also reverted to feminine characteristics, contrasting black morality, gentleness, and benevolence with white violence and avarice.[96]

Stewart's benevolence is not apparent in his narrative. He is callous toward Betsey, his first wife, purchased for $350. Betsey cooked and cleaned for him without complaint, but she angered him because she lied—about what is unclear, possibly the paternity of her three children—even after Stewart tried to elicit the truth by beating her with birch rods and hickory sticks.[97] His beating of Betsey suggests how enslaved persons tyrannized over those they could subdue. Though Stewart never mentions animal abuse, Stroyer's narrative describes the ever-present iconography of the whip, ready to be used on hostlers and horses. Morgan too recounts evidence for Jamaican slaves' brutal treatment of cattle and dogs, both objects of caprice and cruelty.[98] Stewart sold Betsey and the three children back to Major Puckett for what he paid for her in order to buy a horse, reasoning that Puckett got the bargain: four for the price of one. In Stewart's original purchase of Betsey, he similarly appealed to Puckett's pocket, noting that the money would show returns in the children they could raise.[99] In this way Stewart acknowledges both the wider practice of slave breeding and his complicity in it. Though historian Michael Tadman repudiates provocative abolitionist rhetoric claiming the widespread existence of slave stud farms, he, along with Johnson and Pellom McDaniels, describes how planters undertook other forms of slave breeding to augment their labor force. Kentucky slaveholders regularly advertised "good breeding stock," as they would stallions and broodmares.[100] Stewart's abuse of Betsey shows that he thinks of her and the children as animals, reverting to the comparisons often used by his masters. Like a horse, he suggests, "she must ha' come of a bad breed, an' a colt is mos' apt to take arter de dam, anyhow; I better git shet of de whole gang of 'em, an' try a new cross."[101] Soon afterward he married his second wife, Mary Jane Mallory, in Paris, Kentucky.

In the end, although Stewart obtained a large house and could ring a bell to call the overseer and stable workers, he remained enslaved, passed down from Judge Porter to his brother after Porter's death. That he never purchased his own freedom shows both how the privilege of caring for elite horses sustained the system of slavery and how Stewart's agency was structured by dominance.[102] Troye's paintings depicting slave hostlers and horses are consequently fraught with the contradictions of southern slaveholding society in the decades leading up the Civil War. This is the landscape in which Troye found himself, in stables where blooded Thoroughbred horses and black human bodies mingled. In his attempt to introduce his American patrons to a mode of animal portraiture picturing what he saw and experienced in the world of racing during the first half of the nineteenth century, Troye created provocative, contradictory images of animals and humans whose identities are mutually bound to and shaped by the other, but who both warrant recognition.

EIGHT

"More Than a Horse"

The Cultural Work of Racehorse Biography

KRISTEN GUEST

> The *raison d'etre* (if I may be allowed a French phrase on a very English subject) of the thoroughbred horse is twofold. He is in the first place, and essentially, a racehorse, and in the second a sire. On the Turf he supplies the public with the material of an amusement which has become in England a necessity; and at the stud he performs a duty no less serious—that of getting sound and handsome stock. He must have the monopoly of speed, and he must have that quality peculiar to high breeding which enables him to impress his own stamp and image on his progeny. For these two purposes, and these alone, is he of supreme value.
>
> —Wilfrid Scawen Blust

> If animals have a biography, if they are some "body" and not some "thing," what are our ethical obligations to them?
>
> —Clifton P. Flynn[1]

In her biography of Northern Dancer, Muriel Lennox ends an account of the life and career of the top-producing racehorse sire of the twentieth century with a chapter that asks how we assign economic value to a stallion who was "more than a horse" and "more valuable than gold."[2] Concluding her survey of Northern Dancer's breeding career, Lennox describes the response of Charles Taylor, owner E. P. Taylor's son, to an offer to purchase the horse, then twenty years old, for $40 million. Explaining his decision to decline the offer, Taylor replies, "There are those who believe that everything has a price—but not Northern Dancer."[3] This view of Northern Dancer as a being who transcends attempts to assign quantifiable value is buttressed by a biographical narrative that repeatedly asserts the stallion's status as a self-aware subject. "As I looked into the eyes of this remarkable animal," Lennox tells us in the opening passages where she "interviews" him in his Maryland paddock, "I realised the question was not whether he could communicate, but whether I was capable of hearing."[4]

Since the eighteenth century, biography and autobiography have helped to produce and circulate the idea of human subjectivity as a matter of agency and self-possession and have done so, as Erica Fudge points out, by systematically excluding animals. As she explains, "to write a 'life' is not just to present a series of 'facts' but to bear witness to that individual's potential to construct a life-story of him- or herself; to communicate through language the subject's own self-understanding (or misunderstanding)."[5] Traditionally regarded as possessions that lack the "self-awareness and self-will" of autonomous individuality, Fudge contends, animals have been placed in perceived opposition to our understanding of human identity as a state of self-knowledge.[6] Insofar as she recognizes Northern Dancer as a subject, Lennox complicates the traditional function of the genre: Northern Dancer is credited not only with the lineage and career that Fudge identifies as central to human biography, but also with the unique, self-knowing identity that underpins modern ideas about human selfhood. If her aim in according Northern Dancer subjective status is admirable, however, the resulting narrative—about a horse who is "more than a horse"—skirts the complex relation between self-possession and objective value by identifying the champion stallion as an exception who transcends the conflicts central to animal identity. In identifying the horse as a special, humanized subject, in effect, she both anthropomorphizes him and uses him to mediate contradictory aspects of human identity.

In what follows I consider how Thoroughbred biography, a genre that has flourished in America, Great Britain, and Australia since the early 1970s, works to manage our uncomfortable awareness of the ways humans simultaneously embody subjective consciousness and inhabit the world as economically determined objects. In the eighteenth and nineteenth centuries, Deirdre Lynch, Nancy Armstrong, and Regina Gagnier variously assert, human narratives of subjectivity such as autobiography, biography, and the novel addressed anxieties about economic determinants of identity by envisioning the development of the self as a reward for the innate, demonstrated merits of exceptional individuals.[7] As recent scholarship of "things" makes clear, however, not only may objects (and animals) have biographies, the existence of these biographies shows that human subjects are similarly situated in a social system where aspects of the self (from labor to DNA) are objectified and assigned economic value.[8] If human identity is subject to the effects of capitalist systems that frame and shape its conditions of existence, moreover, human relations with animals under the conditions of economic modernity have also, as Derrida suggests, imposed forms of violence that provoke feelings of shame—the affective products, I propose, of our attempts to evade uncomfortable knowledge about ourselves.[9]

As a subject of biography, the Thoroughbred racehorse is well suited to manage such tensions in human identity. Since its inception, Donna Landry writes, the breed has been uniquely connected to ideas about human identity. Not only is the Thoroughbred considered special—insofar as "ideas about going fast implied an impatient intelligence at work and some notion of equine agency"—it also comes to figure as "a higher, nobler kind of self for the humans who became obsessed with them."[10] Within this discourse the Thoroughbred becomes a figure expressive of human fantasies of transcendence—a superior, aspirational being. At the same time, the Thoroughbred is also an ambiguous figure that offers reminders of the permeable relation between subject and object, individual and possession. Rebecca Cassidy suggests that racehorses are "polysemic": "Not animal, not person, not object, not subject, not entirely artificial and not entirely natural."[11] As Katherine Dashper and Thomas Fletcher further note, "racehorses occupy a liminal position, on the boundaries between 'human' and 'animal,' at once valued for their individual characters and abilities yet also discarded and traded according to market demands."[12]

In contemporary racehorse biography, I argue, the convergence between these two aspects of Thoroughbred identity reveals conflicts related to modern subjectivity and the economic frameworks in which it is produced. In Lennox's biography, for example, Northern Dancer is repeatedly positioned as a unique individual—for Taylor a part of the family and for Lennox a bona fide subjective presence; yet the story of his life unfolds, paradoxically, as an account of his escalating value. Indeed, he becomes a subject who seemingly exceeds attempts to assign value only in the context of economic benchmarks of his success. Even Taylor's conclusion, that Northern Dancer is a horse who exceeds quantifiable value, is qualified by his recognition that $40 million "might not have been enough for him at the time."[13] Despite its view of Northern Dancer as a self-possessed individual, then, Lennox's narrative ultimately reaffirms the entanglement of racehorse subjects in their economic conditions of existence when it characterizes its subject as "more valuable then gold." Indeed, Lennox's insistence that her subject is "more than a horse" represents an attempt to imagine an alternative status, even as it reminds us that Northern Dancer's life is determined by his position as an economic object within the Thoroughbred industry.

In Thoroughbred biography, I contend, such contradictions offer us the opportunity both to engage with conflicts central to contemporary notions of human identity and to consider the effects of economic frameworks on animals' lives. Indeed, if Thoroughbred biography articulates fantasies of individual transcendence over one's material conditions of existence by appealing to aspirational notions of exceptional selfhood, it also makes visible the conflicts implicit in our desire for "pure" individuality as it shifts between anthropomorphizing its subjects and documenting their status as valuable possessions. While human ideas about selfhood are mediated on a symbolic and ideological level by racehorse biography, moreover, the genre also uneasily negotiates questions about animal experience. Veering between interiorized notions of anthropomorphized individuality and representations of the horse as an ideally disinterested animal figure—noble, honest, innocent, and pure—much equine biography obscures questions about the experience of animals within the breeding and racing industries.

Thoroughbred Subjectivity and Human Biography

Since the 1970s, the genre of racehorse biography has enjoyed significant popularity in the United States, England, and Australia, all major centers for the global Thoroughbred racing and breeding industries.[14] Informed in part by the rise of televised media coverage of Thoroughbred racing, modern iterations of the genre have also benefited from the adapting of best-selling equine biographies such as Laura Hillenbrand's *Seabiscuit: An American Legend* or William Nack's *Secretariat* into major motion pictures. Recent Thoroughbred biographies detailing the careers of both historical and contemporary racehorses—from Eclipse and Man o' War to Barbaro and Black Caviar—chronicle the lives of exceptional equine athletes. The genre attempts to negotiate the vexed relation between subjectivity and economic value by positing, as Lennox does, that exceptional horses transcend the economic conditions that structure their lives. Typically, racehorse biographies chronicle the material factors considered central to success in the breed, such as pedigree and conformation. In tracking the ways these exceptional horses demonstrate these advantages, however, these narratives argue that champions also possess distinct and distinguished qualities of character. Biographies thus address the central concern of breeders, owners, and the betting public—who all have historically focused on a range of physical traits and material conditions in order to predict winners. They also try to articulate intangible qualities, such as the will to win and the resilience to overcome obstacles, that personalize champions as individuals.

The relation between Thoroughbred biography and the parent genre of human biography illustrates to some degree how specific ideas about human identity have evolved alongside the development of the Thoroughbred breed and the racing industry. Modern versions of autobiography and biography that emerged in the anglophone world in the eighteenth century focused on "a model of the heroic life," positing an idea of autonomous, progressive selfhood associated with exceptional individuals who transcend the limitations of their birth.[15] As products of a time when traditional limits such as position or wealth were unsettled by social shifts toward an ideology of the individual as a self-determining being, autobiography and biography offered narrative forms for representing selfhood as a psychologized, innate possession. As Felicity Nussbaum suggests in her discussion of eighteenth-century autobiography, the self was increasingly understood as "free, responsible, and the agent of its own actions."[16] But if biography elaborates the ideal of an autonomous human subject who transcends the social, ideological, and material restrictions that limit and shape the development of identity, scholarship has increasingly recognized the ways it also contests the ideology of modern subjectivity.[17] Nussbaum, for example, notes that autobiography and biography situate the "published self as property in a money economy."[18]

From the eighteenth century onward, biography and autobiography used this model of selfhood to represent the lives of a range of subjects. In the nineteenth and early twentieth centuries "great men"—usually military heroes, politicians, or, increasingly, captains of industry—became popular biographical subjects, but more marginal fictional and nonfictional subjects—including women, slaves, animals, and objects—were also represented.[19] Early equine biographies took several forms, but from the outset they evinced special interest in the Thoroughbred racehorse. Many authors include fictional elements in their chronicles of the lives of famous horses, as in both Eugene Sue's nineteenth-century account of the life of the Godolphin Arabian and, in the twentieth century, Walter Farley's *Man o' War*. Such novelized biographies chart the careers of famous horses, but they balance details of pedigree, physical traits, and (where applicable) racing statistics against accounts of their subjects' unique personalities and important human or animal relationships. In effect, they represent their equine subjects as self-possessed individuals.

Alongside such popular texts, the emerging Thoroughbred industry began to document the lives of leading champions in more specialized terms. An early example, *A Short History of the celebrated Race-Horse, Eclipse*, published in 1835 by Bracy Clark, chronicles the career of the eighteenth-century sire who dominated racing in his lifetime and whose name anchored the pedigrees of subsequent generations of Thoroughbreds.[20] By the early nineteenth century it had already become clear that Eclipse was the progenitor of an important and influential bloodline, and the timing of Clark's publication—almost fifty years after the stallion's death—suggests the role pedigree increasingly played in the nascent breeding and racing industries. From the mid-nineteenth century onward, volumes documenting the racing careers of significant breeding stallions offered resources for both breeders and a betting public concerned with distilling the genealogy and physical traits associated with racing success.[21] Such accounts were informative and economically focused, highlighting the horse's traits, bloodlines, successful offspring, and details of specific races rather than representing him as an anthropomorphized self.

Modern racehorse biography brings the focus on selfhood central to semifictional narratives together with the documenting of pedigree, conformation, and racing statistics central to publications aimed at an industry readership. In doing so it makes use of the polysemic associations that have come to characterize the breed, representing the horse in ways that envision it simultaneously as a recognizably humanized character, an idealized animal, and a material object of significant economic value. This process of representation is facilitated by metaphoric language that encourages multiple, nonexclusive understandings of the equine subject. In what follows I consider the function of this language, examining particularly the ways biographical representation positions the racing champion in terms that are simultaneously, and ambiguously, human and animal, autonomous and objectified.

Representing Equine Character

In Thoroughbred racing the metaphor "the eye of eagles" connotes the ineffable, mystical quality of a champion and is frequently invoked to describe the equine biographical subject. For American author John Taintor Foote, who coined the phrase in 1916, "the eye of eagles" signifies "an air of freedom unconquerable. The eyes seem to look on heights beyond our gaze. It is the look of a spirit that can soar."[22] In the days before his record-breaking win in the Belmont Stakes, for example, Secretariat is described as having "a presence to him that the others did not have, a sense of greatness, that horsemen used to call the 'look of eagles.'"[23] The expression suggests human recognition of exceptional horses who are attributed inborn human desires and quirks of personality that explain their success. References to this special quality recur throughout Thoroughbred biography. Even as a filly, Jane Schwartz notes, Ruffian stood out from other horses. "It was more the way she held herself, a certain presence, that made people turn and take a second look."[24] The first time she saw steeplechase champion Best Mate, trainer Henrietta Knight recalls, he "stood out": "He seemed unperturbed by the underfoot conditions and walked proudly through the mud with his head held high."[25]

In racing biography as in human biography, looking "inside" is done by examining documents, interviewing the horse's handlers, and, where possible, directly observing the horse. Both Lennox and Nack spent time with their subjects, while memoirs by trainers, such as Henrietta Knight's *Best Mate: Triple Gold* or Ginger McCain's *Red Rum: A Racing Legend*, recount the horse's career and character from an entirely firsthand perspective.[26] The portraits subsequently produced vary among individuals, but taken collectively they emphasize the qualities of humanized self-awareness and personality evident among great champions. Secretariat, for instance, was "an amiable and gentlemanly colt" as well as a prankster who "did a passable imitation of his own groom." By "personality and temperament," Nack writes, he therefore "became the most engaging character in the barn."[27] Northern Dancer, by contrast, was "a real devil" who "wanted little to do with training," an aspect of his personality that is directly connected to his success as a racehorse. As Lennox concludes, "these characteristics, both physical and mental, were what made him extraordinary."[28] Despite his notoriously difficult personality, however, the stallion is described as habitually gentle with Winnifred Taylor (E. P. Taylor's wife) and even allows himself to be petted when Mrs. Taylor brings a young blind boy to visit him, standing "as quiet as an old cart-horse" the whole time.[29] Such accounts, which highlight the complex, humanized personalities of their biographical subjects, suggest that exceptional horses are self-knowing beings capable of situational choice. In context, their temperaments are depicted not as a matter of instinctual behavior, but as suggesting psychologized depth.

If racing biographies focus on anthropomorphized notions of personality in the characters of exceptional horses, they also connect biography's interest in the self-possession and self-awareness of human character with the desire to win that makes Thoroughbred champions. From Ruffian's earliest races, jockey Jacinto Velasquez observed, "She was a horse who knew what she was doing."[30] Even as a filly, Schwartz notes, she was "aggressive, independent, and very self-possessed."[31] As a result of her exceptional character, Schwartz's biography reports, from the outset of her career Ruffian was in danger of running herself to death. The tragedy of Ruffian's breakdown during a race and subsequent euthanizing is thus represented as the outcome of her conscious, overpowering desire to run rather than as the result of breeding, training, or instinct. Despite her catastrophic injury, Schwartz narrates, Ruffian fights her jockey and continues to race on three legs: "She went on running, pulverizing her sesamoids, ripping the skin of her fetlock as the bones burst through, driving the open wound into the stinging sand of the Belmont track, tearing her ligaments, until her hoof was flopping uselessly, bent up like the tip of a ski, as she pounded down the track on exposed bone, running on and on."[32]

Portrayed here not as a matter of instinct but as self-expression, Schwartz voices what she sees as Ruffian's desire—"*Let me run!*" The line is repeated both through a lengthy account of the injury and later, when recounting the filly's death, as freedom from her broken body: "That's all she had been asking—*let me run!*" (315).[33]

Seabiscuit, by contrast, "was almost too quiet, too docile," with an expression "that hinted at devious intelligence." Early trainers wondered "if this horse might be just as obstreperous as his sire, only much more cunning in his methods."[34] As a result of his "cunning," Seabiscuit did not become successful until his handlers recognized that he could not be forced or bullied into running but had to choose to win.[35] Allowed to exercise his intelligence, moreover, Seabiscuit displayed a capacity not just for speed but for overmastering his competitors by "psychological warfare": taking "sadistic pleasure in harassing and humiliating his rivals, slowing down to mock them as he passed, snorting in their faces, and pulling up when in front so other horses could draw alongside, then dashing their hopes with a killing burst of speed." "Those unfamiliar with horses might scoff at the notion of equine pride as silly anthropomorphism," Hillenbrand notes, "but the behavior is unmistakable."[36] Such assertions recur frequently in Thoroughbred biographies, where the individual will of exceptional horses is connected with deep resentment both at the use of the whip (to the point of refusing to run) and the ineffectiveness of external factors such as assigning heavy weights to slow them down. Running, for Thoroughbred champions, is represented as a form of self-expression related to ideas about intelligence and self-awareness that are distinctly human.

Thoroughbred Character and the Paradox of Value

As figures parsed in human terms in Thoroughbred biography, exceptional horses come to represent the fantasy of identity as an ideally free, inborn possession—and as a mark of individual superiority. Yet, as in human biography, the qualities associated with the exceptional racehorse become tokens of an individual's ability to transcend material conditions of existence only when secured by the validation of economic worth: the speed records, career winnings, and value for sale or syndication that anchor expressions of Thoroughbred character and cause them to become objects of public attention. Indeed, without such economic signifiers we would have merely ordinary animals whose independent, genial, or ungovernable temperaments explain only their failure to distinguish themselves as objects of biographical attention. In the field of Thoroughbred biography, in effect, aspects of character exist in tension with the economic forces they are supposed to transcend, and the genre makes significant, if sometimes strained or even critical, efforts to reconcile them.

Although the Thoroughbred industry may accede to, support, or participate in personalizing racehorses in the press, books, and films, such concerns are always ultimately subordinate to the management of a horse's value and earning potential. As Andrew Barton Paterson remarked of Australian champion Phar Lap in 1931, "Phar Lap is not only a racehorse—he is a business, and a very profitable and important business at that. Phar Lap, Unlimited."[37] Nowhere is this focus more evident than in the inevitable moment in the biographies of champion stallions when the horse is withdrawn from racing—a point where the idealization of running as agency or self-expression is instead subordinated to the economic demands of syndication and breeding. Describing Secretariat's retirement, for instance, Nack notes that "already the best years of his life lay behind him": "At the age of three he was being consumed by the industry that had raised and made him worth ten times his weight in gold."[38]

Secretariat's biography chronicles his developing personality alongside his escalating net worth, illustrating the troubling interconnection of selfhood and economics. Between his two- and three-year-old years, Nack relates, the Chenery family undertook extensive consultation about Secretariat's potential value. In purely economic terms, the family were advised, the colt should be syndicated or sold, since his chances of losing value exceeded the gamble that his worth would rise if he won the Triple Crown. He was therefore syndicated for breeding at $190,000 per share before his three-year-old racing season, with a "world record" valuation of $6,080,000.[39] Following his spectacular win in the Belmont that clinches the Triple Crown, however, Secretariat's worth escalates. Despite shareholders being offered up to half a million dollars for a single share, "Secretariat, like his sire [Bold Ruler], is virtually not for sale."[40] In becoming superlatively valued, in effect, the stallion exceeds his status as an economic unit, becoming, as Nack suggests, "a cultural phenomenon"[41] or, to borrow Lennox's phrase, "more than a horse."

Similar accounts recur in the biographies of other racehorses. Best Mate's owner, Jim Lewis, for example, has described the three-time Cheltenham Gold Cup winner as "a priceless Ming vase or a Kohinoor diamond," characterizing the horse as a unique possession and so both infinitely valuable and beyond price.[42] If Best Mate is likened to a work of art, however, he is also recognized as "a valuable commercial commodity" whose economic potential must be protected by trademark.[43] The conflict negotiated here, between notions of the champion racehorse as an individual, a commodity, and a trademarked image to be circulated and reproduced, reflects the complex ways Thoroughbred subjectivity is imagined in racehorse biography in tension with anthropomorphized status as "character."

Perhaps most centrally, representations of great horses as individuals make use of the "polysemic" cultural view of the Thoroughbred to reconcile or displace conflicts central to modern notions of identity more generally. On the whole, biographies that document the apotheosis of their subjects into cultural figures who enfold conflicting notions of character and commodification address the problematic knowledge that economics shapes and limits individual agency by returning to a view of Thoroughbreds as idealized animals who are somehow above such matters. While the maelstrom of public acclaim swirls around him during his Triple Crown year, Nack reports, Secretariat is "composed and collected to the point of indifference."[44] In context, Nack and other biographers suggest, winning represents something pure for the horse, who runs not for money or fame, but rather for running as an end in itself. Contemporary press coverage of Ruffian's final race, for example, characterized the filly as "a victim of her own gallantry."[45] The Thoroughbred's will to run is thus represented, paradoxically, as something quintessentially human and as an ideally "pure" animal impulse.

Such characterizations recur in racing biography, identifying the exceptional horse not only as a disinterested participant in the racing industry, but also as ideally honest and detached from the complexities of human contexts. One reason "the public has embraced these heroes," Linda Hanna suggests, is "their innocence and sincerity."[46] Discussing the public's response to Barbaro's euthanizing after racing injuries, journalist Sally Jenkins asserts that—unlike many human athletes—the colt "never lied to us" and was "an honest, blameless competitor."[47] Great horses are also imagined to be noble in ways that compensate for our own failings, as Nack points out of Secretariat, who remained "oblivious to all but the sensate world within his immediate grasp," winning at a time when Americans were confronting the political corruption of the Watergate scandal.[48] Such qualities inspire people, Thoroughbred biographers recurrently insist, lifting them imaginatively above the economic and social conditions under which they struggle to define their own identities. Describing Red Rum's effect on the British public, for example, Ginger McCain notes that in the 1970s "Ordinary men and women were somehow able to identify with Red Rum, to relate to his humble origins, to understand the harsh rigours he endured in his life, and to rejoice and take hope from his brilliance. He inspired them in a way few other creatures were able to do, and in a very dramatic and positive way."[49]

During a time of economic slowdown and self-questioning in Great Britain, in effect, the horse who was famously stabled behind a used-car showroom and trained on a local beach offered people the prospect of transcending accidents of birth.[50] Phar Lap similarly became a national icon for struggling Australians during the Great Depression, while the diminutive Seabiscuit's improbable rise to national attention in America anchored identification with an empowered "little guy" against the forces of power and money.

A Matter of the Heart: Anatomizing the Ineffable

Perhaps the most pervasive metaphoric quality associated with the character of the racing champion is "heart": the will to win, to overcome adversity, and to persevere. It is a quality that lends itself to human identification and cross-species characterization, as in the case of Australian soldiers whose demonstrations of courage in World War II were celebrated by comparison to the famously large "heart" of Phar Lap.[51] In the history of racing it is also a quality that has persistently been literalized in preoccupation with the actual heart size of exceptional horses, knitting together human notions of selfhood and idealized animal qualities. From the time of Eclipse, whose body was necropsied, to twentieth-century examples such as Phar Lap and Secretariat, the literally large heart has been identified as a physical attribute of greatness. With the rise of genetic science the hypothesis of an "X factor"—a heritable chromosome that produces a larger than normal heart—has become a point of interest for breeders, owners, and the betting public seeking insight into the next generation of champions. Marianna Haun, the journalist whose research into racing pedigrees first prompted the theory, suggests that the notion of heart "originally was meant to describe a personality characteristic—something real, but immeasurable, the ability that made a horse dig deep and find the courage not to give up until he crossed the finish line victoriously." "Today," she continues, "thanks to the truly great heart uncovered at the autopsy of the amazing Thoroughbred Secretariat, it is known that great heart really is a physical description of an extraordinary heart found in certain Thoroughbreds, Quarter Horses and Standardbreds that has passed down the female line on the X chromosome from the legendary Eclipse, foaled in England in 1764."[52]

Beyond its genetic interest, the preoccupation of the Thoroughbred industry with the large hearts of champions suggests not only a desire to refine the breeding process and predictably produce champions, but also a concern to distill reproducible aspects of identity—to look inside the horse's material body to find and quantify the secret of greatness in the same way that biography attempts to look inside his character. Discussing the 1932 discovery that Phar Lap's heart was twice the normal size, Dr. Martha Sear of the National Museum of Australia wrote that "scientists who did the dissection were seeking to understand not only what had killed Phar Lap, but what had made Phar Lap one of the most remarkable racehorses that the world had ever seen."[53] Similar impulses informed the postmortem on Secretariat, which, according to attending veterinarian Thomas Swerczek, revealed a heart "almost twice the average size, and a third larger than any equine heart I'd ever seen. And it wasn't pathologically enlarged. All the chambers and the valves were normal. It was just larger. I think it told us why he was able to do what he did."[54]

Anatomizing racehorses is, of course, a rude return to the economic and material frameworks we look to them to lift us beyond. The process speaks, moreover, to the ways that animals, even idealized, anthropomorphized ones, retain their deeply rooted status as objects. At this moment at the end of a champion's life, in which the animal threatens to disclose itself as fully animal once more, Thoroughbred biography and the racing industry often turn again to the idea of the Thoroughbred champion as a humanized subject. Nack's 1989 *Sports Illustrated* essay commemorating the death of Secretariat (and included as an appendix to his biography of the stallion) is suggestively titled "Pure Heart." Nack begins with the postmortem discovery that the champion's heart was, literally, spectacularly large, but he does so only as a prelude to an extended consideration of the humanized qualities we connect to his greatness. Understood in the terms Nack suggests, Secretariat is both the horse who gives everything when he runs, and thus is "all heart," and the horse whose heart is pure. "Heart," in the terms evoked by Nack and other biographers, thus bypasses engagements with the material realities of horses' lives (as athletes and as breeding stock), instead reflecting on the ways their character connects them to us. Great horses not only inspire us, biographies imply, they also elicit our best and purest feelings and so lift us out of the material contexts that shape our identities.

Such heroic views of heart as something that connects us to great horses are particularly evident in biographies that take as their subjects horses who die of catastrophic racing injuries. Linda Hanna identifies Ruffian's continuing to run on three legs as a matter of "heart and spirit . . . pulling her on."[55] Similarly, Barbaro is eulogized for what his handlers described as "bottomless heart": "He obviously raced for pleasure, and he ran with such dynamic abandon that he made circling a track seem an impetuous act." Discussions of Barbaro's heart are related specifically to his anthropomorphized personhood; as Jenkins points out, "anyone who watched Barbaro run in the Derby felt that they saw traces of a distinct character": "His character wasn't a matter of wishful projection, it existed, and was quite vivid to those who cared for him."[56] Heart, indeed, is the metaphorical site at which character and animal purity decisively come together to block uncomfortable reminders that Thoroughbreds—even racing champions—are material bodies circulating within an industry, and they achieve this end by shifting our attention from the realities of economic and material conditions of existence to the interior, sentimental, and aspirational realm of human feeling.

To a certain extent the industry colludes in such blockages. In the era of modern racing, "heart" and greatness are typically recognized after death in ways that conform to and encourage a distinctly human sense of exceptionality. Retired racehorses who become successful breeding stallions live in rich environments, with elaborate stables, lush pastures, and dedicated human attendants. When great horses die they are buried at the track with funeral ceremonies and marked graves, like Ruffian and Barbaro, or interred in the cemeteries of breeding farms reserved for outstanding performers. Both Secretariat and Man o' War, for instance, had formal funerals and were buried in oak caskets draped with their farms' racing silks, and both are commemorated by headstones.[57] Such horses are also memorialized in obituaries, commemorated with public statues and memorials, and accorded special status as biographical subjects. These practices complete the conceptualizing of the horse as anthropomorphized individual, as do "personal appearances" by retired champions at tracks and on television and formal "retirement" ceremonies that mark the passage from the track to the breeding establishment. Public demonstration of the human ability to feel deeply for horses is central to such activities, and taken together these practices humanize not only the horses singled out as special but also the industry that produces them. It also, not incidentally, elides the fates of "ordinary" Thoroughbreds who fail to find success on the track or, later, in the breeding shed. These casualties of the industry—who include racing champions such as Ferdinand, who ended his life in a Japanese slaughterhouse, as well as the many unstoried Thoroughbreds whose fates are determined by an economic calculus of loss and gain—become less visible when their lives are set against the unfolding drama of the exceptional champions who are dignified as subjects of biographies.

Conclusion

The focus on exceptional individuals is not unique to Thoroughbred biography. Indeed, as Dashper and Fletcher note in their survey of the scholarship on icons, the represented lives of human and animal sporting celebrities offer readers imaginative relief from limited circumstances and encourage feelings of "meritocratic hope."[58] As Leo Lowenthal notes in his study of mid-twentieth-century biography, the growing attention to sporting figures and stars shifts the focus from biography as a primer of self-making to biography as a compensatory narrative.[59] Under the conditions of modernity not everyone can become an icon, but the special status sporting icons enjoy offers "ordinary" people the prospect of participating vicariously in moments of triumphant self-making. Biographies of Thoroughbred racing champions add to this mix narratives that blend human qualities with idealized aspects of animal character, offering a focal point for human aspiration in the chronicles of exceptional horses. Such accounts divert our attention not only from the economic limitations that shape and determine human existence, but also from questionable practices within the racing industry related to animals and people—both the overproduced racing and breeding stock who often end up in slaughterhouses and the grooms and exercise riders who work for subsistence wages. By focusing on the successful individual rather than on those who fail to become storied, racing biography represents the economic conditions that frame the industry in the most palatable light.

If, as I have proposed, they work to subordinate questions of the horse's value to matters of heart, integrity, and character, such narratives also systematically mute questions about the distribution of economic success among the human figures in these stories by highlighting the immaterial value of having been part of a larger story. As biographer Lawrence Scanlan notes of Secretariat's groom Eddie Sweat, the "reward" for caretaking a horse who was regarded as beyond monetary value was not economic but emotional: "He had formed a remarkable bond with the greatest racehorse who ever lived," Scanlan asserts, "and you can't put a value on that."[60] Such views effectively reverse estimates of the horse's exceptionality in terms that place him beyond economic worth by suggesting that, for humans, some emotional experiences exceed economic value. In framing such equivalances, Thoroughbred biography registers the tension at the core of modern formulations of subjectivity, between the idealization of identity as self-determining and the influence of social and economic contexts in which that identity unfolds.

PART THREE

National Identity

NINE

The Politics of Reproduction

Horse Breeding and State Studs in Prussia, 1750–1900

TATSUYA MITSUDA

Breeding Horses for War

In the mid-eighteenth century, European states encountered the need to create a new stud system to maintain a horse population commensurate with increased military demand.[1] During the Seven Years' War (1754–63) in particular, major states suffered from an overreliance on remounts from traditionally rich horse-breeding regions of Europe.[2] During the war, Prussia had to pay double for its horses and suffered from a severe lack of remounts for the army, falling short of demand by approximately 3,400.[3] Owing to its reliance on imports from Hannover and Holstein, Austria-Hungary later experienced a similar shortage and had to disband seven regiments of cuirassiers between 1769 and 1775.[4] Such experiences exposed the inadequacies of early modern studs, which were essentially small operations where individual farmers, nobles, or courts catered to their own small clientele.[5] Neither was "purity" held in high regard: breeders in premodern studs kept a mixture of wild and domesticated stock, which meant producing quality horses was a matter of haphazard coincidence rather than a deliberate policy.[6] The contemporary belief that climate and soil mainly determined the quality of offspring also cast a long shadow, and the breeders' animal husbandry skills were considered relatively unimportant. Those concerned with breeding in the late eighteenth century came to regard this passive stance as an error in need of reform. To address problems of volume, self-sufficiency, and consistency, they thus envisioned state studs on a large scale.[7]

One of the first countries in Europe to establish state studs was France, in 1665 under Jean-Baptiste Colbert.[8] After the French Revolution, state studs were temporarily abolished because of their association with absolutism, but in 1806 they were reestablished and modernized by Napoleon.[9] In Prussia a state stud system emerged in the late eighteenth century when Count Carl Lindenau erected what would later become provincial state studs (*Landgestüte*).[10] By the mid-nineteenth century the country boasted three principal studs (*Hauptgestüte*) at Trakehnen, Neustadt/Dosse, and Graditz—all converted from court studs in the previous century. These central studs were flanked by thirteen provincial studs at Trakehnen, Insterburg, Gudwallen, Lindenau, Döhlen, Marienwerder, Zirke, Leubus, Celle, Dillenburg, Warendorf, Wickrath, and Traventhal. Principal studs were influential because they housed select breeds of stallions (and mares, although to a lesser extent) that served as "seeds," or sources, for the entire domestic equine population. Operating in concert with the principal studs, provincial studs were less powerful and served the needs of smaller geographic areas. Based on monitoring the general equine population, both the principal and the provincial state studs would dispatch government-approved stallions to depots within areas of particular need. The state thus could dictate the mating, or "covering," of mares whose most suitable offspring could be used on the farm for a few years, then bought back by the state for the army. In 1890, 2,340 government stallions covered 121,959 mares across Prussia, producing a large pool of potential warhorses.[11] Occupying the top of the equine hierarchy, the stallions that state studs sent to farmers thus had a powerful impact on the types of horses actually bred and reared.[12] By controlling sites of reproduction, state studs dominated equine politics in continental Europe, whereas in England a state stud system failed to materialize because of the influence of private individuals.

Taking Prussia as an example, this chapter examines two challenges the state studs faced over the course of the nineteenth century. During the first half of the century, the threat was foreign. The English model, which relied on racing as the indicator of a horse's quality, presented a challenge to the position, expertise, and worldview of state stud officials after the Napoleonic Wars. Military horsemen invariably assumed these positions, and I contend that this structural bias explains the emergence of a preference for saddle horses. Encouraging the breeding of lighter saddle horses was a way of meeting the increased demand from the cavalry and, to a lesser extent, the artillery, where horses doubled as remounts.[13] However, the narrow emphasis on the army's requirements created tensions within the wider society. Faced with the demands of industrialization, especially in the west of the country, the state studs eventually succumbed to pressures from agriculture, industry, and commerce to breed heavier draft horses suitable for use in transport, haulage, and construction. Encompassing a much broader spectrum of interests, people, places, and horses than might commonly be supposed, the equine politics of the Prussian warhorse expanded beyond the narrow logistics of procuring enough horses for the battlefield. Indeed, the presence of horses in virtually all walks of human life—from agriculture to sport—meant that the state's actions in breeding warhorses had an unavoidable effect on other areas of equine society.[14] Recognizing this reality, this chapter considers how "horsepower"—both symbolic and literal—became contested.

The Threat of the English Model

At the beginning of the nineteenth century, Johann Christoph Justinus, a low-ranking stud inspector in the Austro-Hungarian court, expressed his enthusiasm for the English model of breeding horses.[15] His involvement with the Austro-Hungarian army during the Napoleonic Wars convinced him that English hunters and thoroughbreds were superior warhorses, and his books, published in 1815 and reprinted posthumously in 1830, attempted to explain why English breeding had triumphed in battle.[16] Together they represent the most systematic German treatise on the merits of horseracing as the best way of measuring the quality of horses:

> [The Thoroughbred racehorse is] the most noble breed, the epitome of equine excellence. It is around [the Thoroughbred] that the turf has become a science, and it is the racecourse that has managed to maintain and popularize the breed and through which the most complete system of horse breeding has been realized. The Thoroughbred, which was introduced from the lands of the Orient, has been enlarged, improved upon, and acclimatized through knowledge and dedication. Now the question remains whether other countries should introduce it and whether they should also make use of horseracing so as to maintain and popularize the breed?[17]

For Justinus, however, it was not just a matter of the Thoroughbred itself; rather, the system that had made the Thoroughbred possible was key to understanding its success:

> The development of racing, which astutely understands how human nature works, stimulates and challenges the passion of the aristocracy and the rich, excites the competitive spirit in the folk and the poor, brings together and unifies all classes, invites the lower elements to see themselves united under

> a common goal with the higher elements, allows the lower orders to triumph over the sovereign, entertains the landowner, the competitor, and the spectator—it is a public spectacle where splendor, wealth, and sloth all have their place.[18]

In short, horseracing had the potential to raise the nation's breeding standards because it involved everyone. Since debate would naturally arise over why a particular horse won while another lost, racing educated the public on important matters of "horseflesh." "Reasons would be looked for, searched, known and finally spread," Justinus explained, "so that equine knowledge becomes general knowledge."[19] That contrasted with the situation in countries such as France and Germany, where aristocrats, cavalry officers, and riding masters pontificated on equine quality "in a tangled mass of unused and hardly used books"; in England, Justinus noted, horse breeding had been elevated to a "popular science" (*Volkswissenschaft*).[20] Thanks to racing, the entire English population talked about the quality of horses in pubs and clubs up and down the country.

A major reason Justinus felt attracted to the English model was that he resented the control stud directors (*Landstallmeisters*) exercised over breeding policy. Compared with continental Europe, where former cavalry officers monopolized the state studs, in England they were blissfully absent. His attack focused on three areas—knowledge, practice, and ideology—that maintained the status quo. First, Justinus criticized stud officials who claimed a scientific basis for their expertise. Pointing out that the publications German equestrians cited were mostly copies and reprints of older hippological works, he noted that these authors were reluctant to accept innovation.[21] Second, Justinus criticized hunting as a way to improve the quality of horses, not least because of the overt emphasis placed on the rider's ability rather than on the performance of the horse. "Even if hunting does have its benefits in testing the rider's courage and skill as well as the quality of horses," he argued, "it nonetheless cannot be defended from the appearance that it is merely a playful recreation of young people whose purpose is to show off both themselves and the horses rather than actually contribute to breeding."[22] Finally, Justinus dismissed the ideology that elevated the breeding of saddle horses into a pursuit seen as qualitatively different from other forms of livestock breeding. "Those who make horse breeding their profession," he observed, "believe out of half-baked pride that their art is something better and higher than breeding cattle, sheep, and pigs."[23] Remarking that pigs and chickens did not have state-appointed studs, Justinus explained that equestrians were so infatuated with riding horses that they considered horse breeding sui generis and the horse, by extension, almost a superanimal.

For all his efforts, Justinus's pleas to reorganize Prussian horse breeding based on the English model encountered sharp resistance in the German states. Many of the ripostes came from various *Landstallmeisters* who had a vested interest in protecting their position, expertise, and worldview. Some traveled to England between 1815 and 1830 to see for themselves how it was done there, rushing to print their impressions. Most German writers ridiculed what they saw, and the head of the Prussian Stud Administration, Carl von Knobelsdorf, quipped that the English love of horseracing typified "the moral history of a strange kingdom."[24] Undoubtedly, English horseracing was a traditional pursuit that shared characteristics with classic racing events such as those held at Munich and Siena, where the aim was to gamble, win, and take part in frivolities.[25] However, the same writers could not take seriously a pursuit that appeared to be nothing more than entertainment: Prussian stud directors believed they were engaged in the more serious business of protecting the country.

Three features of the English model particularly irked them. First, stud officials objected to the way money or commercial interest had hijacked a reputable pursuit. Pointing out that "English horseracing is the biggest betting game in the world," Carl Friedrich Wilhelm von Burgsdorf, the Trakehnen stud director, expressed his disappointment that the English had all but retreated from breeding "noble" horses.[26] Echoing a similar sentiment, Freiherr von den Brincken, a Prussian riding master (*Rittmeister*), observed, "The reputation, which has been gained either through having won prizes at some famous racing event or for having successfully gambled large sums of money, is almost the sole criterion that decides the capability of stud horses in England."[27] Second, stud officials poured scorn on the credibility of private breeders. In 1831 Karl-Wilhelm Ammon, the Munich stud director, implied that they were amateurs:

> The private horse breeder usually treats horse breeding as a secondary concern—or part-time job [*Nebenerwerb*]—that is grouped with other agricultural practices. From this it is clear that he cannot seriously pursue either a theoretical or a practical study of horse breeding. By contrast, the stud director lives for his discipline and is taught comprehensively about breeding from the time he is young.[28]

Third, stud officials alleged that the English undervalued the horse's appearance and chose speed as the main criterion for measuring its quality. Such thinking was unacceptable to an equestrian like Burgsdorf, who insisted on the importance of conformation: from his perspective, "good proportions, consistency in build and pace, purity of bones, smartness, and beauty" were more important.[29] Because these attributes were accorded a subordinate role in racing, England was no longer considered capable of producing quality horses. During his visit to England in the mid-1820s, Burgsdorf thus found only four "good" horses out of the six hundred he encountered.

> [The horses] were at times not the right color; at other times they were not for sale, since they were busy or were too precious for breeding since they were winners of the Derby stakes. But true racing characteristics (or crumpled front feet) were to be found all over the place: full of faults . . . and totally exhausted when young so that they would retire early to lead lives in sickness.[30]

That the English model made horse experts obsolete had much to do with German stud officials' hostility toward horseracing. In contrast to the arrangement where state studs formed the focal point for breeding, English breeding offered the masses "ownership" of, and "access" to, horses, decentering the place of authoritative knowledge. Because speed, not appearance, was privileged, the public could also be excused from inspecting horses for themselves; instead, they merely had to consult the race results and bloodlines recorded in the *General Stud Book*. Any decision about quality could thus be reached without ever leaving home, and there was seemingly no need for lifelong experience, proximity to horses, or specialist knowledge. One of the few advocates of the English model, Friedrich von Biel, accurately noted stud officials' maneuvers "to shut out the public" as reflecting fears that "all principal, court, and provincial studs will become redundant."[31]

More fundamentally, the English model was perceived as an affront to the art of horsemanship. Before visiting England, Brincken had had high hopes, not least because he believed he was visiting a country that boasted a rich equestrian tradition. His expectations were quickly dashed:

> In a country where to move anywhere requires horses, where riding has become a national custom, where only the most impoverished go on foot over long distances, where foxhunting has turned into a popular pursuit of the rich, and where horseracing has become a national pastime—it is all the more galling indeed to discover in such a country that horsemanship has been neglected.[32]

Nowhere was the debilitating effect of this clearer than at Rotten Row in London's Hyde Park. At first glance, members of high society who rode immaculately turned-out horses did look as though they were engaged in serious horsemanship. But appearances could be deceiving, Brincken remarked, because speed had ominously taken precedence; exposed to the influence of horseracing, riders succumbed to the fashion of mindless galloping. Proper horsemen were not so heretical: they would let the horse know who was in charge, lead it gracefully in the desired direction, and effortlessly allow the creature to release the correct amount of power in proportion to the rider's aims.[33]

During his sojourn, Brincken witnessed the passing of the Cruel Treatment of Cattle Act (1822), one of the first pieces of animal welfare legislation, which indicated how far horsemanship had deteriorated in England. (The act did not cover cruelty to horses.) Rather than express his indignation in humanitarian terms, he concluded in equestrian terms that the need for a law signaled that English gentlemen were forgetting how to ride their horses properly, making riders cruel.[34] Even the positives Brincken drew from his experience received qualification. For example, he singled out foxhunters for praise but went on to point out that their horses were usually worn out quickly because the riders—oblivious to the basic tenets of horsemanship—did not know how to ride so their horses could go the distance.[35] Not only was the English model a threat to the way horse breeding was conducted, it also seemed to threaten the ideology that favored the saddle horse.

The Promise of the East

For critics of the English model, the deserts of Arabia—in particular Mesopotamia, the banks of the Euphrates, and the Syrian plains—offered an alternative.[36] Criticism of the English model did not extend to the Eastern foundations of the Thoroughbred–the Godolphin Barb, Darley Arabian, and Byerly Turk–because advocates believed the success of the English horse had little to do with its ancestry.[37] German skeptics of the Thoroughbred inverted the narrative, pointing to the racecourse as the source of contamination. One simply needed, they implied, to set the clock back. Therefore importing purebred Arabians to improve the quality of existing stock was the solution.

One such advocate, Röttger von Veltheim, held that the German states should refrain from importing English Thoroughbreds and procure pure Oriental horses instead.[38] Although he initially thought it would be sufficient to import such horses from either Russia or England or to purchase preselected horses shipped from India, he later advocated direct imports.[39] What changed his mind was John Lewis Burckhardt's influential accounts of travel to inner Arabia, which revealed that quality horses were mainly found in rural rather than urban areas, particularly among the nomadic desert tribes.[40] Convinced by this account that genuine Arabs could no longer be purchased at the usual commercial trading centers, Veltheim backed launching expeditions to trade directly with the Bedouins and Wahhabis.

The German preference for Arab horses was not just patriotic sentiment; it was also based on their being saddle horses first and foremost. Looking for the "real thing" among desert tribes reflected fears that towns and cities were detrimental to breeding riding types. Heavier breeds were in increasing demand in industrialized society, while the lighter breeds declined. By searching out rural enclaves, opponents of the English model hoped to find an environment in which commerce, entertainment, and industry were secondary. Brincken believed that the desert and nomadic life were beneficial to the horses. Placed in warlike conditions, the Arab horse was also subject to a sterner test of its qualities:

> Designed to test the dexterity and skill of both man and horse, the war games that several Persian natives practice on horseback sometimes exceed our powers of comprehension. But in the view of reliable eyewitnesses, the games certainly amount to evidence that the Bedouins of the Arabian desert know how to work their horses. Thus it would not be unreasonable to say that while such practice contrasts with our own systematic art achieved within the manège, it achieves similar honorable ends.[41]

For supporters of the English model, however, Arab horses represented something quite different. For Biel, secretary of the Racing Club in Mecklenburg where, in 1822, the first Thoroughbreds were raced, the Arab horse was costly, unreliable, and romanticized. Importing Arabs directly from the East took time, effort, and patience, he maintained. One expedition conducted by Russians bore witness to the spiraling costs, and persuading owners to part with their prized possessions was difficult. After three years of concerted effort, the Russians managed to purchase a paltry five stallions and two mares.[42] Where is the sense, Biel asked rhetorically, in taking on "endless" risks and costs when the English had already perfected the system?[43] Arab horses were also of unreliable quality, he claimed, and their bloodlines could not be guaranteed because of a lack of documentary evidence. Complete reliance on appearance or expert opinion was risky, in contrast to the English Thoroughbred, whose bloodlines were meticulously recorded in the studbook.[44] Because information about Thoroughbreds was readily available and transparent, supporters argued, the English breed was to be preferred.

Critics also took issue with proponents' romantic views of the Arab horse. "Europeans in general tend to believe everything that comes from the Orient to be pearls and gems," Biel complained, adding that the reality was far different.[45] Instead, he argued that Arab horses' breeding and rearing were vicious: since they were left hungry from birth, made to carry "barbaric" stirrups and rods that damaged their bodies, and ridden mercilessly, it was a wonder, Biel concluded, that "a perfect horse could be found in Arabia."[46]

What was the result of the debates about the relative merits of the Arab horse and the English Thoroughbred? One consequence was a general reluctance by stud officials to accept the Thoroughbred and the institution of horseracing in the first half of the nineteenth century. In 1828 Carl von Knobelsdorf, head of the Prussian Stud Administration, set up societies that deliberately encouraged breeding military horses rather than those founded to support horseracing.[47] At Trakehnen, the principal state stud in Prussia, the emphasis on breeding "riding types" (*Reitschlag*) ensured that the import of Oriental breeds prevailed in the first three decades of the nineteenth century.[48] Stud officials were not completely hostile to the Thoroughbred, however, not least because of their difficulties in procuring Arab horses. In 1830 Karl-Wilhelm Ammon expressed his willingness to accept Thoroughbreds as long as the "misuses and defects [due to the racecourse] are completely removed."[49] He thus distinguished between the horse and the racecourse, which explains why in 1844 the state owned 244 of the 1,539 Thoroughbreds registered in Prussia.[50]

In 1866, however, the state became serious about both Thoroughbreds and flat racing.[51] After the appointment of Count Georg von Lehnsdorf as head of the Prussian studs, the principal stud at Graditz in Saxony acquired sixty Thoroughbred stallions.[52] At this point the state began to compete seriously in racing. Of course, there were earlier successes: there are reports that Trakehnen horses began winning prizes in Berlin, Königsberg, and Insterburg from 1848 onward. From the late 1860s, however, Graditz Thoroughbreds began to steal the show by dominating the field.[53] Both breeding societies and the German Jockey Club (Union-Club) pleaded with the state either to pull out of racing or to compete abroad rather than at home.[54]

Growing interest in flat racing did not alter the German preference for the steeplechase.[55] From the time thoroughbreds first raced in Doberan, Mecklenburg, in 1822, horseracing based on the English model struggled.

In 1842 the Westphalian Society for the Breeding of Thoroughbreds (Der Westfälishe Verein für Vollblutzucht), which had tried to promote the breeding of Thoroughbreds through flat racing, was disbanded. One major cause of its failure was the pervasive criticism of racing as frivolous entertainment; members of the society could not quite convince the public that racing contributed seriously to the breeding of horses for the national interest.[56] Thus supporters of the English model needed to rethink their tactics. Finding it difficult to attract audiences for flat racing, in 1869, the *Sporn* (the official journal of the Union-Club) decided to organize steeplechase events.[57] Despite the Union-Club's attempts to pique the public's interest in the horse rather than the rider, it was largely unsuccessful.

During the 1870s there was controversy surrounding the introduction of professional jockeys to replace the amateur military officers who typically competed in steeplechasing.[58] For advocates of flat racing, the participation of amateur horsemen who refused to carry weights skewed results because horses raced under unfair conditions.[59] In 1881 a Prussian commission commented that "jockeys on the whole ride better and more evenly than gentlemen, and precisely the situation in which individual gentlemen ride so much better than the others would . . . lead to races becoming not a test of the performance of horses but a test of the rider."[60] Despite such efforts at reform, officer riders continued to be popular and refused to act as mere technicians subordinate to the racehorse. Instead, they insisted on competition between unequal individual riders and on the utility of the steeplechase as training for war. One of the most celebrated equestrians of his day, Kurt von Tepper-Laski, explained the attraction of the steeplechase:

> The knightly passion of combat between men, the concentration of all powers, unfettered devotion to risk in the hope not to perish but to conquer, the straining of the mind to outsmart the opponent through skill and deceit, either through the right pace or through skilled negotiation of obstacles, and above all to receive from the Most High fame in the form of prizes—this is why officers ride in races.[61]

The Rise in Popularity of Heavier Horses

For some time, the influence of state studs and the preference for breeding warhorses stifled demands from the wider society. One of the first regions to challenge state dominance in this regard was the Rhine Province. When the Napoleonic Wars ended, it was quick to question the disproportionate emphasis on remounts, and local agricultural societies pressured Berlin to send stallions that catered to the real needs of farmers.[62] With the foundation of the *Landgestüt* at Wickrath in 1839, these pressures increased. One letter received by the *Oberstallmeister*, the head of Prussian studs, demanded stallions "that would be big, strong, and weighty."[63] Two decades later, the stud director at Wickrath received an appeal for "the highly regarded and urgently requested [Flemish] Brabant stallions."[64] These early pleas for heavy breeding stock fell on deaf ears, and the preference for *Campagnepferde*, or riding horses, was upheld well into the 1850s.[65] The situation differed little in the other thirteen *Landgestüte* operating in Prussia at this time.[66]

Circumstances began to change in the 1860s, however, under two related pressures. First, breeding heavy horses became a lucrative business. In the 1850s, heavy horses in the Rhine Province had fetched between 80 and 100 talers.[67] By the mid-1860s prices had markedly increased: cold-blooded horses commanded between 200 and 300 talers.[68] Such increases were an incentive for private breeders to invest in heavier horses. Second, the inability to breed sufficient cold-blooded horses domestically led to an increase in imports. One study published in 1865 reported that five thousand to six thousand working horses had to be purchased from neighboring Belgium and the Netherlands,[69] producing an annual loss to the local economy of 1 million talers. Such pressures, in addition to increased demands from industry and commerce, resulted in Wickrath's eventual acquiescence. From 1875 to 1883, sixty-seven Belgian heavy stud horses arrived, and by the end of the nineteenth century the ratio between light and heavy stud horses increasingly favored the latter.[70] For example, whereas in 1876 it had stood at 48:1, in 1890 it was 89:75, and by 1910 it had reached parity at 200:202.[71] As table 9.1 shows, the shift from light to heavy horses was replicated across Prussia, where the share of heavy horses overall jumped from just 36.03 percent in 1898 to 48.64 percent in 1911.

By the late nineteenth century the trend toward breeding heavier types finally began to influence the traditional remount breeding regions of East Prussia. The state of affairs led Richard Schoenbeck, a breeder of remounts, to fear for the security of his country: "Though we are at present able to satisfy demands of the cavalry domestically," he warned, "if the breeding of cold-blooded horses were to continue apace, it would be difficult to satisfy demand in the event of war."[72] Proposals to divide Prussia into remount and heavy horse breeding areas—in order to protect saddle horse breeding from the free market—did little to allay his fears that private breeders would choose their self-interest over patriotic duty. They would willingly respond, he predicted, to industrial, commercial, and agricultural demands for heavy horses. His ultimate charge was an old one: in the event of war,

Table 9.1. Proportion of light and heavy horses in Prussia, 1898–1911 (%)

	1898		1911	
	Light	Heavy	Light	Heavy
East Prussia	90.69	5.11	73.53	22.26
West Prussia	94.76	5.24	88.19	11.81
Brandenburg	71.55	24.81	53.80	46.20
Pomerania	80.82	15.82	80.15	19.85
Posen	95.77	3.30	92.18	7.82
Silesia	70.83	28.07	54.89	45.11
Saxony	33.87	63.97	8.54	91.46
Schleswig-Holstein	85.10	11.10	58.05	41.95
Hannover	69.00	22.61	84.73	15.27
Westphalia	55.39	40.32	46.86	53.14
Hesse-Nasau	47.29	50.03	21.49	78.51
Rhine Province	15.45	81.38	1.10	98.90
Hohenzollern	80.00	20.00	—	100.00
Average	61.60	36.03	55.45	48.64

Source: Oskar Knispel, *Die Verbreitung der Pferdeschläge nach dem Stande von 1911* (Berlin, 1915), cited in Rudolf Hompertz, "Pferdezucht und Pferdehandel im deutschen Wirtschaftsleben" (dissertation, University of Cologne, 1922), 47.
Note: Mixed breeds have been omitted from this table.

breeding heavy horses did little to protect the country. By contrast, remounts were a matter for the state.

Such sentiments, which privileged remounts over other types of horses, may have been convincing in the first half of the nineteenth century, but they cut less ice later in the century. Countering Schoenbeck's argument, Heinrich von Nathusius, a supporter of cold-blooded horses, rejected attempts to label non-remount breeding as unpatriotic, noting that contributions from the sector generated wealth for the national economy. Bolstered because horse breeding then fell under the Ministry of Agriculture and not the Ministry of War, Nathusius argued that horse breeding should consider the broader interests of society.[73]

In East Prussia, private breeders made a breakthrough in 1898 when the Ministry of Agriculture agreed that while the state would not actively encourage breeders to deal in heavy horses, it would not prevent them from doing so.[74] Why did East Prussian private breeders, who in the past had dutifully obeyed the state, change their minds? First, they increasingly saw the economic benefits of breeding heavy horses. Looking at the situation in the western provinces, farmers recognized that remounts had little market value outside the military. Their efforts were helped by the establishment of cooperatives that freed them from relying on landowners by providing direct funding to invest in ventures they saw as fit to pursue.[75]

Private breeders also experienced a shift in the nature of agriculture. Previous arrangements had benefited both the farmer and the military, since the horses farmers bred and reared could be offered to the army as remounts after several years' use on the farm. As agriculture became more intensive, however, breeders no longer saw any benefit in this setup. Bureaucrat Otto Gagzow explained, "The light remount horses were not able to pull on their own—in teams of four—the turnip plow and other heavy farming equipment, nor could they carry the turnip plow over badly maintained highways."[76]

Finally, the loss of skilled laborers to the industrial regions affected the quality of saddle horses. Dietrich Born, an East Prussian landowner, explained that breeding lighter horses was a delicate undertaking:

> Every experienced farmer will know that strong, round, apt horses are as easily cared for by a laborer, while lighter, temperamental noble horses must be fed and cared for with greater attention, and that such animals are quickly corrupted in the hands of inexperienced workers and consequently perform badly.[77]

A study published in the *Journal of German Agricultural Breeding* confirmed this assertion. In East Prussia, there were 11.49 equine-related accidents for every 10,000 horses; in the Rhine Province, where heavy horses made up the majority, the figure was just 4.37.[78] Partially lame draft horses could at least fetch some money on the market, but saddle horses with defects had almost no market value.

When Leonhard Hoffmann, a veterinarian in Stuttgart, surveyed German horse breeding in 1902, he noted that a romanticized view of the horse had given way to a more rational perspective that favored heavy horses over light ones, economic need over military dictates, and calculation over patriotism. "What could one possibly want," Hoffmann asked rhetorically, "in any area of business, from agriculture to haulage, from saddle horses?"[79] If breeders were "to breed the most noble Spanish carousel horse, which had fetched enormous sums in its time," they would "do as badly financially as those who, over fifty years ago, filled their stables with Arab horses."[80] Lighter horses were worth less, "since they can be of use neither for agriculture that uses deep plows nor for industry that requires suitably serviceable horses."[81] Only in the military could saddle horses find employment, a preference that had made "German horse breeding backward with regard to present circumstances."[82]

Highlighting the favoritism the state had traditionally lavished on saddle horses, Hoffmann accused it of not "having the right to demand that everything be wasted only on the so-called warm-blooded horses."[83] Increasingly, breeders were escaping from the clutches of the state by helping themselves—through breeding societies—so that they might not be tempted away from their core interests of breeding for "heavy transport."[84] Breeders then had to face the fact that they could no longer operate within a world dominated by the "ideals, aesthetics, and passions" of equestrians, "but in place of all these sentiments the reckoning farmer and breeder should have a calculating mind and brain."[85] Horse breeding, in other words, was no longer the "noble" pursuit it had been a hundred years earlier.

Dividing a Precious Resource

Despite the temptation to view breeding warhorses as a narrow preoccupation limited to ministries of war and breeders of remounts, the Prussian experience shows that equine politics involved virtually everyone with an interest in benefiting from "horsepower." Over the nineteenth century, a broad debate erupted over how a precious resource should be produced, divided, and managed. Throughout the first half of the century, state horse breeding policy could afford to ignore wider interests. Indeed, the state could do so because to some extent the interests of farmers in East Prussia and those of the state overlapped, since lighter breeds could be useful in both agriculture and war. As industrialization transformed horse breeding, however, the military penchant for lighter breeds attracted increasing criticism. Although the system of state studs had developed in the mid-eighteenth century as a response to the demands of war, horse breeding could not forever remain in the hands of the military alone. Beginning with the Rhine Province, and eventually even in East Prussia, a broadening of equine politics took place as private breeders demanded and produced heavy horses better suited to new farming methods. Those engaged in commerce and industry likewise called for heavier breeds that could be employed in transport, haulage, and construction, helping to shift equine politics away from the breeding of lighter types.

It was not simply the triumph of economic demand that dictated this shift in breeding practices, however, for international social and cultural influences also played a part. Rivalry with England and the threat an English model of horseracing posed to interpretations of the quality of horseflesh also determined the direction of equine politics. One result of this tension was the Prussian rejection of English Thoroughbreds in favor of Arab horses within the state studs; another was the privileging of steeple-chase racing over flat racing. Both results illustrate that military influences remained strong throughout the nineteenth century, but they also show how traditional sentiments about horsemanship chafed against new ideas about the expertise of the general public. For advocates of flat racing, objective data for comparing horses could be achieved only with wide public involvement, while opponents claimed that the English model was no true test of horsemanship under the conditions experienced in war. Both English and Prussian models show how priorities—military and civilian, public and private, riding and driving—were negotiated differently during the twilight years of what one distinguished student of equine history has called the "late equine period."[86]

TEN

"Horsemeat Is Certainly Delicious"

Anxiety, Xenophobia, and Rationalism at a Nineteenth-Century American Hippophagic Banquet

SUSANNA FORREST

SOUP
Consomme a la Equine. Broncho Bullion.

MEATS
Roast Sirloin of Stallion with Brown Gravy.
Fried Filly a la Soubise.
Old Mare Boiled, with Horseradish.
Boiled Gelding a la Francaise

VEGETABLES

PASTRY
(Thoroughbred) Pudding
Nuts—Horsechesnuts

DRINKS
Ice Water. Hard Water. Soft Water. Well Water. Hydrant Water.
Water.
Coffee. Mares' Milk.

On March 5, 1898, students and professors of the Kansas City Veterinary College gathered with guests in a restaurant on Twelfth Street to eat a horse. This act of consumption, normal in much of Europe and Asia at that time, became the first story on the front page of the *Kansas City Journal* the following day. "HORSE MEAT FEAST," began the headline of a story that ran for a column and a half, "BANQUET AT WHICH HORSE MEAT IS THE

STAPLE. SERVED IN VARIOUS STYLES. KANSAS CITY VETERINARY COLLEGE MAKES A STARTLING MOVE." It was illustrated by a pen-and-ink sketch of a mustachioed and aproned German restaurateur standing behind a table of dishes labeled "Old Mare Boiled," "Boiled Gelding" and "Roast Sirloin of Stallion."[1]

Behind the horsemeat feast lay a very specific historical context, in which each actor played his part: veterinarians, their physician guests, the German waiter, and the horse, "a bay . . . five years old," "fresh from the plains." At the time, horse slaughter for human consumption was technically legal in most parts of America but socially suppressed by a dominant narrative in which the nation was white, Anglo-Saxon, and repulsed by horseflesh. The hippophagic banquet was a European innovation—an exercise in didactic, performative consumption—and, with the folksy touches of "broncho [*sic*] bullion" and "well water," each participant at the Kansas City feast attempted to Americanize an activity their press had long since characterized as a curious, perverse, and even effete foreign practice linked to poverty, war, and social breakdown.

Participants doubtless believed the time was ripe for Americans to overcome their "superstition" and begin to eat horse: although the working horse and mule population was still rising, peaking in 1915, the advent of the electric streetcar and automobile signaled the beginning of the end of horse power, freeing the workhorse for alternative uses;[2] the once boundless western ranges were filling with cattle farmers who wanted the grasslands cleared of feral horses to make way for more beef; and an American horsemeat industry had emerged and was struggling to develop. These Kansas City vets made an educated example of themselves for this most public experiment. By doing so, they were attempting to simultaneously reverse horsemeat's long-established foodway in the West—as a shameful, unclean meat sold by subterfuge and eaten in desperation—and substitute one with shallow roots planted by earlier men of science seeking to improve the lives of the working classes. Against this ran the current of other historical factors: rising concern about animal welfare and anxiety about food that was increasingly industrialized, unrecognizable, and removed from its source.

The Taboo

For every attempt to explain the taboo on horsemeat in one neat shot, there is a countervailing argument. As Sylvain Leteux suggests, horsemeat is "a taboo in constant evolution,"[3] and there is no untangling its original roots. By the nineteenth century, European and American anxiety about horse flesh was very real, and in America this distaste persisted long after consumption had been legalized and to some extent normalized in the Old World, where it had even begun to be seen as a health food. To understand why the entirely legal 1898 Kansas City banquet was "a startling move," it is necessary to examine the history of the taboo.

Archaeological records show that horses were commonly eaten across Europe and Asia in Neolithic times and earlier. At the beginning of the Holocene, driven by a changing climate and perhaps human hunters, wild horses retreated to Iberia and the Eurasian steppe, where they appear to have first been tamed in northeastern Kazakhstan about 3500 BCE.[4] The domestic horse arrived in Mesopotamia from the steppe as "the ass of the mountains" in the Akkadian period (2350–2150 BCE), and by 2000 BCE horses were used for chariot warfare. At this junction the taboo first emerges from an intertwined combination of functionalist and structuralist reasoning: thanks to their role in battle, horses were both too expensive and too prestigious to eat.[5] A trained horse was worth twice as much as an ox, and a single horse might be exchanged for an entire flock of sheep. Unlike free-roaming, scavenging goats and sheep, the horse also required cultivated, expensive grain as fodder.[6] In landscapes where horses were more economically and easily kept, such as the steppe and northern Europe, horses continued to be eaten and sacrificed, but the Mesopotamian ass of the mountains had no dual role, unlike the ox, who was converted into beef when his prime working years were over.

The first clear reference to avoiding horsemeat comes from a piece of Babylonian wisdom literature found in the library of Ashurbanipal (668–631 BC) in Nineveh, which Wilfred Lambert believes originated in the Kassite period (ca. 1531–1155 BCE), featuring a pampered talking horse who says, "my flesh [is not] eaten."[7] This horse defines himself against a humbler ox by pointing out that "[close to] king and counselor my stall is located," while servants maintain his "magnificent drinking fountain" and bring him leafy plants to eat. By the time Deuteronomy was composed nearly a thousand years later, the horse was not just too expensive to eat, but also unclean. Although not mentioned by name in the list of prohibited meats, he is automatically excluded by neither chewing the cud nor having a divided hoof. The horse may live alongside man with other domestic animals like the cow, sheep, and goat, but he alone is indigestible.

Neither the Greeks nor the Romans (with the exception of the Veneti) were open equivores, although the Roman poor did eat horse flesh purchased from knackers.[8] The distinction between a butcher, who prepares legitimate meats for human consumption, and a knacker, who breaks down the inedible horse into grease, bone, hide, tendons, and animal feed, is another critical factor in the evolution of the horsemeat taboo, one that partially explains how an expensive animal became, on death, a revolting cheap meat fit only for dogs, chickens, and pigs. The horse's meat was a by-product of the end of its working life, and since that flesh was not desirable, the horse was worked till it dropped, bringing the suggestion that its meat was aged, tough, and inedible—chosen only by the desperate poor.

Beyond the walls of Rome, hippophagy was a practice of uncivilized barbarians like the Slavs, Teutons, and Celts, set in opposition to clean-eating, civilized Roman citizens. As Christianity spread across Europe in the wake of the Roman Empire, hippophagy and the closely linked practice of horse sacrifice were singled out. In AD 732 Pope Gregory III wrote to Saint Boniface, telling him he should stop his pagan German subjects from eating both wild and domestic horse, since the flesh was "impure and detestable."[9] While some scholars believe Gregory's letters were either fabricated or of little actual importance in the centuries that followed,[10] missionaries from Russia to Iceland introduced at least a nominative taboo on hippophagy. In ninth-century Ireland it required three and a half years' penance, and in one Icelandic saga a good Christian king under pressure to eat horse flesh makes an elaborate compromise by merely sniffing at a cloth placed on the handle of the meat kettle.[11]

From the Middle Ages onward, horses were increasingly used for a broader array of tasks beyond riding and pack work as wagons and later carriages were used more frequently and agricultural implements improved—making the horse more economical than the slow ox—and human power was replaced with horse power in early industrial tasks like milling, mining, lifting goods, operating pumps, and processing raw material. The number of horses correspondingly increased, and both their cost and their exceptional status among livestock continued to be factors. The earliest veterinary and farrier manuals were dedicated to the horse alone, emphasizing its value and status as a companion to both farmer and knight.[12] The Babylonian talking horse had a direct descendant in the noble medieval warhorse, the "most suited and handsomest, most courageous and strongest to withstand troubles and most able to serve the man."[13]

For all this, the body of the horse—whether it drew a dung wagon or carried a king—still represented a considerable quantity of red meat. Disposal of this flesh was associated with, and created opportunities for, illicit practices. Public taboo thus masked a private, illegitimate practice of occasional consumption, made easier because horsemeat closely resembles beef and is impossible to detect when mixed with other meats. While there are many mentions of horse corpses being left in ditches or fed to pigs, some body parts made their way into human dishes, and not just in times of desperation like famine, revolution, or war. It is hard to imagine thrifty European peasants overlooking the rare boon caused by old workhorses dying. Francis Bacon mentions horsemeat as inedible, which of course means it was known and its unacceptability was a given. Keith Thomas mentions a ballad from seventeenth-century Europe about a man giving his neighbors a pasty made of horse and making them ill.[14] Sailors in the Spanish navy were fed on barrels of preserved "red deer" that was in fact from foals.[15] At the same time, the taboo on horsemeat was enforced more aggressively by church and state, again for perhaps both functionalist and structural reasons: on the one hand, guilds and associations of butchers were well organized and influential, and they resented being undercut by knackers peddling cheap flesh. On the other hand, church and aristocracy recognized the higher status of the horse—a threat to the animal was a threat to them.[16] A Frenchman was beheaded for eating horse flesh during Lent in 1629, causing Voltaire to protest, "Had he been a rich man, and had spent two hundred crowns in a supper of sea-fish, suffering the poor to die of hunger, he would have been considered as a person fulfilling every duty."[17] The century that followed saw numerous government strictures in France on the sale of horsemeat for human consumption.[18]

Meat and Rationalism

The hippophagic revolution that began at the end of the eighteenth century sought, in true Enlightenment style, to strip hippophagy of illegality and superstition and present it as a rational practice for the good of mankind. Following Voltaire, the physician Mathieu Géraud's 1786 essay on the management of urban waste touched on the illegal sale of horsemeat, often passed off as beef or mutton at a low price. He noted that "the ancients and the Tartars of today, the soldier and the citizen, who eat these animals, are not inconvenienced by it," so why shouldn't butchers openly sell it?[19] The ox was vanishing, and more conventional meats were priced beyond the reach of the poor.

In the Middle Ages red meat had come to have an importance beyond its poundage: wealthy English and the military in particular ate increasing amounts of beef, which not only "represented land-based wealth and all the power that came with it" but was also believed to endow one with physical strength. At banquets, "social rank determined which cuts of beef a diner received."[20] Géraud was proposing a new, cheaper beef for the growing urban proletariat: on the eve of the French Revolution, he suggested cake, of a sort, for all.

It was war that introduced European civilians and armies en masse to horsemeat. During the Napoleonic Wars, Denmark became the first European city to legalize the sale of horsemeat when Copenhagen was besieged by the English in 1807.[21] Meanwhile, French army surgeon Baron Larrey fed wounded soldiers horse broth as an antiscorbutic, publishing his findings on his return to civilian life. More voices were added to the rationalist chorus, with treatises and reports issued by doctors and zoologists and committees of inquiry formed by municipal authorities. Pro-hippophagists followed the pattern established by Géraud. The Industrial Revolution of the nineteenth century once more accelerated the number of horses required for transportation, agriculture, and industry, so the hippophagists calculated the number of horses killed annually whose flesh could go to workingmen.[22]

These apologists included prominent physicians, veterinarians, and other men of science like the head veterinarian of the French army, Émile Decroix, or the director of the Paris Natural History Museum, Isidore Geoffroy Saint-Hilaire. "There are millions of French people who do not eat meat . . . and considering this misery, each month millions of kilos of good meat are given to . . . pigs or dogs, or even thrown to the streets all over France!," Saint-Hilaire wrote.[23] The recasting of horsemeat as a healthy food was the most dramatic reversal of the perception of uncleanliness about meat northern Englanders colloquially called "knackerine." In scientific journals and newspaper editorials, pro-hippophagists explained that because the horse was a "clean" herbivore, its meat was purer than that of omnivorous pigs or farmyard fowl that gobbled anything. Unlike cattle and pigs, horses were free of tuberculosis and tapeworm, and their meat was rich in iron. The German chemist Justus von Liebig pronounced it higher than beef or mutton in "creatine," a substance found in mammalian muscle.[24]

In the 1840s, hippophagic banquets were held by doctors in German states and Scandinavia.[25] In Berlin in 1847 one was interrupted by a group of assailants rumored to be butchers angry at the threat to their livelihood, who severely beat the hippophagists. By the following year, however, horsemeat was so well established as a healthy food that Berlin doctors offered horse-broth baths for children.[26] German states gradually legalized the sale of horsemeat for human consumption, and in 1847 Austria and Belgium followed, then Switzerland in 1853, and Norway and Sweden in 1855. Humane societies and hippophagic clubs began to sponsor butchers specializing in horsemeat in poorer areas of towns. Meat was distributed free to the poorest.[27] In a concession both to the butchers and to public anxiety about "horse beef," the new *boucheries chevalines* or *Pferdemetzgerei* were segregated from conventional butchers, bound by strict standards and inspection systems.

Antihippophagists "with significant Catholic and noble elements" endeavored to protect the horse, arguing "that horsemeat marked regression of civilization" and comparing hippophagy to cannibalism.[28] The old structuralist sentiment that the horse should receive the care due to its privileged status also found a new twist with the animal welfare movement. Knackers' yards were notorious for emaciated, lame horses foraging desperately for food, so newly founded humane societies argued that old horses would be treated better if they had secondary value as meat animals. In his *Letters concerning Nutritional Matters, and Above All, Horse Meat,* Saint-Hilaire, a member of the Société Protectrice des Animaux of France, suggested: "Let [the working horse] rest, put him up somewhere, feed him so that he's not a loss; and above all, . . . heap no more blows on him," "because to beat him would be to add to his distress a damage to ourselves: we risk spoiling the merchandise."[29]

And what about the other subjects of this philanthropic effort, the poor? As one English antihippophagist pointed out, "The privileged and wealthy classes are to have a monopoly of beef and mutton, and the poor, politically excommunicated working man is to content himself with the flesh of the horse." Berliners may have taken to *Pferdefleisch,* but Parisian servants did not trust the meat their masters proffered, believing it was diseased. Only the siege of Paris in 1870 finally converted them. The English preferred to dine on frozen beef and mutton from Argentina and New Zealand, and when Decroix offered a prize for London's first horse butcher, there were no takers.[30]

Selling Hippophagy

In the nineteenth century horsemeat was a foodway with a complicated history and notorious reputation, promoted by an educated group who attempted to lead by example and introduce it from the top down. The hippophagic dining clubs of 1840s Germany became more elaborate public performances in France and the United Kingdom, written up in amused detail in newspapers and journals. One, at the Grand Hotel in Paris in 1856, convened over a hundred "of the most distinguished literary and scientific men . . . including 24 physicians, 8 veterinary surgeons, 16 editors and men of mark," including industrialists, bankers, agronomists, Gustav Flaubert, Dumas Père, the inspector general of veterinary schools, and the chief of a police prefecture.[31] Since horsemeat was reputed to be tough and stringy, the flesh of carriage horses was lavishly prepared and the resulting menus also printed in the press. At the Langham Hotel in London in 1868, dishes included "purée de destriers" served with amontillado, Pegasus filet, sirloin stuffed with brussels sprouts "centaur style," lobster mayonnaise made with "Rosinante oil," jellied hoof with cherry liqueur, and—the apotheosis of mock beef—a 280-pound baron of horse carried in by four cooks, to the accompaniment of "Roast Beef of Old England" played on the trumpet by a real beefeater.[32] Guests were usually informed about the nature and price of the horses they were eating or even shown photographs. The banquets were exclusively male events.

As with so many aspects of the pro-hippophagy campaign, these displays were fraught with contradictions. Hippophagists stressed the cleanliness of the horse as a meat source, but that raised the specter of unclean meat. Émile Decroix ate the meat of diseased and paralyzed horses to show that it was safe, but this was hardly an enticement, even if it had no ill effects. Campaigners talked about humane ends for old cab horses, but that conjured up the familiar sight of suffering horses in the street. These wealthy and influential men called horsemeat a solution to poverty, thus stigmatizing it as a meat of the poor and desperate, even as they ate it in dainty dishes that were beyond the means of the people they thought would benefit most from it. Price rather than taste appears to have been the foremost concern of most Europeans, and when the price of horsemeat rose in the 1950s as the last workhorses were turned into sausage, appetite for it declined.

Horsemeat in America

America represented a more challenging potential market for horsemeat than Britain, having inherited European Christian values that predated the rationalist hippophagists. After the initial experimentation of the colonial period, the country was both increasingly conservative about food and too large and socially diverse for a national cuisine. American tastes were essentially British, though Americans ate more of everything,[33] and that plenty distinguished their cuisine. It included above all a desire for meat, which–thanks to an apparently endlessly fertile, underexplored landscape and ambitious farmers–the country produced in abundance. An Englishman crossing America in the 1820s reported that no American but a "free negro" would eat offal or animal heads—the European peasant's brawn and sweetbreads were out of the question. "There are few things in the habits of Americans, which strike the foreign observer with more force than the extravagant consumption of . . . meat," confirmed one commenter.[34]

In the last decades of the nineteenth century living standards rose rapidly, and with them the demand for the best cuts of meat at low prices.[35] If meat, and especially beef, was a source of national identity, then horse, at least in the mainstream narrative, became its opposite: an un-American food. American "prejudice" against eating horsemeat was not out of step with the resistance hippophagy met in Europe, but America went on publicly resisting despite massive immigration from nations that ate horse, and despite the same social factors: growing urbanization, industrialization, and an ever rising number of working equids.

In the 1840s horsemeat is mentioned as part of wilderness narratives: missionaries, miners, and pioneers were sometimes reduced to eating their horses out of desperation. They also took along dried horsemeat for Native Americans, who were sufficiently "other" to be considered suitable recipients. While some equid meat was eaten during the Civil War, there was no major conflict that would have caused a situation like the Siege of Paris, and the 1860s saw the opening of vast new territories for cattle ranching. Giant herds of beef cattle were driven to railheads and transported to new industrial meatpacking centers like Chicago and Cincinnati, then distributed to major cities by refrigerated railcars. Kansas City was one such prosperous "cow town," with stockyards and packing plants. Mass production and competition made beef affordable to most: "Where in the old country do you find a workman that can have meat on his table three times a day?" asked a German immigrant in the 1890s.[36]

The United States did experience substantial economic depressions in the 1870s and 1890s, but horsemeat was not required. Fluctuations in the cattle fodder market caused beef prices to rise on occasion, and these increases were bitterly resented—sometimes even causing riots—but they did not result in the opening of legitimate *boucheries chevalines*.[37] By the mid-nineteenth century, even pork was eclipsed by beef on the national menu; one commenter stated, "We are essentially a hungry beef-eating people, who live by eating."[38] There was no role for poor man's beef.

The horse's position was also increasingly distinctive among domestic animals. Steers, sheep, or pigs were once driven live into the centers of American cities and slaughtered in butchers' yards, but after the 1880s they began to arrive jointed and frozen in refrigerated railcars. It was part of general change in Western meat consumption toward what anthropologist

Noelie Vialles describes as "sarcophagy"—the consumption of flesh that is not recognizable as belonging to a particular animal, as opposed to zoophagy, in which your dinner is a visual reminder of exactly what you are eating.[39] The only animals that filled the streets were horses, who—rather than living on a distant, imagined grassy range—sweated, excreted, and suffered before the eyes of citizens. America joined the English animal protection movement, opening its own Society for the Prevention of Cruelty to Animals in 1866. In 1890 the organization began widespread distribution of over a million copies of Anna Sewell's 1877 novel *Black Beauty*—billed as "the *Uncle Tom's Cabin* of the Horse"—giving an immediate voice to the cab horse.[40]

Yet America was fascinated by hippophagy in Europe. As early as 1856, rogue Democrat supporters tried to goad German immigrants in New York by implying that their bologna was made of horse.[41] The consumption of horsemeat became a lens through which to view the shortcomings of the Old World so many Americans had left behind. The spectacle of European hippophagy undermined rationalists and entrepreneurs who tried to bring horsemeat to America. Every time they cited the example of other nations who were hippophagic, they were pointing to barbarians or to Old World populations dogged by war or revolution, unable to afford more legitimate meat. Indeed, many popular narratives used nonconsumption of horsemeat to distinguish Americans from brutal, impoverished, or effeminate foreigners.

Foreigners

Through the second half of the nineteenth century and the early twentieth century, American foreign correspondents reported on European hippophagic banquets, butcher shops, and abattoirs. Dispatches range from brief wire reports to detailed essays syndicated across the country. Decroix and Saint-Hilaire were household names. Generally, even when these pieces acknowledged the practical advantages of hippophagy for Europeans, they did not recommend its adoption by Americans. Horsemeat was never linked to an American patriotic narrative but was regarded as a practice associated with a continent long left behind.

Ida Tarbell visited an abattoir in 1890s Paris that she described as "a chamber of horrors": "I have looked into the revolutionary prisons of Paris and upon the guillotine with less shivering than I felt in this place." Despite her belief that "if [the horse] had a voice in deciding his fate he would raise it emphatically in favor of the sausage"—rather than mistreatment by "poor hucksters, teamsters, jacks-of-all-trades"—she left before the fatal blow was delivered to a broken-down Percheron: "It was too much like assisting at the execution of a friend."[42]

In 1893 Frank G. Carpenter, another prominent journalist, wrote a long feature on the horsemeat trade in Berlin. While praising German hygiene standards and inspections as superior to those in America, he describes the death of a "magnificent black carriage horse" as "more like a murder than anything else," its "fine eyes" shining "piteously with pain for a second." Under the headline "How the Germans kill, cook and eat the noblest animal known to man," he described how children "ravenously" devour bowls of "horse-bone soup" and the wife of a horse butcher—a monster carving up a sausage in the accompanying illustration—has "cheeks fat and rosy on a diet of horse meat."[43]

As Maureen Ogle writes, "In the late nineteenth century, widely accepted theories linked food to national power and racial superiority. . . . [If] diet and national might were linked, it was crucial to understand which food delivered strength and health," because "meat-rich diets had made Europeans and Americans masters of the planet." In contrast, the "rice-eating" Chinese and "Hindoos," as one typical essay phrased it, were an "inoffensive collection of people from whom not much could be expected."

Nineteenth-century America subscribed to Justus von Liebig's theory that meat was the only food that actually made the human body generate new flesh, but they could not embrace his scientifically derived conclusion that horse could be more nutritious than cow, for "beef reigned supreme."[44]

"We are aware that the meat is consumed, to some extent, in France, Belgium, Germany, and Russia, but it has never, until very recently, been used as a food by anyone of the white race in the United States," fulminated the *New York Sun* in 1894 on the "abomination" of horsemeat. "It is not here as it is in those countries of Europe, where many poor people are unable to buy even the cheapest of meats, and are glad to get anything that is eatable."[45] After all, what sort of flesh was built from horsemeat? The Berliners' rude health had an ogreish quality. Tarbell was unusual in ascribing positive qualities to hippophagy, pondering, "If we are what we eat, as some wise men argue, will France acquire vigor, persistency, patience, steadiness, in proportion as she eats the animal which is the personification of all these qualities?" However, her refusal to describe her own horsemeat meal "à la Geoffroy Saint-Hilaire" made it clear: this need not apply to Americans.

France needed the horse's steadfast qualities after a century of social breakdown, revolution, and war. When prices rose and Parisian women hurled horse sausages at butchers in Les Halles Centrales in 1870, reports reached America, along with word of the price of *Pferdefleisch* in Vienna. Over their breakfast eggs, Americans read about student "horse communities" in Russia that bought a horse to eat communally, among whom "so many Nihilists have been found . . . that the horse meat eaters are liable to prosecution by the government."[46] Twenty-two years later some students were said to be "addicted."[47] By 1905 American commenters even blamed Japan's defeat of the Russian army on the Russians' preference for vodka and horsemeat over tea and rice.[48] The Japanese fed horsemeat to their prisoners, with Carpenter sampling some but finding it impossible to chew.[49]

What if this tainted substance—brought about by social degeneracy and also a cause of it—came to America? Reflecting on the collapse of the antebellum southern states in 1868, an Illinois newspaper spoke of the "manly fortitude" of white men "paralyzed by oppression" as the agricultural system collapsed: "Horse-meat is eaten in France and England, and pronounced *charmant—magnifique*. If the negroes catch the idea, farewell to all the plow animals; even the toughest old mule will have to succumb."[50]

American Horse Eaters

Behind this phobia lay a more rational fear of substances closer to home. America might have more meat than Europe, and a sophisticated industrial production system, but it also lacked consistent federal laws for inspection until 1890. From 1879, attempts had been made without success to introduce bills tidying up the food production process; states fought for their right to legislate independently, or else commercial interests intervened.[51] From the 1850s, successive scandals involving tainted, adulterated, or rotten food rattled the public. The meat industry was thought to be fixing prices, and butchers were suspected of adding illicit or spoiled meat to sausage or ground meat. Various unregulated additives were developed to make food look fresh. One of the driving forces behind the introduction of federal legislation was the advent of oleomargarine, a blend of beef tallow and cottonseed oil much mistrusted, for obvious reasons, by the US dairy industry.[52] Rumors arose that in England this fake butter was made from horse bones mixed with waste butter and coloring, sold at a hefty markup.[53] "The devil has got hold of the food supply of this country," proclaimed Senator Algernon S. Paddock, who pushed through the first comprehensive food and drug bill in 1892.[54]

Horsemeat, with its well-established association with uncleanliness, poverty, and contamination, was unlikely to succeed in such an atmosphere. The horse's public suffering was transmuted into the meat itself:

"The horse sweats; the Ox does not; and the meat of the horse seems impregnated with an odor of perspiration," the *New York Times'* man in Paris informed his readers after dining on horse flesh in 1875.[55] Horsemeat was morally and literally tainted. Far from delivering the horse from suffering, the diner consumed his sweat and struggle. One horsemeat tourist reported in 1870:

> I had the cholera, nightmare and sea sickness, all at once, and all night. . . . It makes me belch and heave to write about it, twelve hours after. Every piece of meat I see now transforms before my eyes from the tenderest beefsteak into the stringy, coarse, strong, indigestible stuff which—ugh, I shall never allude to it again as long as I live.[56]

Noting that envelope flaps were coated in glue made from "old nags," one newspaper columnist suggested that licking an envelope could cause death from "some taint of animal poison."[57]

Occasionally editorials promoted horsemeat's virtues over other meats. "Maryland and Virginia highland horses are hardly less wholesome than Illinois distillery hogs," argued Felix L. Oswald, MD, author of *Household Remedies*, although he conceded that "even the Dixie darky, who consumes those hogs by the barrel, would probably deem it an insult to invite a friend to a lunch of cold horse-steaks."[58] When horsemeat surfaced in butcher shops and cheap restaurants, it was greeted with horror and threats of legal action. A butcher in Philadelphia was tried for adding horsemeat to the "black sausages" he sold in neighboring beer shops in 1857,[59] and when a butcher in Cincinnati served his customers equine bologna in 1870 one paper described the event as "an atrocity."[60] A New Jersey butcher who joked that he had sold a lady horse instead of beef sirloin had to cover his customer's $30 medical bill when she got sick,[61] and in 1896 a German butcher in Pennsylvania was arrested for selling horse bologna and rib roasts as beef.[62]

Yet many individuals attempted to launch legitimate horsemeat businesses, finding markets in immigrant populations and exporting canned meat to Europe. These entrepreneurs came largely from hippophagic European countries like Switzerland, Austria, France, and Denmark, and they included some of the eight million Germans who arrived in the United States in the nineteenth century, many of whom found work as butchers or in the industrial stockyards. Foreignness is emphasized in accounts of their work, and their ventures tended to end in scandal, economic failure, or being shut down by state or municipal authorities.

Henry Bruckman, a "thrifty young" recent German immigrant, pleaded ignorance of the law when he was found slaughtering horses on a "lonely site" near Chicago in 1890. He argued that he was butchering them only to feed to his pigs, but his wife said they were eating the meat themselves and supplying willing neighbors. Although Bruckman protested that he would never use sick horses, he was suspected (wrongly) of selling horsemeat under false pretenses to cheap "foreign" restaurants, part of a "Queer Traffic" of "Old Broken Down Street Car Steeds and Animals that Long Only for Death."[63]

Henry Bossé, a "Patriotic Frenchman," turned his back on Chicago when he was refused a license, instead opening an abattoir near New York in 1889 making smoked horse sausages for export. The health committee intervened after locals claimed their horses wouldn't go within a mile of the plant and after calls for nonhorse sausages dropped at nearby restaurants. The press reported in detail on the clean shop floor, and Bossé ate raw beef sirloin for his audience, but the inspectors refused to sample his wares, giving him three months to relocate.[64] In 1891 a packing company in nearby Newton Creek was discovered to be shipping canned "crippled horses" to Europe under the label "family beef," leading to direct intervention by the secretary of agriculture, Jeremiah Rusk.[65] In 1895 the Indiana legislature was poised to block the sale of horsemeat "as a marketable commodity" after an investigation that found three Chicago plants producing horsemeat for food in Belgium and France were killing the "old, worthless, disabled, halt, maimed and blind." This unregulated horsemeat market in Chicago threatened Packingtown's reputation.[66]

Yet, despite disgust and ostentatious xenophobic revulsion, the homegrown entrepreneurial spirit was fired when faced with another source of American abundance. The grasslands of America, rapidly filling with beef cattle, were also inhabited by an estimated two million feral horses. Some were owned by individuals who raised horses for sale, others were unclaimed mustangs or broncos descended from escaped domestic horses. They were so cheap that they were a more economical pig food than corn. All were eating grass that could feed beef cattle. By 1894 Montana's state veterinarian proposed that the state's 100,000 feral horses be canned for export.[67] A $3 horse, it was claimed, was worth $30 to $40 once tinned .[68] One rancher struck it rich, selling up to 7,000 horses to a packing plant.[69]

By the time of the Kansas City banquet, however, American horsemeat canners were closing their plants. There was not much margin in the conventional meat business thanks to the demand for low prices, and horsemeat packers were not exempt: they sold every other by-product of horse slaughter but relied on meat to make a profit. Europe proved a difficult market, since not only did its natives prefer fresh horsemeat to canned, they were also concerned about the threat to their own meat industry from American beef, pork, mutton, and horse. Tariffs were levied on American meat, and European consuls raised questions about American hygiene and inspection standards compared with their own. Horsemeat was once again the focus of these allegations. In August 1895 Richard Martin, a Chicago man, was visited by the French and German consuls on suspicion of shipping diseased meat. Germany barred US horsemeat exports that year.[70]

By the time the secretary of agriculture introduced inspections for horsemeat and issued an official stamp—which was distinct in both shape and color from the stamp used for other inspected meats—Belgium had closed its ports to American horsemeat. That autumn, Democrats spread rumors that a failing Oregon plant was going to be purchased by "foreign capitalists" if a Republican won the presidential election, for "they expect the present hard times to continue, and therefore the demand for horsemeat will increase."[71]

A Banquet in Kansas

No one asked the Kansas students their motives for holding their banquet at this seemingly inauspicious time. A report on an earlier hippophagic banquet mentioned that its host had eaten horse at his graduation from veterinary college and at other gatherings of New York veterinarians, suggesting that America's vets had made a tradition of copying Saint-Hilaire and Decroix.[72] The Kansas City college was founded only in 1891 and did not offer a three-year course till 1896. In 1895 it had fewer than thirty students.[73] Perhaps when the students christened the horsemeat dinner their "first annual banquet" they were trying to equal older, more prestigious colleges.

Their motive might also be found in their choice of horse "fresh from the plains." Instead of eating a used-up workhorse, they chose a feral horse who would have been a threat to local beef grazing. The open range system in Kansas ended after a severe blizzard in 1886, and—as elsewhere in the West—the space for wild horses was vanishing.[74]

The students faced opposition both from members of college staff and from local restaurateurs and hoteliers. The best businesses in town were unwilling to alienate customers "by preparing such a banquet," and the vets paid double the fee of a restaurant on Walnut Street, only for the chef to "balk" just hours before the meal, after the horse had been killed and butchered. So it was that the "little German restaurant" with the mustachioed waiter stepped in.

Guests included local doctors, students, and faculty members, including Dr. Charles H. Sihler, formerly in charge of the US Bureau of Animal Industry, and Dr. Sesco Stewart, who had organized the bureau's inspections for trichina in pork. There were two "long tables" set with "flowers, celery, catsup bottles, salt cellars," and printed menu cards. The Kansas City banquet shared with its predecessors and with many newspaper reports of hippophagy a certain collegiate humor. The single bay horse became stallion, filly, mare, and gelding. It was fried, served (nodding to Saint-Hilaire and Decroix) "a la Francaise," with horseradish, as a consommé and "bullion," boiled and roasted. The dessert course was full of puns: "(Thoroughbred) pudding" and "chesnuts" [*sic*], with mares' milk to follow. Instead of fine wines—Kansas was officially a dry state—a variety of water was served, from "hard" to "well."

The high spirits that prompted the students to organize the banquet and devise the amusing menu faltered at the first hurdle. When confronted by "Broncho Bullion" and "Consomme a la Equine," diners reached instead for celery sticks. Some tried to return their soup claiming they had oversalted it, but they were swiftly handed new bowls. Finally, laughter and "bantering" overcame the awkwardness, and people began to eat.

The meat course was served on platters and "resembled beef very closely." "By the time the waiters had placed the meats before the guests everyone was in a persuasive mood—persuading each other that horse meat was certainly an important article of food if only people could place their prejudice to one side." "Why," the author of the piece noted, "in France certain classes of the people subsist almost entirely on horsemeat."

Much emphasis was placed on the fact that the horse was "perfectly sound" and "had never had a halter on in his life." Hal C. Simpson, who had purchased the horse at a local market, stressed that he had "always been permitted to roam at will on the plains" and had thus been selected "because he would be more likely to be without a blemish or any of the diseases known to tame horses."

Dr. O. W. Krueger, a prominent local doctor, pronounced the horse "as tender as any meat I ever tasted," while student H. E. Rice added lemon to his fried filly and pronounced it "delicious." Each guest was called on to speak about the horse as superior to cow, and a few commented that a deliberately fattened domestic horse might have been less tough. "It bucked and kicked enough to make it as tough as shoe leather," commented a member of the purchasing committee, and someone joked that as long as it didn't buck once eaten he would be happy, causing much laughter.

At the close of the meal, the president of the college, Dr. Charles H. Sihler, informed guests that he had examined the horse before it was killed and found that "he had a bad case of tuberculosis, his glands were in a horrible condition, and his liver in a bad state." There was, he went on, an abscess on the horse's left hip. As the guests' faces registered horror, Sihler grinned and pointed to his own plate, emptied and scraped clean.

It is unclear from the *Kansas City Journal*'s piece whether Sihler was joking or telling the truth, but the meal did end with the resolution that a horsemeat banquet would be held every year: "'Horsemeat is certainly delicious,' was the unanimous statement."[75]

After the Meal

The Kansas City banquet did not launch hippophagy in America, or even in Kansas. The embattled industry was dealt a fresh blow when the Second Boer War began and British army agents began to buy up range horses to ship to South Africa, driving up their price. Although some firms struggled on, it was no longer a growth area. Another high-profile scandal hit in 1899 when it was alleged that rancid canned meat supplied to US soldiers in the Spanish-American War was horsemeat. The highly publicized "Beef Court" inquiry featured experts testifying that "a compound of horsemeat, carpenter's glue, tallow and common salt, would show the same results under chemical analysis as those shown by canned roast beef."[76] Although the inquiry found that the meat was poorly canned beef overheated in the Cuban climate, this made little difference to horsemeat's public reputation. When Harvey Washington Wiley slaughtered a horse to develop a test for calculating the percentage of horse as an admixture with other meats, the *Washington Weekly Post* mocked his efforts as "the Kimberley diet"—referring to the starving, besieged Boers—calling the work "nauseating to the man who would as soon partake of fricasseed humanity as to eat the flesh of his four-footed friend."[77]

Chicago was hit by yet another panic in 1902 when papers reported that "15,000 maimed, crippled and diseased horses" were slaughtered in the city annually, their meat carried off in butcher carts under cover of night.[78] The country was gripped by a "beef famine" that suspicious Americans blamed on the greed of the beef-packing industry rather than a poor corn harvest. "Grave doubts," wrote the *Indianapolis Journal*, "are beginning to fill the minds of citizens as to whether the prime beef which they are eating from day to day is really beef or possibly only horsemeat." Although a cleanup was attempted, state authorities lost control over food hygiene thereafter, as big beef packers pushed for federal inspections that would enable them to once again sell meat to Europe. In 1906 the Federal Meat Inspection Act was signed, stipulating mandatory inspections of horses before and after slaughter.

Conclusion: American Hippophagy at Last

Within ten years Americans in large numbers would turn openly to hippophagy. What finally overcome taboo, anxiety about stringiness or disease, love of horses, and pride in devouring good cuts of meat wasn't a drive for health or sophistication, or the efforts of domestic economists to educate the poor. It was simply a bare butcher's counter. With World War I, government-inspected meat exports rose and shortages kicked in. "Food will win the war," proclaimed Herbert Hoover's Food Administration, asking Americans to observe "meatless Mondays." Old canning plants reopened and went in pursuit of mustangs too small to be sold to European cavalries. For the first time hippophagy took on a patriotic role. "Food savers" in a Minnesotan "feeder's club" ate not just horse but dog and muskrat.[79]

One Swiss-owned market in New York sold 1,800 pounds of horsemeat in the first week it was open.[80] St. Louis housewives "returned again and again" to buy horsemeat,[81] and a New York jazz club served "cab horse cutlets with whine [*sic*] sauce."[82] In 1917 two butchers in Kansas City sought permission to sell horsemeat[83] after the state investigated the possible sale of canned mustang shipped from Idaho.[84] Chicago held out against a legitimate horsemeat business, protecting its reputation to the last. New York was reportedly consuming 10,000 pounds a week by 1918, and Professor Dean Horace Hoskins of the State Veterinary College in Ohio advised housewives' collectives to stop clubbing together and just buy horsemeat instead.[85]

Yet after the war, in the 1920s the horsemeat industry faltered before remaking itself as a convenience pet food business. Horses were still going into cans, but they were emptied onto the plates of dogs, not humans. The "taboo in constant evolution" reacted once more to historical and economic circumstances, returning horse to its long-established roots as an outcast meat. The educated example of the veterinarians and physicians of Kansas City, Newark, and New York was once more sidelined as ordinary

Americans returned to the red meat they knew best: beef. In 1919 the *Bisbee Daily Review* summed up the dietary reversion with a boastful dose of patriotism: "Mr. American Citizen" didn't want whale, horse, noodles, or cheap cuts of meat "French style,"

> No Siree, he wanted his pork chops well, and his steak rare, and his French fried, and his eggs, and four slices of bacon. Butchers tell us that when pork chops were $.50 per pound they sold as many pounds as they did when they were $.30. And those who insist that an honest-to-John Yank can be nourished on coolie grub, or on mush, beans, boiled hoofs and horns, or the third cutlet from the tip of the cows tail can guess again. He doesn't even care for fish except once in a while. Wherever food prices may climb Mr. American Workingman will be found ascending right along side; breathless and disheveled, perhaps, but there.[86]

ELEVEN

Circus Studs and Equestrian Sports in Turn-of-the-Century France

KARI WEIL

Riding has a long and illustrious history in France, where military might depended—until well into the nineteenth century—on a famous cavalry and an aristocracy that prided itself on horsemanship.[1] This changed over the course of the nineteenth century with the decline of the French military and the transformation of riding into a bourgeois pastime and sport. Writing during the Second Empire, the popular journalist Albert Cler wrote that while it was once considered "la partie la plus essentielle de l'éducation surtout pour la noblesse . . . l'équitation est tombée de nos jours dans une complète décadence" (the most essential part of education, especially for the nobility . . . today equitation has fallen into complete decadence).[2] Increasingly popular for men of various means and for their *lorettes*, or mistresses, riding became a deceptive signifier during the century: a symbol of longed-for aristocratic habits and bodily comportment, even as the practice of riding and driving horses became both means and metaphor of bourgeois ascendance, if also moral derision. Equestrianism is thus one area that reveals the bourgeoisie's inconsistent attitude toward the aristocracy in France, where, as Robert Nye and others have noted, an aristocratic code of honor was esteemed by successive generations of bourgeois men despite their professed belief that talent rather than blood determined individual worth.[3]

Contradictory as a marker of class, horsemanship was even more volatile in its gendered connotations. The rise of the easily mocked Sunday rider (usually a man), coupled with the growing number of skilled woman riders, brought new fears about "women on top."[4] With the annexation of the Bois de Boulogne as a kind of horse playground for "le tout Paris," the question of who was mounting whom became the focus of gossip that cut across class lines and threatened male supremacy. Despite (or because of) the strictly gendered rules of equitation, whereby only men could ride astride while women rode sidesaddle, equestrian metaphors carried an erotic charge that linked fears about changing class relations to fears about changes in gendered behavior. Equestrian practice and its representation thus bring to light the instability of what were deemed basic bodily distinctions of class and gender.

The ambiguous status of riding is linked especially to its emergence as sport and, as such, to a merging of bourgeois and aristocratic worlds. As Eugen Weber has noted, the word sport had an "equivocal sound" in France owing to its associations with both riding and the more vulgar practices of racing and betting.[5] Equestrianism underscored the ways sport itself both was built upon and clashed with markers of aristocratic behavior. Essentially, sport was seen as a means to show (if not show off) one's physical and, by extension, moral capacities. Indeed, sport was said to inculcate the moral properties historically identified with the ruling classes and with horsemanship—will, courage, and virility—but to do so through forms of bodily display that were considered markers of a lack of decorum.[6] How, given the growing popularity of sport, could one show one's honor without seeming to need to? Or did the meaning of bodily display change by the end of the century to allow for a noble spectacle of the male body and, by extension, the man on horseback?

The eighteenth-century natural historian Georges-Louis Leclerc, Comte de Buffon, had called the horse "the most beautiful conquest of man" and celebrated the noble image promoted by man and horse together.[7] A necessary catch phrase of Second Empire Paris according to Cler, Buffon's statement regarding the noble image of the horse clashed with the crass and undisciplined image of the contemporary "horsey set" that was more interested in consumer display than in military or moral conquest.[8] Perhaps, then, it is not surprising to find, toward the end of the century, efforts to restore the symbolism of the horse and of horsemanship as a noble and virile ideal—efforts that nevertheless raised new fears about changing relations of class, gender, and sexuality. This is especially apparent in the discourses surrounding the founding and reception in 1880 of the Cirque Molier, established by, and primarily for, aristocratic men who were also the primary performers. Much turned on the notion of the Thoroughbred, or *pur sang*, to which these men were compared, but whose meaning was ambiguous. Translated literally as "pure blood," "thoroughbred" could refer to a proto-fascist notion of a pure race and a product of noble birth. But the Thoroughbred horse was in truth a product of cross-breeding, and its powerful image was understood to be more a matter of training than of blood. The image was thus also available to the bourgeoisie, who joined the aristocracy in efforts to reveal their talent through bodily display. As a result, equestrianism also worked against the normative masculinity it was said to promote by tainting the image of the horseman with the destabilizing effects of objectifying the male body for a male gaze.

Horsemanship: From Aristocratic Spectacle to Bourgeois Spectator Sport

Already in the 1830s Stendhal noted the changing symbolic function of riding. Whereas in our post-Freudian century we imagine little girls dreaming of a horse between their legs, Stendhal makes it clear that in Napoleonic France this was the dream of adolescent boys.[9] Julien Sorel, son of a carpenter and the "hero" of *Le rouge et le noir* (1830), is one such cavalier who is "au comble de la joie" (at the height of joy) when allowed to ride in the king's *garde d'honneur*, and as the horse rears he imagines himself a hero of the Napoleonic army. Mounting a horse is a sign both of Julien's (social) mobility and of his virility—confirmed by the women who watch him on horseback: "Il voyait dans les yeux des femmes qu'il était question de lui" (He saw in the women's eyes that it was all about him).[10] But we find that "heroes start falling off their horses in French literature" in the aftermath of the Revolution. A subsequent fall while riding with Count Norbert makes Julien realize that he might better impress Norbert's sister Mathilde with humor than with riding.[11] More important, the novel makes it clear that in the years following Napoleon's defeat and retreat, the hero on horseback is no longer born, or made in battle, but is produced in lessons. The only heroism that can't be bought, Mathilde claims, is the death penalty (289).

In *Le rose et le vert* (The pink and the green), written seven years later (1837), Stendhal's narrator describes, with a touch of nostalgia, certain gendered distinctions of riding and watching that are still prevalent in Prussia. Men take pleasure in a daily parade on horseback up and down the streets of Königsberg, knowing, without having to see, that curious women watch their every move from behind covered windows.

> La curiosité des dames est aidée par une ressource accessoire: dans toutes les maisons distinguées l'on voit, aux deux côtés des fenêtres de rez-de-chaussée élevé de quatre pieds au-dessus de la rue, des miroirs d'un pied de haut, portés sur un petit bras de fer et un peu inclinés en dedans. Par l'effet de ces miroirs inclinés les dames voient les passants qui arrivent du bout de la rue, tandis que, comme nous l'avons dit, l'oeil curieux de ces messieurs ne peut

pénétrer dans l'appartement, au travers des toiles métalliques qui aveuglent le bas des fenêtres. Mais s'ils ne voient pas, ils savent qu'on les voit et cette certitude donne une rapidité particulière à tous les petits romans qui animent la société de Berlin et de Koenigsberg.

[The curiosity of the women is aided by an accessory resource: in each reputable house one finds on either side of the ground-floor windows, elevated four feet above the street, foot-high mirrors attached to a small iron arm and slightly inclined toward the inside. By the reflection of these inclined mirrors, the women see the passersby who arrive at the end of the road; at the same time, as we have said, the curious eyes of these men are not allowed to penetrate the apartment because of the metallic sheets that cover the bottom of the windows. But if they don't see, they know that they are seen, and that certitude gives a particular rapidity to all the small novels that animate the societies of Berlin and Königsberg.][12]

Riding has come to have different meanings in France under the July Monarchy than it does in Prussia, and the difference between these two nations is presented in the language of spectacle and its relation to knowledge-power. In Prussia being a spectacle is still an honorable distinction for a man. Prussian men could parade with the "certitude" of being both watched and desired, the very certitude that also animates their novels. Such certainty was harder to come by in Paris, where the incipient commodification of the horse created unexpected changes in its expression of class and gender codes. Indeed, by the time Stendhal wrote the *Le rose et le vert*, the Parisian upper classes had all but abandoned the once obligatory parade down the Champs-Élysées to avoid mixing with the crowds. In 1847 the French author Delphine de Girardin claimed it was now "la mode" not to join the promenades.[13] While in the novel's opening a Prussian general who has returned from Paris tells of the only Frenchman with whom he could strike a friendship—one "dont le rôle ou *l'individualité*, comme ils disent, est de briller par ses chevaux de voiture" (whose role or "individuality, as they say, is to shine by virtue of his carriage horses) (9)—we also learn that the Frenchman was ready at any moment to gamble away his ideals of love and beauty (10). Paris, unlike Prussia, is a place where ideals can be bought and sold and where noble masculinity, no longer situated in the blood, can easily be gained or lost. Whereas in Prussia equestrianism is still a sign of heroic, virile undertakings, in Paris the horse has become a sign of surrender to "la vie de café."[14] The physical mastery represented by the spectacle of the horseman has ceded pride of place to the economic mastery represented by the horse bettor or breeder.

For Stendhal, however, Julien Sorel's inadequacy as a rider comes with a compensatory gain in ironic vision that presages changes in the representation of male bodies more generally. Whereas Prussian customs celebrate what D. A. Miller has referred to in another context as the "pleasurable visibility of the male body as such," Julien's situation is representative of a shift in the role of the French novel's hero after the Revolution and the fall of Napoleon, such that the Parisian male body disappears as spectacular object and increasingly finds its power in a disembodied gaze upon others.[15] Riding may thus be one of the last activities to succumb to the "great masculine renunciation" described by psychoanalyst J. C. Flugel and the change "from (passive) exhibitionism to (active) scoptophilia (erotic pleasure in the use of vision)—the desire to be seen being transformed into the desire to see."[16] The compensatory pleasures of seeing over being seen as described by Flugel help explain the rise of riding as spectator sport during the century, especially as such pleasures were projected both onto the woman rider as a specular object and onto the horse. Frenchmen, as Stendhal suggested, were thus able to "briller par ses chevaux" (shine by their horses) as well as by their women.

Whereas the French school of riding had been dominated by haute école dressage as developed by and for the military, a different, more forward seat and relaxed style of riding imported from England became increasingly popular, especially among women. "Anglomania" was thus blamed for everything from men's losing control of their horses to the masses attempting to "sais[ir] les rênes de l'État" (seize the reins of the state).[17] A "real man," moreover, no longer had to ride in order to "know" horses. The eye of the "véritable amateur," as Charles Baudelaire suggests in his poem "Un cheval de race," could recognize the still "delicious" Thoroughbred "même attelé[s] à un carosse de louage ou à un lourd chariot" (even hitched to a rented coach or to a heavy wagon).[18] The Société d'encouragement pour l'amélioration des races de chevaux en France (Society for the Encouragement of the Betterment of the Breeds of Horses in France) and the Jockey Club (founded in 1833 and 1834 respectively), transformed a passion for riding horses into a passion for judging their conformation and betting on them. According to Anne Martin-Fugier, "Avec le Jockey-Club, le monde s'installe dans le Boulevard. Ce cercle, en prônant une vie fait principalement de chevaux et de divertissements, opérait la jonction entre le grand monde et le monde du spectacle" (with the Jockey Club, high society took its place on the Boulevard. This circle, by promoting a life composed principally of horses and entertainment, functioned as the link between high society and the world of spectacle).[19] Horseracing, especially, turned watching instead of riding into the privileged activity, transforming horse enthusiasts into spectators and making the Thoroughbred the privileged object of their gaze.

Women and horses were also entwined as objects of spectacle in the French circus, which grew during the century.[20] Originally developed for the display of military maneuvers on horseback and haute école dressage, during the nineteenth century the circus became a form of chic entertainment. With four circus halls by midcentury, Paris was the capital of what was called the "temple de l'équitation."[21] The hippodromes were, in principle, barred from presenting haute école riding, but later in the century the programs of these two equestrian arenas grew more difficult to distinguish. Moreover, competition from the music halls and other new forms of popular entertainment meant that equestrian performances had to make way for clowns, jugglers, and acrobats who, when they did perform with horses, did so to show off their own agility and bodily mastery (or exaggerated lack of it) rather than the horses'. Acrobatic numbers on horseback increasingly became the provenance of a special type of *écuyère* who, instead of mastering the horse, used the animal as a stage on which to display her femininity. For many, the popularity of the *écuyère* whose image appeared on posters all over fin de siècle Paris marked a clear decline in the classical ideal the circus was founded on, a decline evinced by the loss in popularity of the horse—the original raison d'être of the circus.[22] In 1874 Victor Franconi, the last of the great *écuyers* of the nineteenth century and founder of the hippodrome of the Place de l'Étoile, lamented that a mule whose "dressage" consisted of throwing anyone who tried to ride him had become the hit of his circus. "Un mulet remplit ma salle, alors que le cheval ne fait plus recette" (a mule fills my hall while the horse is no longer the winning ticket).[23]

If the circus's replacement of haute école with the *écuyère*'s acrobatics can be seen as the logical outcome of a century that put woman in the role of spectacular objects, the replacement of horsemanship by the burlesque spectacle of a mule throwing its rider may be read as both social-sexual and political satire: a nightly reenactment of France's military defeat by Germany. Here it is important to remember the association of military glory and the horse around which the circus originated in France. The point is not only that haute école dressage was derived largely from military maneuvers, but that it produced an erotic identification between man and horse that confirmed the rider's virility. As historian of the French circus

Henry Thétard explains, "La haute école est la suprême sorte de dressage puisque l'écuyer fait corps avec son élève et peut, par son contact permanent, non seulement lui imposer des pressions, des coértions violentes, mais aussi lui transmettre, lui infuser son fluide dominateur" (Haute école is the ultimate dressage because the rider is one with his student and can, by his permanent contact, not only use pressure and violent force, but also transmit to him his dominating fluid).[24] Thétard describes the perfection of oneness with one's horse in specifically gendered terms:

> l'homme pétrissant avec les jambes cette masse puissante et chaude qui cherche à dérober à ses ordres par tous les moyens, à fuir l'emprise de la volonté qu'elle redoute. Quand enfin la bête abdique, s'abandonne, mi-lasse, mi-confiante, quel triomphe enivrant, quelle fierté joyeuse pour la vainqueur qui a conquis l'empire d'un être.
>
> [the man, kneading with his legs that powerful and warm mass that seeks to escape his orders by any means, to flee the hold over her will that she fears. When finally the beast abdicates, gives in, half weary, half confident, what an intoxicating triumph, what joyous pride for the victor who has conquered the empire of a being.][25]

No wonder that even as more women successfully performed dressage, representations of the *écuyère* rarely show them astride their mounts except in mockery of the noble equestrian. The equestrienne as clown was epitomized by Lulu, Félcien Champsaur's celebrated star of the circus and a short novel, whose most famous image showed her riding a pig.[26]

If the circus had once celebrated France's military might, by the end of the century it appeared to be an arena for the parodic display of masculine impotence and animal domination, hence an illustration of many of the psychosexual maladies said to affect the French nation after its 1870 defeat. How then are we to interpret the fact that, at the same moment the circus became a form of entertainment for the display of feminine (and feminized) bodies and human impotence in the face of the animal other, it also became the provenance of a new breed of performer: the aristocrat?

The Aristocratic Circus: Purebreds on Show

In March 1880, Ernest Molier founded the amateur Cirque Molier in a wing of his *hôtel particulier*, which he converted into a riding school to satisfy his lifelong "passion for horses." The performers chosen were friends, members of the French aristocracy including the Comte de La Rochefoucauld and Baron de Bizy, and the audience was chosen by personal invitation.[27] What and whose pleasures were piqued by the athletic performance of these purebreds? Or was the question one not of pleasure, but of necessity—a need for the aristocracy to take back its provenance and to contest claims of its demise? If this was the hope for many, it was a risky business. On the one hand, the demanding physical exercises of the circus allowed the aristocracy to assert its capacity to govern. On the other, because "these men transgress codes of class and gender decorum," many found their performances "embarrassing."[28] The title of Daniel Lesueur's 1892 novel *Névrosée,* in which a culminating scene at the amateur circus precipitates the heroine's physical and moral decline, points to the ways the desires and pleasures of the circus are symptomatic of the degeneration of the fin de siècle.

Reception of the amateur circus was mixed, and it was alternatively regarded as symptom of and cure for the maladies of the time. As Molier himself reported, the press saw his project as advancing either "the regeneration of the human race or its demoralizing."[29] Taking the latter position, *Le Radical* (May 25, 1886) claimed that this is what the aristocracy does when it fails at everything else, calling it "the beginning of the end."[30] A letter in *La Tribune* lampooned in political terms the "humiliation" of a duke proving himself on the trapeze or a count on horseback:

> Voilà les soutiens du trône et de l'autel! Les voilà! Et c'est pour cela que je ne peux arriver à garder mon serieux quand je lis, au lendemain d'une soirée orléaniste, que . . . tout est prêt et qu'il n'y a plus qu'à souffler sur la République. Les sympathiques d'Orléans allant à l'assaut de nos institutions avec une troupe de clowns titrés!
>
> [Here are the supports of the throne and the altar! Here they are! And that is why I can't stay serious when I read, the day after an Orleanist evening, that . . . all is ready and that we have only to breathe on the Republic. The sympathizers of Orleans are assaulting our institutions with a troupe of titled clowns!][31]

One of the more sustained criticisms came from *Le Figaro* in 1886, when journalist Henry Fouquier railed against Molier's assault on the "santé moral" (moral health) of the country: "Ce qui domine, en effet, les représentations ad ostentationem, qui n'ont rien de commun avec l'entrainement national des temps antiques, c'est le désir de paraître, ce désir de paraître qu'Agrippa d'Aubigne reprochait déjà à la noblesse de son époque" (What in effect dominates the endless representations that have nothing in common with the national training in ancient times is the desire to be seen, the desire to be seen with which Agrippa d'Aubigne already reproached the nobility of his time).[32] For a noble to put on a leotard and perform for "les filles à la mode" was, for Fouquier, democracy taken to extremes. He adds, "C'est le mal français par excellence, qui gâte les meilleures choses, qui donne au patriotisme même cette allure de cabotinisme, dont ont tant souffert ceux qui ont suivi, dans l'histoire, la sévère régénération de la Prusse après Iéna" (It is the number one French disease that spoils the best things, that gives even to patriotism the allure of showing off, and from which have greatly suffered those who followed in history, the severe regeneration of Prussia after Iena).[33]

Enthusiasts, by contrast, saw Molier's circus as a means for the aristocracy to prove themselves not through the number and elegance of their homes, but by the strength and agility of their bodies. "Charmé de la résurrection du muscle dans les classes dirigeantes," wrote Henri de Pène of the *Paris-journal* (1881), (charmed by the resurrection of muscle in the ruling classes), they saw the exercises as a way to renew the tradition of aristocratic sportsmanship. Physical exercise, one writer for *Le Temps* claimed, was what the present generation had wrongly abandoned and what the country needed to regain:

> Les mêmes plumes qui accusent la dégénérescence de la société moderne sont mal venues à stigmatiser les sports, qui la retrempent au moins au physique. Non déplaise aux malheureux affligés de cet esprit atrabilaire que nous considérions comme l'apanage des vielles filles jauniés dans le célibat, le spectacle d'assauts d'armes chaudement disputés, du travail de Haute-École, de courses d'obstacles, d'exercises gymnastiques, de luttes nautiques, de tout ce qui exige une dépense d'énergie morale et de vigueur matérielle, est autrement salutaire pour leurs spectateurs que les chansons idiotes de cafés-concerts et le décolletage plastique des féeries; en fortifiant ceux qui s'y livrent, ils propagent l'attrait de ces passe-temps virils, qui font ces hommes solides dont la patrie a besoin.
>
> [The same pens that condemn the degeneration of modern society do wrong to stigmatize sports that put that idea to the test, at least physically. With all due respect to those malcontents who are afflicted with that bilious attitude we consider to be the privilege of old maids jaundiced by celibacy, the spectacle of hotly disputed assaults of arms, of the work of haute école, of jumping

> courses, of gymnastic exercises, of swimming contests, of all that requires an expenditure of moral energy and material vigor, is otherwise salutary for the spectators than the idiotic songs of the café concerts and the plastic, plunging necklines of fairies; by fortifying those who do it, they propagate the attraction of those virile pastimes that make the kind of solid men our country needs.]

Such reviews attest that the amateur circus prompted conflicting views about the propriety of the body that were both class- and gender-based. While its equestrian focus promised to restore chivalric relations between men and women, its presentation of half-dressed male bodies challenged codes of class and gender decorum. Although it was originally planned as a performance of men for male friends and lower-class mistresses, the question of women's participation presented itself almost immediately, since the spectacle of aristocratic men in tights was considered acceptable only if they were accompanied by women. As Molier explains,

> Puisque nous étions amenés à donner une véritable représentation de cirque, il nous fallait des femmes. Quelques-uns ajoutaient même que sans femmes, nous aurions l'air bêtes: peut-être allaient-ils un peu loin. Enfin, l'élément féminin étant jugé indispensable, restait à résoudre la terrible question: dans quel monde allions nous chercher nos collaboratrices.
>
> [Since we were determined to present a real circus show, we needed women. Some even said that without women we would seem silly: maybe they went a bit far. In any case, the feminine element having been judged indispensable, it was left to resolve the frightful question: From which world would we find our female colleagues?][34]

Understanding that respectable men would not allow their wives to participate, they hired professional women from among Molier's students and the Cirque d'été. Such women performers displaced men as the sole object of attention, thus obscuring any signs of pleasure men gained by gazing at male bodies. The "femmes du monde" insisted that they be permitted as spectators, a wish granted only for special performances in 1882.[35]

A painting from James Tissot's *Femmes à Paris* series titled *Les femmes du sport* (The sporting women) (1883–85; fig. 11.1) depicts a scene from Molier's circus and reveals the ambivalent gender dynamics of the viewer's gaze. At the center of Tissot's composition are seemingly unprofessional male performers, including a trapezist listed in the original catalog as

Figure 11.1. James Jacques Joseph Tissot, *Women of Paris: The Circus Lover, 1885*. Oil on canvas. Juliana Cheney Edwards Collection, 58.45, Museum of Fine Arts, Boston. Photograph © 2018 Museum of Fine Arts, Boston.

the Duc de la R (presumably the Duc, or Comte, de La Rochefoucauld), whom Molier mentions among his performers.[36] His monocle and the handkerchief tucked into his leotard are mocking reminders of his class, and he seems to enjoy his position of "to be looked at-ness," which nevertheless garners little audience response. The men in top hats talk to each other or look beyond in a bored daze; the women above them look toward the audience to see who is there. The most compelling gaze is that of a woman in pink in the foreground, who stares out at us, bringing us into the scene. Her "brazen" gaze, as Tamar Garb describes it, reinforces the ambiguous boundaries between spectacle and spectator, class and gender.[37] Although "De la R" has a bird's-eye view, his monocle and wandering eye point to his impoverished gaze. The precariousness of his position is exaggerated by his widely spread legs and the illegible gender of his crotch, to which our gaze is directed. The only male gaze with any weight is that of the gentleman whose line of vision directs us to the buttocks of the second trapezist. This view from behind, or "behindsight," to use Lee Edelman's term, creates a "disorientation of positionality" that suggests the aristocracy's apparent, if disavowed, sodomitic fantasies.[38]

For aristocratic men, the pleasure of being looked at may be what the contemporary horseman and historian Baron de Vaux called the "prétexte de déchéance" (pretext of decadence) through which the "vie élégante" passed each year, if not also a means to retrieve the status of object of the gaze that had to be renounced after the Revolution.[39] Vaux's notion of pretext hints at the way such decadent display paradoxically secures the aristocrat's social position by distinguishing him from the bourgeoisie's fearful avoidance of decadence. In *The Politics and Poetics of Transgression*, Peter Stallybrass and Allon White demonstrate how elements of the carnivalesque—defined as spectacles of the body, the animal, and the grotesque—persisted into the nineteenth century in certain liminoid or "low" practices from which the bourgeoisie distanced themselves, claiming to be different. Such distancing, in turn, meant that the bourgeoisie produced the low as "a primary eroticized constituent of its own fantasy life."[40] Molier's circus offered a strategy for subject formation different from the "degenerating" aristocracy of the fin de siècle by producing a new form of carnival in which upper-class men could participate with impunity. This is carnival not as revolt, but as an expression of "social promiscuity," controlled by the "by invitation only" audience.[41]

Such promiscuity and disdain for bourgeois propriety is the focus of Daniel Lesueur's novel *Névrosée* (mentioned above), written during the twelfth year of Molier's performances. But Lesueur also shows how the acceptability of promiscuous display is inflected by gender. Warned against any association with carnivalesque outlets, aristocratic women face a particular danger that their male counterparts are spared. At the core of the novel is a critique of the atrophied state of the aristocracy, whose talents are no longer productive or reproductive; the main character suffers a miscarriage owing to misguided intellectual pursuits and neglect of her body. The penultimate scene takes place at the Cirque Laurencie (modeled on Molier's circus), where the Vicomte Norbert d'Epeuilles, an equestrian performer, uses his talents to seduce women and particularly his married cousin, Étiennette. Untrained in the passions, she begins to succumb to his advances even as she is equally drawn by "une curiosité âpre et malsaine" (fierce and unhealthy curiosity) toward a female performer wearing boy's clothes.[42]

Despite a misogynistic and homophobic didacticism that warns women against straying from their domestic duties, Lesueur's narrative puts the circus at the center of its story about degeneration, education, and breeding, themes linked through an equestrian focus. Like her cousin, Étiennette shows unmistakable signs of aristocratic heritage and is said to be a thoroughbred or pureblood: "une d'Epeuilles pur sang."[43] This heritage, however, is useless to her in the modern world, much as Norbert has no use for the glorious military skills he now uses in the circus. Étiennette's downfall begins when she poses for Norbert in an *amazone*, or woman's riding habit, though she has no intention of riding.[44] Nénette and Norbert are figures of a degenerate aristocracy, whose showy exteriors conceal a moral vacuum that is exteriorized by their taste for the circus. Even if they are barred from performing, the novel suggests, the risks of the circus are greater for women. Lured by men into this world, they come to know the "angoisse des passions sans en connaître les assouvissements" (the anguish of passions without knowing their appeasement) (312). Unlike their male counterparts, they are punished for taking part in its pleasures. Disgusted (like Molier himself), with the "moers plates et bourgeoises" (boring, bourgeois customs), Nénette is torn between the desire to see and the desire to separate herself from the women riders "qui, elles, du moins, connaissent le changement, l'imprévu, le caprice, et parfois le danger" (those women who, at least, know change, spontaneity, caprice, and sometimes danger) (259). Upper-class women, in other words, experience the carnivalesque in a particularly conflicted manner, as Peter Stallybrass and Allon White explain:

> Placed on the outside of a grotesque carnival body which is articulated as social pleasure and celebration, the female bourgeois subject introjects the spectacle as both the pathos of exclusion ("why can't that be me?") and as a

> negative representation which becomes phobic precisely through the law of her exclusion, the interdiction which defines her difference ("You must not be *that*").[45]

The result for Nénette is a particularly modern neurosis, if not hysteria, that ends in her suicide.

Animal Training and Physical Education: Building and Breeding Strong Bodies, Minds, and Nations

In linking degeneration and horsemanship, Lesueur (pen name for Jeanne Loiseau) may show the influence of her lover and longtime companion, popular scientist Gustave Le Bon. Known most widely for his writings on crowd psychology, Le Bon wrote extensively on matters of education, race, and—perhaps surprisingly—equitation. For Le Bon the scientific training of horses offered a model of modern education: "Au point de vue de la psychologie et de l'éducation, sur la façon de pénétrer dans la cervelle des êtres inférieurs, sur les moyens de transformer des mouvements conscients en mouvements inconscients, sur le mécanisme de la persuasion et de l'obéissance, le cheval m'a beaucoup appris" (From the point of view of psychology and of education, on the means of penetrating the minds of inferior beings, on the means of transforming conscious movements into unconscious ones, and on the mechanism of persuasion and obedience, the horse has taught me a great deal).[46]

Le Bon went further than some in his analogy between education and animal training, but he was not alone in connecting the horse to theories of education. By the end of the century metaphors of horses and horsemanship surfaced in relation to the new sports and hygiene movement, which was critical of the French education system that emphasized intellect at the expense of moral and physical training and produced "only rhetoricians and dilettantes and so few men of character, will and action."[47] References to riding as the most noble of sports (and to Buffon's statement that the horse is the most noble conquest of man) helped advance the idea of riding as a means to combat the ills of modern life. In an essay published in 1896, "L'équitation en France," the Baron de Vaux reminded his readers that of all bodily exercise,

> l'équitation est le plus noble, celui le plus propre à développer l'état physiologique de l'homme, à diminuer les tares héréditaires, engendrées par la tuberculose, l'alcoolisme, l'imperfection du développement des enfants des

> grandes villes, de la dégénérescence de la race. . . . En outre, n'est elle pas le meilleure antidote contre toutes les affections qui atteignent les hommes de cabinet, les bureaucrates; contre le surmenage intellectuel de nos jeunes générations . . . contre la déchéance physique de notre race.
>
> [Equitation is the most noble, the most suited to develop the physiological state of man, to diminish hereditary defects engendered by tuberculosis, alcoholism, the imperfect development of children in large cities, the degeneration of the race. . . . In addition, is it not the best antidote against the ills that attack men who sit in offices, the bureaucrats, against the intellectual overload of our young generations . . . against the degeneration of the race.][48]

In 1908 the founders of the physical culture or hygiene movement, Drs. Georges Rouhet and Edmond Desbonnet, shifted attention from riding to the horse itself with the publication of their controversial *L'art créer le pur-sang humain* (The art of creating a thoroughbred human). The appeal of the title, which the founder of the modern Olympics, Pierre de Coubertin, called "appetizing," belied its ambiguity.[49] What is a thoroughbred human? Is it made or born? Evoking a Darwinian notion of the thoroughbred as the "fittest" for survival, the title addressed the hopes and fears of aristocrats who defined themselves by their blood but looked down on the notion of sport. Rouhet and Desbonnet suggested to readers that that the English had succeeded "à créer véritablement une nouvelle race de cheval pur sang" (in truly creating a new race of Thoroughbred horse) and that the same method could be applied to humans:

> Si nous voulons obtenir une race de pur-sang humain, il nous faut user des procédés employés pour obtenir un pur-sang cheval. Créons d'abord des individus forts et robustes qui seront,—que la pudibonderie courante me pardonne le terme—les étalons de la race future.
>
> [If we want to obtain a race of thoroughbred humans, we must use the procedures undertaken to obtain a Thoroughbred horse. Let us first create strong and robust individuals who will be—if current prudishness will pardon the term—the stallions of the future].[50]

Whereas literary analogies between Thoroughbred and human were common in the 1830s, they often linked "pur sang" with women of good breeding.[51] In the hygiene movement, however, the thoroughbred human was to became a poster boy for a cult of youth, beauty, and health. Turning

Figure 11.2. *A Human Thoroughbred* (Un pur-sang humain): "product of the Desbonnet method." From Georges Rouhet and Professeur Desbonnet, *L'Art de créer le pur-sang humain* (Paris: Berger-Levrault et Cie, Éditeurs, 1908), lxxii. Courtesy of the New York Academy of Medicine Library.

the body into an object of rigorous scientific investigation, Rouhet and Desbonnet offer a rehabilitated image of the thoroughbred by transforming its showiness, presumably cleansed of erotic and lascivious potential, into a kind of mechanical motor, the mark of efficiency and productivity (fig. 11.2).

In this Rouhet and Desbonnet were heirs of Étienne Jules Marey, who put the horse at the center of the newly emerging conception of the body as an "animal machine," the title he gave to his 1873 study of human and animal motion. Not meant to deny animal sensation (in the tradition of Descartes), the analogy of the animal machine was meant to inspire a particular approach to the horse (and human) as motor, in order to determine its optimum efficiency of movement.[52] Rouhet and Desbonnet's thoroughbred men were also to be designed for efficiency of movement, illustrating the neo-Lamarckian belief that race is the result of function, not of environment or breeding. Breeding would of course have a role, but it was seen to follow from the aesthetic function satisfied by the thoroughbred: "Les hommes forts et beaux, par une affinité naturelle qu'une morale fausse, irrationnelle et funeste a seule pu faire dévier, iront vers les femmes belles et fortes, comme l'abeille se tourne vers la fleur et la fleur vers le soleil" (Handsome and strong men, by virtue of a natural affinity which only a false, irrational, and harmful morality could cause to go astray, would go toward beautiful and strong women, as the bee turns to the flower and the flower to the sun)(lxxii). Natural selection, for Rouhet and Desbonnet, is helped along by beautiful bodies, perfected through rigorous training to "sport logique et de fécondité certaine" (logical sport and certain fecundity) (lxxv).

Metaphorical associations of the Thoroughbred horse inflected visual representations of thoroughbred humans. Photographs of male bodybuilders sat alongside photographs of classical statuary in *La culture physique*, the journal Rouhet and Desbonnet founded in the 1880s. Together, aristocratic and classical codes of aesthetic purity and authenticity redeemed the spectacle of the male body, making it available to a larger audience. Representatives of the physical culture movement were photographed in poses of classical sculpture not only to prove the effectiveness of the method, but also to underscore the nobility of their bodies. This classical ideal was already in place in Molier's circus history, which includes a snapshot of La Rochefoucauld in the pose of a classical athlete, frontally lit according to the convention for photographing classical sculpture (fig. 11.3).[53] Like the image of the Thoroughbred, whose animal body is mechanized through photographic representation, the Greek athlete warns, by comparison, of

Figure 11.3. *Le Comte Hubert de La Rochefoucauld.* From Ernest Molier, *Cirque Molier, 1880–1904* (Paris: P. Dupont, 1905), 26. Archives and Special Collections, Thomas J. Dodd Research Center, University of Connecticut.

the weakened, degenerative state of the contemporary Frenchman and offers an image of what the body could become through proper hygiene.

If in the early part of the century riding well was a sign of one's nobility and riding Thoroughbreds could compensate for one's own less than pure bloodlines, the physical culture movement at the end of the century insisted that nobility, like race, was not a given. Rather, it was a product of culture, the result of a system of physical education for which there was no replacement. Rouhet and Desbonnet's method was criticized by more conservative sports enthusiasts like Pierre de Coubertin, who faulted the notion of the thoroughbred human for focusing exclusively on the (animal) body to the neglect of the moral and psychological capabilities that distinguish man from animals. "Après avoir dans l'homme négligé l'animal humain, on est arrivé à ne plus tenir compte de ce fait prépondérant que dans l'animal humain . . . il y a l'homme" (After having neglected the human animal in man, we have come to neglect the very significant fact that in the human animal, there is man).[54] But Coubertin's objection also betokened his resistance to the thoroughbred as a signifier of the possibility of creating a new, pure race. While paying lip service to neo-Lamarckian ideas by suggesting that certain sports, "practiced by former generations, imprint themselves on the race," he declared himself a colonial fanatic who believed in the inequality of races and found the idea of the thoroughbred human contrary to his faith in "colonial progress."[55] For Coubertin, sport was above all a means to strengthen the French race and build its resistance to the forces of degeneration. As distinguished from merely training the body, a sport like equestrianism produced a healthy nervous system because it trained body and mind together. Rejecting the analogy between man and horse, Coubertin put the rider back on top, beginning his *Essays on Sport Psychology* with a metaphor of horsemanship: "Considérez le sport hippique et voyez comme il donne bien l'image de la vie" (Consider the equestrian sport and see how it gives an image of life). Similarly, in a 1906 essay he notes "L'âme—esprit et caractère—est un cavalier qui chevauche le corps, animal plus fort que lui et à la merci duquel il se trouverait s'il ne le maniait avec un art suffisant pour diriger et dompter cette force" (The "esprit"—mind and character—is a cavalier that straddles the body, an animal stronger than he and at whose mercy he would find himself if he did not control it with an art sufficient to direct and tame that force).[56] In a series of essays titled "Equitation and Life," "Spurs," and "Dressage," Coubertin repeatedly returns to horse and rider as metaphors for the "moral" governance of mind over body and to riding as the ideal sport for shaping real men: "Rien de plus virilisant pour l'homme que le contact du cheval" (Nothing makes man more virile than contact with a horse).[57]

According to Le Bon, it is because France has ignored the psychological principles of education—for horses and for humans—that it is "incontestablement le pays du monde où les chevaux et les enfants sont le plus mal dressés" (incontestably the country in the world where horses and children are the most poorly trained).[58] In *The Crowd*, published the same year as his book on equitation, Le Bon describes one of the principal characteristics of the present age as "the substitution of the unconscious action of crowds over the conscious action of individuals."[59] Crowds tend to swamp conscious, rational, and individualizing capabilities with the homogeneous and unconscious effects of heredity or "historical race." Race, here, is something like Coubertin's uncontrolled horse and refers not to the body per se, but to the hereditary forces and even convictions that are stored in the body. These include moral, religious, and political convictions that, Le Bon writes, "become so fixed in the soul that everybody accepts them without discussion."[60] Insofar as the crowd is a place of racial domination, it functions regressively to return men to what Herbert Spencer had described as a homogeneous past, if not also to a state closer to animals. One cannot erase one's race but, as Le Bon wants to show through his own experience in training horses, one can train the unconscious to strengthen its resistance to crowds and the dangerous influence of heredity.

In his chapter "The Psychological Bases of Dressage," originally published in 1894, horses stand in for students. Le Bon states that

> toute éducation doit avoir pour but de transformer les actes conscients en actes inconscients. . . . La moralité elle-même ne se crée pas d'une façon différente. . . . Qu'il s'agisse de dresser le cheval ou son cavalier, la méthode est toujours la même: répéter les associations jusqu'à ce que la manifestation de l'un des signes provoque fatalment l'exécution de l'acte associé à ce signe.
>
> [all education must have as its goal the transformation of conscious acts into unconscious acts. . . . Morality itself is created in the same way. . . . Whether it is a question of training a horse or his rider, the method is always the same: repeat the associations until the presence of one signal fatally provokes the act associated with that signal].[61]

Indeed, he claims, such education is usually accomplished more quickly in animals than in humans because reason often thwarts the accumulation of hereditary reflexes that allow morality to become unconscious.

If for Le Bon sport is basic to education, it is not because it engages what distinguishes man and animal, but because it exercises the kinds of "nonrational forms of logic that are shared by man and animal."[62] Le Bon demonstrates little of Coubertin's concern for safeguarding man's distinction from animals. Thus he writes that "les chevaux sont un peu comme les peuples et comme les enfants" (horses are a bit like crowds and children),[63] and for this reason the principles of dressage apply to all three. Unlike horses and crowds, however, some children can grow out of their animal-like state because they have the capacity for reason and will benefit from an intellectual education. Those who are of "inferior" races, or are women, as we have seen in *Névrosée*, are destroyed by higher learning.[64] In "L'éducation actuelle des femmes" (Women's education today), Le Bon writes that

> de par les lois de l'hérédité, don't l'action séculaire a différencié si profondément les races humaines, le cerveau de l'homme civilisé continue à évolué après l'enfance, alors que celui du nègre, de même que celui de la femme, est condamné à ne point dépasser un certain niveau.
>
> [by the laws of heredity, whose secular effects have profoundly differentiated the human races, the civilized human brain continues to evolve after childhood while the Negro's, and the woman's, is condemned to never go past a certain level.][65]

To give inferior beings more than basic moral training, for Le Bon, is to put training and the moral judgment it enforces at risk. In the case of women, it turns them into neurotics. Whereas Coubertin opposed women's participation in sport fearing it might make them unnaturally virile, Le Bon opposed women's intellectual education: "Cette éducation les menace d'une décadence physique profonde, et, par suite, nous menace aussi dans notre descendance" (That education threatens them with profound physical decadence and, as a result, threatens us also in our descendants).[66] In the end, both ideas turned on the notion that women's best qualities are natural, not acquired. Hence their education should concentrate on bringing out essential characteristics.

If the concept of the thoroughbred human was anathema to both Coubertin and Le Bon, it is not simply because it foregrounded the body and bodybuilding, but also because it promoted the possibility of mixing races to create a new "pure" one. Coubertin and Le Bon offer a far more conservative notion of the purebred in their view of woman as the embodiment of racial stability and the guarantor of its "natural" evolution. This view was echoed by the *French Woman*, one of the first sporting magazines for women (1902–4), whose goal was to find and promote physical activities that would "enseigner à mes amies lectrices à demeurer ce qu'elles sont si bien: des françaises de race, c'est à dire la femme naturellement noble" (teach women how to remain what they are so well: French women of breeding, that is to say, the naturally noble woman).[67] For Coubertin and Le Bon, if not also for Rouhet and Desbonnet, women were the born thoroughbreds of French society. Just as women should encourage men's progress by "rewarding them with their applause" (as Coubertin suggested), their stability and imperfectability prompted men to perfect and cultivate themselves.[68]

In a passage often cited by theorists of gender, John Berger describes the conventions used to distinguish between the social presence of men and of women: "men act and women appear."[69] By the beginning of the Third Republic, one might also have written the statement in terms of class: men of the bourgeoisie act and aristocrats appear—admitting thereby the risks of feminization attendant upon the aristocracy's showy exterior. I suggest, however, that the aristocracy's participation in the physical education movement of the turn of the century, and by extension Molier's circus, worked to efface the boundaries between action and appearance—at least in terms of class. Appearances, the aristocracy would come to profess, like the sleek lines of the Thoroughbred, are the result not only of bloodlines, but also of training and hard work. Amateur training, whether for the circus or for the Olympics, may not be productive in a strict utilitarian sense, but it could be said to produce a race of potent, or potentially useful, bodies. Through discipline and hygiene the spectacle of the male body, whether on horseback or in the gym, would no longer be the sign of idle wealth or of a feminized desire to be seen but, rather, would reflect the physical and moral virility needed to govern both self and others.

TWELVE

Heritage Icon or Environmental Pest?

Brumbies in the Australian Cultural Imaginary

ISA MENZIES

In 2015 the Australian Brumby Alliance outlined how the key principles of the Burra Charter applied to thousands of feral horses (brumbies) in the national parks of Australia.[1] The Burra Charter, more formally known as the Australia ICOMOS Charter for the Conservation of Places of Cultural Significance, outlines the best-practice management of Australia's built (or tangible) heritage. The ABA's citation in this context is based on the belief that "it supports our values, for example, where cultural values conflict, the Charter requires that co-existence of cultural values should always be recognised, respected and encouraged. It is not one culture above another; both have equal value and need to be in balance."[2]

As Laurajane Smith has argued, heritage is not simply about the past. It refers to a process of meaning-making that is manufactured in the present.[3] According to Smith, "heritage" is not the site or the building, but the meanings we ascribe to such material relics.[4] This process of meaning-making is integral to forming identity at community, state, and national levels. In the case of brumbies, this reframing of feral animals as cultural heritage offers an opportunity to consider how such narratives are constructed within the context of the Australian heritage discourse.

In what follows, I argue that the brumby functions as an avatar of belonging for white Australians of Anglo-European descent. While only a relatively few individuals strongly identify their heritage with brumbies, the issue of the horses' ongoing management has been used to garner support from across the Australian community. Drawing on the work of Karen Welberry, I contend that Australia's impassioned "brumby debate" reflects the brumby's role in mediating what Welberry describes as an anxiety of belonging among Australians.[5]

The Brumby Debate

In 2000, the New South Wales National Parks and Wildlife Service began an aerial cull (in which trained marksmen shoot horses from a helicopter) of about six hundred feral horses from Guy Fawkes River National Park in the New England region of New South Wales. The cull ignited community outrage that spread across the globe. The Australian arm of the Royal Society for the Prevention of Cruelty to Animals launched a legal campaign against the National Parks and Wildlife Service, though all charges were eventually dropped. The highly politicized nature of the debate was apparent when the minister for the environment, Bob Debus, banned the aerial culling of horses in New South Wales, instigated an independent inquiry, and commissioned a heritage assessment of the Guy Fawkes River horses.[6]"

"Brumby debate" loosely refers to the ongoing dispute between conservationists and brumby advocates regarding the presence of feral horses in Australia's national parks. A number of issues are debated, including the need for population control;[7] potential management strategies (including advocating or opposing methods such as the passive trapping of horses, ground shooting, aerial culling, fencing, and fertility control); and the veracity of scientific evidence demonstrating the environmental effects of feral horses. Opponents of culling range from those who position the brumby as an Australian icon[8] to animal rights advocates who consider culling brumbies as reprehensible as culling other species not native to Australia, such as foxes and rabbits.[9] The other side of the debate is somewhat more unified, opposing the presence of feral horses in National Parks for reasons of environmental conservation. The effects of horses on Australia's fragile alpine ecosystems, which evolved without the presence of hooved mammals, are well documented and include compacting soil, muddying waterways, introducing weeds, and affecting native animal populations.[10] Australia has the world's largest feral horse population, currently estimated at about one million,[11] though numbers within discrete populations are contested.[12] Also contested is their impact, with many brumby advocates either denying that these horses cause environmental damage or claiming degradation is the work of feral pigs or other introduced animals.[13] Scientific evidence is disputed, and many advocates remain unconvinced of the need to manage feral horse populations.[14]

Since the Guy Fawkes River cull, the heritage significance of brumbies has permeated the debate, though Australia currently has no legislation regarding intangible heritage (heritage not associated with buildings or objects, classified as "tradition"). Yet the construction of brumbies as heritage has become so ingrained in the popular imagination that fifteen years after the Guy Fawkes River cull, the National Parks and Wildlife Service has commissioned a heritage assessment of brumbies in the Snowy Mountains region to inform a new Wild Horse Management Plan.[15] In this context, the discourse of "heritage" has been co-opted to serve the agenda of pro-brumby lobbying groups.

Aside from the issue of heritage, the ramifications of the Guy Fawkes cull continue to be felt elsewhere. Feral horse management policies in a number of Australian states are now heavily influenced by an aversion to lethal strategies.[16] At present, New South Wales and Victoria—which contain the only alpine regions on Australia's mainland—are developing new feral horse management plans. With their shared border falling within the Snowy Mountain range, these peaks collectively form the Australian Alps National Parks, home to the fictional brumbies associated with *The Man from Snowy River*. The horses of the Snowy Mountains are currently at the heart of a heated debate regarding their management.

Unlike other feral species, brumbies transcend ecological terrain, entering the realm of culture[17] and identity,[18] and it is here that discourses of heritage are evident. Environmental anthropologist Nicholas Smith has observed that brumbies are immune to the loathing directed toward feral cats in Australia and are a rare exception to eco-nationalist discourses.[19] Significantly, although brumbies are frequently referred to as "wild horses" by their proponents, and even by the National Parks and Wildlife Service, this term is a misnomer; the only true species of wild horse extant is the endangered takhi (Przewalski's horse), *Equus ferus przewalskii*, native to the Central Asian steppes. Although those opposed to culling brumbies from an animal rights standpoint prefer not to use the term feral,[20] brumbies are the same species as the domestic horse, *Equus ferus caballus*. The name brumby is thought to derive either from the horses left behind by soldier-pastoralist James Brumby when he moved from New South Wales to Tasmania or from an Aboriginal word, *baroombie* or *baroomby*, which purportedly refers to feral horses.[21]

Though the 2000 Guy Fawkes River National Park cull is seen as seminal in the evolution of the brumby debate in eastern Australia, for Dale Nimmo and Kelly Miller the subsequent outcry and mobilization of popular sentiment was "a predictable sequence of events, so congruent with past experiences that it could have been foreseen from past literature alone."[22] As Nimmo and Miller demonstrate, the interweaving of ethical, political, and cultural constraints makes this issue invulnerable to "appeal[s] to institutionalised ecological knowledge."[23] While such "soft" approaches may be difficult for the scientific community to engage with, the brumby debate can be contextualized within the framework of what academic Laurajane Smith has described as the "Authorised Heritage Discourse."[24]

Defining "Heritage": Nature versus Culture

Debate about the presence of brumbies in Australia's national parks illustrates what Simon Cubit describes as "tournaments of value, in which one vision competes against another for acceptance by decision makers, invariably seek[ing] political expression."[25] In the current context, the environmental concerns of those opposed to brumbies in national parks are set against the claim that horses, particularly brumbies, embody significant cultural heritage values for Australia. It is worth highlighting the broader issues of this debate, for, as Cubit and others argue, nature itself is a cultural construct.[26] While the validation of purportedly natural landscapes is enshrined through processes such as UNESCO World Heritage listing, such landscapes are themselves constructed within cultural frameworks.[27] Ideas about nature and culture cannot be isolated from each other. Laurajane Smith draws our attention to questionable uses of the word natural in describing the Australian landscape, pointing out that landscapes perceived as "natural" are in fact the result of 40,000 to 60,000 years of active management by Aboriginal people.[28] Moreover, if nature is a cultural construct, then heritage is certainly so. If we examine the dichotomy between natural and cultural heritage, we find it is artificially constructed. As David Lowenthal argues, the two share many similarities and are frequently managed by the same instruments and institutions, for example, the World Heritage Convention.[29]

The term heritage can itself be understood in a number of ways. Among academics and heritage professionals, it is usually used for either built (tangible) or intangible heritage, both fields that are defined and managed in accordance with relevant conventions and legislation. Outside the professional context, however, "heritage" is defined somewhat more loosely. Laurajane Smith's international visitor research reveals differing interpretations of the word.[30] In the United States the word is strongly associated with family and identity, while in the United Kingdom it suggests a focus on preservation. For Australians, "heritage" is most commonly related to identity.[31] This offers an important insight into the affective power of the horse when it is constructed as "heritage" in Australia.

This chapter uses "heritage" in accordance with William Logan and Laurajane Smith's definition: "a social and political construct encompassing all those places, artefacts and cultural expressions inherited from the past which, because they are seen to reflect and validate our identity as nations, communities, families and even individuals, are worthy of some form of respect and protection."[32] This provides a suitably broad framework and is inclusive of both tangible and intangible interpretations while also emphasizing the political dimensions inherent to arguments about heritage. These latter center on the legitimizing of particular constructions of the past, which are either reinforced or marginalized by approved narratives of identity. Competing discourses wrangle for authority, though the politics of identity are largely invisible, naturalized within what Laurajane Smith terms the "Authorised Heritage Discourse."[33] Narratives that "speak to white Australian mythologies that are so intrinsic to Australian identities that they 'just are' and thus are not subject to reflection"[34]—like the discourse around the brumby—must be closely scrutinized for underlying political agendas.

Narratives of Historical Significance: The Horse as Pioneer

The brumby is frequently conflated with the companion horse, particularly in arguments put forth by brumby advocates. For example, speaking of why she views brumbies as different from other feral animals, Leisa Caldwell, local resident and founding member of the Snowy Mountains Horse Riders Association, explains:

> Our grandfathers did not ride foxes into battle at Beersheba. It was not pigs, deer or cats that transported humans throughout the world for over 8,000 years, and partnered humans in the field for survival. It's not the other introduced animals that still partner humans today in the Olympics. There's no other animal on the planet that has such a relationship or has that interaction with humans. So, horses should be viewed very differently.[35]

Caldwell's argument hinges on the role the *horse* has played in Australian history, and in human history more broadly, rather than on the specific significance of the *brumby*. This bears further scrutiny, since many of the arguments put forth by brumby advocates draw on this conflation. Thus we must examine the history and narratives associated with the domestic horse in order to better understand its relation to the brumby.

One of the recurring narratives relating to the horse in Australia, frequently offered as a rationale for preserving brumbies, is that it is historically significant. In fact, the notion of the horse as a contributor to Australia's economic, technological, and social development underpins many contemporary assertions that this animal is important to Australian heritage.[36] While the horse as a species unquestionably provided an advantage in the colonizing and settling of Australia,[37] it was not feral horse populations that rendered these services. Domestic horses are documented as having been released into the bush by 1804, and by the 1830s feral horses were fairly common in parts of southern Australia.[38] Within a few decades, many considered these animals pests.[39] Given this early separation between feral and domestic populations, one could suggest that brumbies are not descended from the horses that contributed to Australia's economic and agricultural development. As we will see, the history of the horse in Australia is distinct from the history of the brumby.

It is widely accepted that seven horses arrived with the First Fleet in 1788 aboard the *Lady Penrhyn*, having been purchased en route at Cape Town.[40] The stallion Rockingham, imported to Australia in 1797, improved the colony's equine bloodlines,[41] which were further bolstered by the arrival of the stallion Northumberland in 1802, for whom a stud fee of £10 was charged. This fee was considered so exorbitant that even the colony's governor, George King, felt unable to afford it.[42] As an aside, this example demonstrates the significance placed on bloodlines and breeding from the earliest days of the colony and could be viewed as the precursor to Australia's modern-day multibillion-dollar Thoroughbred breeding industry.[43]

The number of horses in the fledgling colony grew steadily. In 1800 there were 173 horses, 105 of them owned by officers. Eight years later, officers owned 227 horses and free settlers owned 666.[44] Interweaving a narrative history of the colony with the growing number of horses and the change in their owners demonstrates not only that the colony's development naturally followed the increase in horses, but that Australia developed a more egalitarian mode of horse ownership.[45] We can then examine the popular notion of Australia's unique relationship with the horse, which is viewed as so intrinsic that some remain unaware that the horse is not native to this continent.[46]

Horses were indeed essential to Australia's development. They prompted technological advances such as improved cropping techniques,[47] and their needs often dictated practices on small farm holdings, such as devoting a proportion of arable land to growing feed crops.[48] Australian cities like Melbourne were built with the needs of horses in mind, including minor infrastructure such as hitching posts and water troughs, and hundreds of businesses that serviced horses contributed to the economy.[49] But these horses, integral to the fledgling nation, were not brumbies. Further, it is worth reiterating that by this time brumbies were already regarded as pests.

Battle is another facet of Australian history where an association with brumbies has been manufactured.[50] During the nineteenth century, "Waler" horses (named for New South Wales, as Australia was broadly known for much of its colonial history) were a profitable export. They proved popular with the British army in India, where they served as remounts. (Remounts were ridden into battle but were not cavalry in the traditional sense; instead, troops traveled in small groups and dismounted to fight, with one member designated to hold the horses.) Although Australians rode Walers in the Boer campaign of 1899–1902, the name has come to be used for the approximately 120,000 horses sent overseas during World War I. After the war there was a push to establish the Waler as a breed. Today the Waler Horse Society of Australia is keen to dissociate Walers from the brumby label.[51] Further evidence that brumbies are not descended from the horses that served alongside the men of the Light Horse Brigade is that these horses were subsequently procured by the British army and continued in military service: only one of the horses sent overseas returned to Australia. The perceived connection between brumbies and Australian soldiers is thus tenuous at best. In spite of this evidence, the feral horses of the Guy Fawkes River region are characterized as heritage horses of "direct descen[t from] Australia's wartime cavalry horses."[52]

Away from the arenas of battle, agriculture, and urbanization, horses proved inadequate for the rigors of heavy haulage and exploration that were essential to Australia's economic growth. Bullocks (oxen) and camels proved more suitable. Bullocks were able to transport much heavier loads than horses, including timber and wool, and camels were pivotal to the exploration of Australia's arid interior and subsequent transcontinental expansion. In spite of these major contributions, however, bullocks and camels remain conspicuously absent from Australia's nationalist discourses. Camels present an interesting parallel to brumbies. Australia is estimated to have the world's largest number of wild camels,[53] which were released into the interior of the continent and bred into healthy populations. Camels have been declared a pest species, recognized as damaging plant and animal communities, and aerial culling and ground shooting are common management practices.[54] In contrast to the brumbies, lethal control of feral camels is carried out without protest.

The camel and the bullock provide interesting counterpoints to the brumby: despite their all having claims to historical significance for their role in Australia's development, only for the brumby are such claims made. This comparison demonstrates that "history" and "heritage" are not the same thing[55] despite dialogue with each other. Positioning the brumby as "heritage" embeds this animal within a narrative of Australian identity operating at personal, local, and national levels.

The Brumby as Heritage

Brumbies have significant power for conjuring romance and myth, and at the epicenter of this phenomenon are the feral horses that inhabit the Snowy Mountains region of New South Wales and Victoria. The particular significance of this population originates with A. B. "Banjo" Paterson's 1890 poem "The Man from Snowy River," in which an unnamed man on his trusty steed rounds up a herd of wild horses. The poem found a ready audience from the outset. It was included in the first compilation of work published under Paterson's own name rather than his pseudonym "Banjo," and the anthology broke all Australian publishing records, selling out its first edition within a week and selling ten thousand copies in its first year.[56] Paterson's literary reach was huge, regarded as second only to Kipling's.[57] Although the poem's popularity may have stemmed from the heroic figure of the Man rather than the latent power of the wild horse imagery, it has come to be associated with brumbies, particularly those of the Snowy Mountains. Since its first publication, "The Man from Snowy River" has never been out of print. The poem has been disseminated through films, a television series, music, an annual "Man from Snowy River" festival, and even the opening ceremony of the 2000 Sydney Olympics.[58] It has come to be recognized as "heritage" through frequent repetition and continued visibility. Thus the Man from Snowy River has become part of Australia's cultural iconography, and the brumbies he is associated with (though they were never called that in the poem) are now also described as part of its heritage.

The history of the brumby diverged from the history of the horse soon after Australia's colonizing. Colonists released domestic horses into the bush from the earliest years of settlement,[59] their distribution loosely following the path of colonial expansion. By the 1840s they had spread across every mainland state.[60] Releasing horses into the wild continued for generations as farm holdings were abandoned throughout the nineteenth century, and in the twentieth century when the remount trade collapsed after World War I.[61] There is anecdotal evidence that the practice continues today, with pastoralists releasing new horses into herds to improve breeding and appearance.[62]

While brumbies may have become particularly associated with the Snowy Mountains, largely owing to the Paterson poem, the wild horses described there are not from the Snowy River or the Kosciuszko region. The author is said to have imagined the action as taking place around Burrinjuck Dam, several hundred kilometers north of the headwaters of the Snowy River. Nonetheless, the brumbies and the Snowy Mountains are continually conflated in the popular imagination. Madison Young of the Hunter Valley Brumby Association states that "everyone who thinks about the Snowies thinks about these wide open spaces, and snow and, to me, when I think about them, I think about the brumbies. . . . [W]hen I think of brumbies, I picture the ones from 'The Man from Snowy River,' the ones running across the mountains."[63] Despite fictitious origins and geographical inaccuracy, the conjunction is so powerful in the national imagination that it may prove impossible to dispel.[64]

The Man from Snowy River was first and foremost a stockman, and this figure informs debates about brumby management. Many brumby advocates have family ties to the landscapes in question and feel they have been unfairly treated through the gradual banning of grazing and recreational riding in wilderness areas.[65] Such legislation has been enacted independently by states across Australia, including the Blue Mountains and Snowy Mountains areas in New South Wales and the central plateau region of Tasmania. In all cases the resulting outcry illustrates Cubit's "tournaments of value"[66] as wilderness values and constructions of nature are positioned in opposition to horses, grazing rights, and a sense of ancestral tradition. For Caldwell and others the brumby is strongly associated with a heritage and identity that are also bound up in the narratives of pastoralism and the figure of the stockman, and the process through which these have had to make concessions to competing values is tantamount to hijacking the community's heritage:[67]

> In the past 50 years the people of the Snowy had their cattle and livelihood taken from the mountains, their towns flooded and much of their history lost. And then the Snowy River riders were prohibited from even riding their beloved horses in the mountains as their fathers and grandfathers did. Once the brumbies are gone, there will be nothing left to demonstrate that our Snowy Mountain history since white settlement even existed.[68]

This coalescence of heritage and identity permeates the brumby debate. Caldwell writes, "Here in the Snowy Mountains, the brumbies are not just . . . an integral part of the high country natural environment, they reflect our history, our ancestors and our culture. That's a heritage that gives us our own identity and sense of belonging."[69] For Caldwell, brumbies are inseparable from the Snowy Mountains: "It's a package deal with us; it's horse-riding in the mountains, it's the mountains themselves, and it's the brumbies, and if it weren't for the brumbies there would be nothing left here to demonstrate that our history even existed."[70]

It is thus evident that the brumby encompasses a wide-ranging terrain of identity and heritage in Australia. Whether aligned with Authorised Heritage Discourse or the subject of tournaments of value, what is ultimately at stake are questions of authority over these disputed narratives. Is the brumby a heritage icon or an environmental pest? If the former, whose heritage does it represent? If the latter, what methods are appropriate for its control and management? And who has the right to make these decisions? With an estimated population of at least one million across Australia, the brumby is unique among feral species for garnering impassioned defense. Support for the brumby does not come only from pastoralists or animal rights advocates but is drawn from all quarters. Through the discourse of heritage, the brumby roams the popular imagination of Australians, particularly those who identify as Anglo-European.

The Brumby and Anxieties of Belonging

Anxieties of belonging are a consistent theme in Australian studies discourse, evincing a national disquiet that scholars identify as symptomatic of the collective uncertainty regarding the moral right of Europeans to occupy the land.[71] It is expressed in varying narratives, from perceptions of the bush as hostile to the construction of animals as avatars of belonging. Peter Pierce sees anxieties of belonging in the image of the lost child, a recurring motif in Australian art and literature.[72] Elsewhere, Nicholas Smith's investigation of eco-nationalist narratives identified European attitudes toward dingos as symbolic of the notion that colonists can become naturalized, a positive and desirable outcome.[73] For Karen Welberry, the brumby helps indigenize European colonists.[74]

If we accede to the widely accepted convention that the natural world is distinct from culture, with the former typically characterized as untouched by humanity and the latter understood as a product of human design and intention, then other assumptions must follow. For example, both nature and culture must be positioned within the same value system, with one or the other inevitably given priority when they are in opposition. Lowenthal points out that when these two values conflict, culture is more likely to be defended, for "however deeply we may love nature, most of us identify more easily with human relics and rise more readily to their defence."[75] If we consider the brumby debate within this nature versus culture dichotomy, then the brumby, a culturally constructed embodiment of the concept of heritage, must be positioned in opposition to nature. On an essentialist level this argument does not make sense. As horse, the brumby is distinctly nonhuman and therefore "natural." But if we replace the brumby in this debate with the figure of the human, then the issue is reframed as one where it is the presence of the (white Anglo-European) *human* that is perceived as contested, rather than that of the *horse*. By repositioning the brumby as a projection of the human, we can see that the animal functions as an avatar of belonging for white Anglo-Europeans in Australia.

Karen Welberry's examination of *The Silver Brumby*—a series of books written by Elyne Mitchell for children but ultimately read by a broader audience—demonstrates the symbolic power of the horse as an agent of belonging. In these books, Welberry argues, the eponymous equines, written so as to be the characters readers identify with, "signally became more 'native'/suited to life in the high country than legitimately native animals and/or indigenous trackers employed to hunt them down."[76] In this context the brumbies are thereby reframed not as feral or pest animals, but as rightfully belonging in the Australian landscape. In Welberry's analysis, these horses epitomize the idea that "the 'best' intruder could 'earn the right' to live in a privileged virgin space through demonstrating the ability to 'read' and survive the landscape more effectively than pretenders to that title."[77] The *Silver Brumby* stories revolve around the silver stallion Thowra, his descendants, and their respective herds. Published over forty years starting in 1958, the stories present Thowra as the hero in his quest to elude capture by humans, though it is Thowra's coloring rather than his environmental impact that provides the impetus for hunting him. The notion that the brumbies carry the projections of white settlers gains credence in that Thowra, unlike most brumbies, is distinctively *pale*. The books have proved hugely popular and doubtless contribute to the sentimental view that many Australians have of brumbies in the High Country.

When they are positioned as embodying an iconic national heritage, it becomes more difficult to consider brumbies interlopers. Instead of compromising native landscapes and wilderness, the brumby becomes a symbol of identity that belongs in the spaces it occupies—spaces ascribed to it by a white settler society. Beginning with Banjo Paterson and percolating through subsequent representations, the brumby as a symbol of Australian identity has been internalized so that it functions as an avatar of belonging for many white Anglo-Australians.

Outside the brumby debate, the horse more generally has featured in the tug-of-war that is community heritage. It appears as a recurring trope in tournaments of value where ownership and land use are contested among non-Aboriginal settler communities. In Tasmania during the 1990s, conflict arose when vast tracts of land in the Central Plateau were reclassified as "wilderness." Disputes centered on access, and the reclassification generated hostility from the local community when it was revealed that the wilderness designation would put an end to riding within the area. Tracing the history of the conflict between environmental managers and the local community, Cubit argues that the Anglo-European residents in Tasmania "saw the plateau as a robust environment with resources that should be used as a living cultural landscape bearing the imprints and stories of their ancestors and as a place where community values and traditions were passed on to younger generations."[78] What Cubit describes is essentially an argument about community heritage. Similar disputes have been repeated in the Blue Mountains[79] and the Snowy River region.[80] In all these examples the local community's definition of heritage, and what it values as significant, is in direct opposition to the values of environmental advocates.

Interesting though limited scholarship investigates the legal elements inherent in such tournaments of value. This work finds that private interests, motivated by self-interest, are more effective than publicly motivated groups or even the state itself.[81] In parallel examples from the United States, New Zealand, and Australia, it appears that graziers have achieved greater access to land than they are legally entitled to by aligning their interests with national iconography.[82] The Australian example of this process, the 2005–6 expiration of grazing licenses in Victoria's Alpine National Park (the continuation of the Snowy Mountains range past the New South Wales state border), ended with federal environment minister Ian Campbell proposing alpine grazing as a heritage activity after an outcry from graziers.[83] This heritage was repeatedly linked to the iconic figure of the Man from Snowy River,[84] a connection that was persuasive for Campbell: "*The Man from Snowy River* and the involvement of mountain cattlemen droving cattle up into the alpine region, which has been going on for 170 years, is without any doubt, in my mind, an absolutely intrinsic part of the Australian story and a part of our heritage."[85] This example demonstrates how self-interest masquerading as heritage might fail on a legal basis but retain its political efficacy and ultimately deliver results.[86]

It is worth noting that such discussions occur squarely within settler culture, and those who frame the brumby as heritage—as intrinsic to personal and community identity—are referring specifically to white Anglo-European identity. None of these constructions take into account an Aboriginal perspective, though many attempt to appropriate recognized understandings of Aboriginal connections to "country."[87] Laurajane Smith argues that there is a perception among rural communities that Aboriginal cultural claims carry political legitimacy. This understanding is predicated on a wish not to recognize such claims, but rather to appropriate them for the political agenda of settler culture.[88] This is apparent in statements like this one made by Leisa Caldwell: "Similar to our Indigenous friends, we too have a profound and unique culture and history in the mountains, and it also deserves preservation, as well as celebration."[89] Comparable rhetoric informed the discourse around expired grazing licenses in Victoria's High Country.[90] Even use of the term "country" in these contexts capitalizes on the commonly understood Aboriginal meaning of the word.[91] Here the discourse of "country" as a spiritual connection to place[92] is appropriated to legitimize narratives of belonging.[93]

The horse is not a singular figure of cultural significance in Aboriginal cosmology,[94] though many Aboriginal people became consummate horsemen and horsewomen through the nineteenth-century pastoral advance.[95] However, it can be understood, alongside other nonnative species, as one of many participants in a complex and interwoven construction of "country."[96] The horse holds greater cultural significance to settler Australians, who are the most vocal in support of the brumby. Much cultural capital has been invested in mythologizing the figure of the stockman, described as a bricolage constructed of the foxhunting gentleman of England, the chivalrous cavalryman of the army, and the knight errant.[97] Despite the widespread mechanizing of farm labor, the image of the mounted stockman continues to dominate cultural representations of Australia.[98] Yet little thought has been given to the darker aspects of this figure, a key player in colonizing Australia and dispossessing the continent's first inhabitants. Environmental historian Tim Flannery emphasizes that

> *The Man From Snowy River* is an archetypal Australian hero–one of the brave Aussies who tamed the rugged land. . . . Yet our worship of the self-reliant stockman neatly side-steps the fact that the men of the cattle frontier were the shock troops in our Aboriginal wars. . . . There is a deep current in our colonial Australian society that resists these simple facts and clings to the great founding lie.[99]

Aboriginal people who occupied the Australian continent for over forty thousand years were systematically dispossessed of their land as settlers arrived in the late eighteenth century, and the identity myth of the stockman evolved, at least in part, to suppress the brutal realities of frontier conflict.[100] The physical displacement of Aboriginal people can be charted alongside the pastoral and agricultural expansion of the colonists, in which the stockman and his horse were integral.[101] The horse gave settlers an advantage over Aboriginal owners, both in the violent physical clashes in disputes over access to land and by permitting the rapid spread of white colonists. Perhaps most significant, the dispossession of Aboriginal people can be charted alongside the concurrent spread of white colonists and the feral horses that followed in their wake.

Concluding Thoughts

This chapter examines what happens when a pest species is reframed as a heritage icon. The dissemination of brumby mythology in poetry, books, films, and popular culture has deeply permeated mainstream Australian culture, creating a strong association between feral horses and national identity. Though it is questionable whether the notion of heritage applies to the brumby, it has been vigorously advanced as such, particularly since the Guy Fawkes River National Park cull. The ramifications of this event continue to influence both community attitudes and the management approaches of those tasked with protecting Australia's national parks. Questions about brumbies' physicality are seldom addressed. Though the destructive agency of feral horses is constantly emphasized by those opposed to their presence in national parks, more practical considerations of the fleshly implications of lethal management strategies (such as what to do with all those bodies) are usually absent from discussions. Conversely, for those who actively frame the brumby as heritage, the intrinsic animal is subordinated to an entirely cultural and anthropomorphized construction—except when images of bloated and rotting corpses are used to incite public opinion against culling.

The Authorised Heritage Discourse provides a useful lens through which the brumby can be reexamined, rendering visible the discourses of identity and power through which constructions of heritage have been invoked, or co-opted, in the service of white Anglo-European settler Australians. Closer analysis of arguments in favor of protecting the brumby reveal a conflation of brumbies with the broader history of the horse in Australia. Once exposed as such, these arguments become tenuous when applied to brumbies. While the brumby debate can be superficially considered as positioning wilderness values in opposition to heritage values, on closer examination we see how these debates are being argued at cross-purposes. For one group of stakeholders the issue is environmental and ecological diversity, while for many brumby advocates the matter is, at its core, about belonging. This ideological disparity is problematic, since any debate under such conditions is essentially unwinnable. Reframing the brumby as heritage simultaneously hides and hints at the underlying issue, which is that, for settler Australians, the brumby has come to function as an avatar of belonging.

Recognizing the significance of this transference would be a significant step forward not only in dealing with the concrete realities of land management concerning brumbies but, on a deeper level, in Australia's race relations and the ongoing, systemic marginalizing of Aboriginal people. Given the role of the horse in their dispossession, it is ironic that today it is the proposed expulsion of the brumby from the Edenic wilderness of the Snowy Mountains (and elsewhere) that triggers pangs of dispossession among non-Aboriginals. Ultimately, to find solutions we must look beyond the current terms of reference of the brumby debate and challenge these deeply held anxieties.

NOTES

INTRODUCTION

1. See *The Wild Horses of Sable Island Gallery*, dutescoart.com/sable-island-story/.
2. Donna Landry, "The Noble Brute: Contradictions in Equine Ideology, East and West," in *Representing the Modern Animal in Culture*, ed. Jeanne Dubino, Jiza Rashidian, and Andrew Smyth (London: Palgrave Macmillan, 2014), chap. 2. For information on Whistlejacket and Stubbs, see also Diana Donald, *Picturing Animals in Britain, 1750–1850* (New Haven, CT: Yale University Press, 2007), 199–204, and John Baskett, *The Horse in Art* (New Haven, CT: Yale University Press, 2006).
3. Donna Landry, *Noble Brutes: How Eastern Horses Transformed English Culture* (Baltimore: Johns Hopkins University Press, 2009), 14.
4. Peter Edwards, *The Horse Trade in Tudor and Stuart England* (Cambridge: Cambridge University Press, 2004), and idem, *Horse and Man in Early Modern England* (London: Continuum, 2007); Pita Kelekna, *The Horse in Human History* (Cambridge: Cambridge University Press, 2009); Kevin De Ornellas, *The Horse in Early Modern English Culture* (Madison, NJ: Fairleigh-Dickinson University Press, 2013); Karen Raber and Treva Tucker, eds., *The Culture of the Horse: Status, Discipline, and Identity in the Early Modern World* (London: Palgrave Macmillan, 2005); Peter Edwards, Karl Enenkel, and Elspeth Graham, eds., *The Horse as Cultural Icon: The Real and the Symbolic Horse in the Early Modern World* (Leiden: Brill, 2011).
5. Clay McShane and Joel A. Tarr, *The Horse in the City: Living Machines in the Nineteenth Century* (Baltimore: Johns Hopkins University Press, 2007); Ann Norton Greene, *Horses at Work: Harnessing Power in Industrial America* (Cambridge, MA: Harvard University Press, 2008); Margaret Derry, *Horses in Society* (Toronto: University of Toronto Press, 2006); Louis A. DiMarco, *War Horse: A History of the Military Horse and Rider* (Westholme: Yardley, PA, 2008).
6. Landry, *Noble Brutes*; Monica Mattfeld, *Becoming Centaur: Eighteenth-Century Masculinity and English Horsemanship* (University Park, PA: Penn State University Press, 2017); Gina Dorré, *Victorian Fiction and the Cult of the Horse* (Farnham, UK: Ashgate, 2006); Sandra Swart, *Riding High: Horses, Humans, and History in South Africa* (Johannesburg: Wits University Press, 2010); Peter Mitchell, *Horse Nations* (Oxford: Oxford University Press, 2015).
7. Anthony Giddens and Christopher Pierson, *Conversations with Anthony Giddens: Making Sense of Modernity* (Stanford, CA: Stanford University Press, 1998), 94; Mar-

shall Berman, *All That Is Solid Melts into Air: The Experience of Modernity* (New York: Verso, 1982), 15.

8. Timothy Mitchell, "The Stage of Modernity," in *Questions of Modernity*, ed. Timothy Mitchell (Minneapolis: University of Minnesota Press, 2000), 8–9.
9. Susan Nance, *Animal Modernity: Jumbo the Elephant and the Human Dilemma* (London: Palgrave Macmillan, 2015), 2.
10. Jeanne Dubino, "Introduction," in *Representing the Modern Animal in Culture*, ed. Jeanne Dubino, Jiza Rashidian, and Andrew Smyth (London: Palgrave Macmillan, 2014); John Berger, *Why Look at Animals?* (London: Penguin, 2009), 260. See also Royden Loewen, "'Come Watch This Spider': Animals, Mennonites, and Indices of Modernity," *Canadian Historical Review* 96, no. 1 (March 2015): 64–69, for details about how modernity's urbanizing tendencies and the rejection of the natural world in exchange for industry and commercialization can be resisted with and by animals.
11. Julie Clutton-Brock, *Animals as Domesticates: A World View through History* (Lansing: Michigan State University Press, 2012), 136.
12. See Donna Haraway, *When Species Meet* (Minneapolis: University of Minnesota Press, 2007), and Karen Barad, *Meeting the Universe Halfway: Quantum Physics and the Entanglement of Matter and Meaning* (London: Duke University Press, 2007), for full theorizing of material feminist ideas.
13. Timothy Mitchell, "Introduction," in *Questions of Modernity*, xi. In addition to Nance see, for example, Kathleen Kete, *The Beast in the Boudoir: Petkeeping in Nineteenth-Century Paris* (Berkeley: University of California Press, 1994); Paula Young Lee, ed., *Meat, Modernity, and the Rise of the Slaughterhouse* (Lebanon, NH: University Press of New England, 2008).

CHAPTER ONE

1. Jacques Derrida, *The Animal That Therefore I Am*, ed. Marie-Louise Mallet, trans. David Wills (New York: Fordham University Press, 2008), 42.
2. Monica Mattfeld, *Becoming Centaur: Eighteenth-Century Masculinity and English Horsemanship* (University Park, PA: Penn State University Press, 2017).
3. Donna Haraway, "Cyborgs to Companion Species: Reconfiguring Kinship in Technoscience," in *The Haraway Reader*, ed. Donna Haraway (New York: Routledge, 2004), 297.
4. Donna Haraway, *The Companion Species Manifesto: Dogs, People, and Significant Otherness* (Chicago: Prickly Paradigm Press, 2003), 32.
5. Jane Bennett, *Vibrant Matter* (Durham, NC: Duke University Press, 2010), 9.
6. Karen Barad, "Posthumanist Performativity: Toward an Understanding of How Matter Comes to Matter," *Signs: Journal of Women in Culture and Society* 28, no. 3 (2003): 801–31.
7. For information on sentiment, sensibility, and society see Ildiko Csengei, *Sympathy, Sensibility and the Literature of Feeling in the Eighteenth Century* (New York: Palgrave Macmillan, 2012).
8. Stephanie Eichberg, "Constituting the Human via the Animal in Eighteenth-Century Experimental Neurophysiology: Albrecht von Haller's Sensibility Trials," *Medizinhistorisches Journal* 44 (2009): 278. For a detailed investigation of Haller's experiments see Hubert Steinke, *Irritating Experiments: Haller's Concept and the European Controversy on Irritability and Sensibility, 1750–90* (New York: Rodopi, 2005).
9. Eichberg, "Constituting the Human," 278.
10. Ibid., 279.

11. Ibid., 283. See Steinke, *Irritating Experiments*, 21–26, for details on how the soul was understood as the root cause of voluntary motion. For information on period debates around the differences and similarities between human and animal rationality, similitude to machines, and the presence of an immortal soul see Ann Thomson, "Animals, Humans, Machines and Thinking Matter, 1690–1707," in *Transitions and Borders between Animals, Humans and Machines, 1600–1800*, ed. Tobias Cheung (Leiden: Brill, 2010), 3–37.
12. Csengei, *Sympathy, Sensibility and the Literature of Feeling*, 101.
13. Ibid.
14. Eichberg, "Constituting the Human," 283–84.
15. For information on Cavendish and his circle see Karen Raber, "'Reasonable Creatures': William Cavendish and the Art of Dressage," in *Renaissance Culture and the Everyday*, ed. Patricia Fumerton and Simon Hunt (Philadelphia: University of Pennsylvania Press, 2005), 42–66; Elspeth Graham, "The Duke of Newcastle's "'Love . . . For Good Horses': An Exploration of Meanings," in *The Horse as Cultural Icon: The Real and the Symbolic Horse in the Early Modern World*, ed. Peter Edwards, Karl A. E. Enenkel, and Elspeth Graham (Leiden: Brill, 2012), 37–69; Elaine Walker, *To Amaze the People with Pleasure and Delight: The Horsemanship Manuals of William Cavendish, Duke of Newcastle* (n.p.: Long Riders' Guild Press, 2010); Tom Addyman, "Riding Houses and Horses: William Cavendish's Architecture for the Art of Horsemanship," *Architectural History* 45 (2002): 194–229; Peter Edwards, *Horse and Man in Early Modern England* (London: Continuum Books, 2007); Peter Edwards and Elspeth Graham, eds., *William Cavendish, 1st Duke of Newcastle, and His Political, Social and Cultural Connections: Authority, Authorship and Aristocratic Identity in Seventeenth Century England* (Leiden: Brill, 2016).
16. Richard Berenger, *The History and Art of Horsemanship*, 2 vols. (London: T. Davies and T. Cadell, 1771), 2:94, 64.
17. Kari Brandt, "A Language of Their Own: An Interactionist Approach to Human-Horse Communication," *Society and Animals* 12, no. 4 (2004): 304, 309.
18. Karen Barad uses "intra-action" to highlight the ongoing plurality, mixing, configuring, and reconfiguring of matter at the atomic level: Karan Barad, *Meeting the Universe Halfway: Quantum Physics and the Entanglement of Matter and Meaning* (Durham, NC: Duke University Press, 2007). For information on understandings of horse-human, and animal-human, relationships today, along with details on some of the ongoing debates, see Paul Patton, "Language, Power, and the Training of Horses," in *Zoontologies: The Question of the Animal*, ed. Cary Wolfe (Minneapolis: University of Minnesota Press, 2003); Vicki Hern, *Adam's Task: Calling Animals by Name* (New York: Skyhorse, 2007); Donna Haraway, *When Species Meet* (Minneapolis: University of Minnesota Press, 2007); Lynda Birke, Mette Bryld, and Nina Lykke, "Animal Performances: An Exploration of Intersections between Feminist Science Studies and Studies of Human/Animal Relationships," *Feminist Theory* 5, no. 2 (August 2004): 167–83.
19. Mattfeld, *Becoming Centaur*.
20. Berenger, *History and Art*, 2:2.
21. Henry Herbert, *A Method of Breaking Horses and Teaching Soldiers to Ride, Designed for the Use of the Army* (London: J. Hughs, 1762), 3.
22. Berenger, *History and Art*, 2:66–67. Berenger defined an aid as "whatever assists or directs a horse, and whatever enables him to execute what we put him to do" (2:63). This included the voice, tack, whip, spurs, seat, legs, and hands.

23. Ibid., 2:3.
24. Ibid., 2:72.
25. Ibid., 2:179.
26. For a list of "disorders" in equine mouth anatomy and the bits necessary for their correction see Berenger, *History and Art*, 2:195–210.
27. Ibid., 2:211.
28. Ibid., 2:10.
29. Ibid., 2:12–13.
30. Ibid., 2:106, 14.
31. For details of how centaurism was understood over the long eighteenth century see Mattfeld, *Becoming Centaur*.
32. Berenger, *History and Art*, 1:36.
33. Donna Landry, *Noble Brutes: How Eastern Horses Transformed English Culture* (Baltimore: Johns Hopkins University Press, 2009), 35–37.
34. Mattfeld, *Becoming Centaur*, 89–90.
35. William Cavendish, *General System of Horsemanship in all Its Branches*, (London: J. Brindley, 1743), facsimile reproduction (North Pomfret, VT: J. A. Allen, 2000), 82; Thomas Blundeville, *The Fower Chiefyst Offices* . . . (London: Wylliam Seres, 1566).
36. William Cavendish, *A New Method, and Extraordinary Invention, to Dress Horses, and Work Them according to Nature* (London: Thomas Milbourn, 1667), 22. Blundeville's text was a translation of the 1550 Italian work *Gli ordini di cavalcare* (The rules of riding), by Frederico Grisone. The bit designs Cavendish so disparages were also originally Grisone's.
37. Cavendish, *General System*, 82.
38. Berenger, *History and Art*, 2:219–20.
39. Ibid., 2:216–17. Snaffles came in many forms during the seventeenth and eighteenth centuries, as the following list of manufactured goods from Staffordshire indicates: "They make also great variety of *bridles*, both *Snaffles* and *Bitts*: such as the *wheel* and *jointed Snaffle*, the *neck-Snaffle*, *wreath-Snaffle*, *prick-Snaffle*, &c. to the *ends* or *sides* whereof belong these fashions, viz. the *Rippon*, *acorn*, *Spoon*, *trumpet*, *bobbing*, and *knob'd end*. They make likewise *Colt-snaffles* and *trenches*, *Cabbinsons* and *Musrolls*; which are all commonly made too by different *persons*, tho' sometimes the same makes them all himself." Robert Plot, *The Natural History of Staffordshire* (Oxford: Printed at the Theatre, 1686), 377.
40. Charles Hughes, *The Complete Horseman, or The Art of Riding Made Easy* (London: Printed for F. Newbery, and Sold at Hughes's Riding-School, n.d.), 29–30; Henry Herbert, tenth Earl of Pembroke, *Military Equitation, or A Method of Breaking Horses, and Teaching Soldiers to Ride* (London: J. Dodsley and J. Wilkie, 1778), 20–21.
41. Berenger, *History and Art*, 2:222, 44.
42. Mattfeld, *Becoming Centaur*, esp. chap. 2.
43. On the subject of riding the great horse see Karen Raber and Treva J. Tucker, eds., *The Culture of the Horse: Status, Discipline, and Identity in the Early Modern World* (New York: Palgrave Macmillan, 2005); Peter Edwards, Karl A. E. Enenkel, and Elspeth Graham, eds., *The Horse as Cultural Icon: The Real and the Symbolic Horse in the Early Modern World* (Leiden: Brill, 2012); Peter Edwards and Elspeth Graham, eds., *William Cavendish, 1st Duke of Newcastle, and His Political, Social and Cultural Connections: Authority, Authorship and Aristocratic Identity in Seventeenth Century England* (Leiden: Brill, 2016).
44. For information on the development of the English Thoroughbred see Richard Nash, "Honest English Breed: The Thoroughbred as Cultural Metaphor," in *The Cul-*

ture of the Horse: Status, Discipline, and Identity in the Early Modern World, ed. Karen Raber and Treva Tucker (New York: Palgrave Macmillan, 2005), 245–72.

45. Landry, *Noble Brutes*, 43.
46. Josephus Sympson, in his *Twenty Five Actions of the Manage Horse* (London: J. Sympson and Andrew Johnston, 1729), 4, summarized this seat thus: it "is like the *Seat* of the *Asiatick* Nations, who are much on Horseback, with *short Stirrups* and light *Saddles*." Also, "Neither is this *Seat* so easily obtain'd; and tho' it may not appear Graceful, as that of the *Manage*, it is found very necessary in our fine Hunting Counties, upon a long Chase, *viz.* to sit light, and humour the Horse's Motions, by inclining the Body; and save his Wind by pulling the *Reins*, more or less, according to the Ground he runs over, which will greatly help him to last the Day."
47. Berenger, *History and Art*, 2:218; Monica Mattfeld, *Performing Centaur: Eighteenth-Century Masculinity and English Horsemanship* (University Park: Penn State University Press, 2017).
48. Berenger, *History and Art*, 2:218–19.
49. Mattfeld, *Becoming Centaur*, 88–89.
50. Landry, *Noble Brutes*, 66.
51. Sympson, *Twenty Five Actions*, 220.
52. Riding a horse was not only about controlling the self and exercising naturally given physiological abilities. Instead, riding illustrated the control and improvement of nature, a central element of Enlightenment ideas on human nature and the formation of the nation. For Berenger, "This truth being established, that there are few if any horses given to man so correct and perfect, as not to have something wrong, something that we would wish otherwise in their shape, limbs, or character, the utility, as well as necessity, of the horseman's art will be clear and evident; and the merit of that art must be confessed, which comes in as a friend to the assistance of nature, which strengthens it where it is feeble, guides and supports where it is weak and uncertain, and always acts so kind a part, as to leave it improved and better than it was, when it was first undertaken": Berenger, *History and Art*, 2:187.
53. Berenger, *History and Art*, 1:36–37.
54. Ibid., 1:201.
55. Cavendish, *General System*, 131.
56. Michel Foucault, *Discipline and Punish* (New York: Vintage Books, 1995), 136; Stephen J. Smith, "Human-Horse Partnerships: The Discipline of Dressage," in *Sport, Animals, and Society*, ed. James Gillett and Michelle Gilbert (New York: Routledge, 2014), 36.
57. Berenger, *History and Art*, 1:201.

CHAPTER TWO

1. Rees Howell Gronow, *The Reminiscences and Recollections of Captain Gronow, Being Anecdotes of the Camp Court, Clubs and Society, 1810–1860*, ed. John Raymond (New York: Viking, 1964), 358.
2. "At Waterloo, over 180,000 men with over 40,000 horses fought on a battlefield no wider than three square miles, and by the end over 50,000 men and 20,000 horses were killed or severely maimed": Gareth Glover, *Waterloo in 100 Objects* (Stroud, UK: History Press, 2015), 14.
3. Since "it is impossible to be chivalrous without a horse," as Noël Denham-Young once observed, the horse's well-being was at the center of honorable military behavior as an ideal, if not always in practice: Noël Denham-Young, "The Tournament in the Thirteenth Century," in *Studies in Medieval History presented to Frederick Maurice*

Powicke, ed. R. W. Hunt, W. A. Pantin, and R. W. Southern (Oxford: Clarendon Press, 1948), 240. From Xenophon onward cavalry commanders have recognized the "utility" of "regard" or affective bonding between soldiers and horses to achieve this end, as noted by Thomas Simes in 1773: "The Officers to take particular care, that the men fodder their horses regularly; that they rub down, and curry them well; and further, that they imbibe a regard for them, and learn to be sensible of the many advantages accruing to themselves, in consequence of the pains they bestow upon them; for which reason it is necessary to be inculcated as much as possible by all Officers, that for the horse to be in good condition, whether in an engagement, or on a march, is of the highest utility": Thomas Simes, *The Military Guide for Young Officers* (London: Printed for the Author, 1773), 97. On close partnerships between horses and riders as definitive of English masculinity on the battlefield and beyond throughout the "long" eighteenth century, see Monica Mattfeld, *Becoming Centaur: Eighteenth-Century Masculinity and English Horsemanship* (University Park, PA: Penn State University Press, 2017).

4. That cavalry was already well on the way to becoming obsolete by the Napoleonic Wars is the argument of John Ellis's classic global history, *Cavalry: The History of Mounted Warfare* (New York: Putnam's, 1978), 158–63.
5. See Donna J. Haraway, *When Species Meet* (Minneapolis: University of Minnesota Press, 2008), 222–23, and Vinciane Despret, "The Body We Care For: Figures of Anthropo-zoo-genesis," *Body and Society* 10, no. 2–3 (2004): 111–34, esp. 116, 122. On horse-human partnerships as affective relationships during World War I and the play *War Horse*'s engagement with these relationships, see Lynda Birke, "War Horse," *Humanimalia: A Journal of Human/Animal Interface Studies* 1, no. 2 (2010): 122–32.
6. Even Ian Fletcher's recent revisionist study of the British cavalry during the Peninsular and Waterloo campaigns does not examine the horses as such: Ian Fletcher, *Galloping at Everything: The British Cavalry in the Peninsular War and at Waterloo, 1808–15; A Reappraisal* (Stroud, UK: Spellmount, 2008).
7. See Dipesh Chakrabarty's essay on Indian jute workers, which "aspires to draw a picture, however incomplete" of the jute workers' conditions but "also intends to account for the gaps in our knowledge"; he argues "that the gaps are as revealing of working-class conditions as any direct reference to them" and that his essay "is thus a history both of our knowledge and of our ignorance": Dipesh Chakrabarty, "Conditions for Knowledge of Working-Class Conditions: Employers, Government and the Jute Workers of Calcutta (1890–1940)," in *Selected Subaltern Studies*, ed. Ranajit Guha and Gayatri Chakravorty Spivak (New York: Oxford University Press, 1988), 179–230, 185.
8. Colonel Sir George De Lacy Evans, in a letter of 1842, apologizes for "gossiping" about specific horses: H. T. Siborne, ed., *Waterloo Letters: A Collection of Accounts from Survivors of the Campaign of 1815* (1893; repr., Barnsley, UK: Frontline Books/Pen and Sword, 2015), 65. Neil Ramsey describes as an "outpouring" the soldiers' writing that Charles Oman first identified: Neil Ramsey, *The Military Memoir and Romantic Literary Culture, 1780–1835* (Farnham: VT: Ashgate, 2011), 1. See also C. W. C. Oman, *Wellington's Army, 1809–1814* (London: Edward Arnold, 1913), 2–3.
9. I am currently preparing a larger study of the significance of Waterloo and its aftermath from an equine and equestrian point of view that will consider French and other non-British representations; as James Tomkinson remarks when introducing his father's posthumously published diary, we learn far more about Baron de Mar-

bot's charger Lisette at the battle of Eylau, for instance, than about his father's charger Bob—or indeed any of the British horses in the Napoleonic Wars—and this may be a matter of "the difference of nationality and temperament": Preface to *The Diary of a Cavalry Officer in the Peninsular and Waterloo Campaigns, 1809–1815, by the Late Lieut.-Col. William Tomkinson, 16th Light Dragoons*, ed. James Tomkinson (London: Swan Sonnenschein, 1894), vii.

10. Ramsey observes that Yuval N. Harari, *The Ultimate Experience: Battlefield Revelations and the Making of Modern War, 1450–2000* (London: Palgrave Macmillan, 2008), 190–93, rather "contentiously" makes a case for the military memoir as the "preeminent form of personal witness narrative to emerge during the period," in part because of its potential coupling of the sentimental with "the other key aesthetic doctrine of the eighteenth century, the sublime"; Ramsey, *Military Memoir*, 3-16, 13.
11. Ian Haywood, *Bloody Romanticism: Spectacular Violence and the Politics of Representation, 1776–1832* (London: Palgrave Macmillan, 2006), 3–6.
12. As reported by Major B. R. Ward of the Royal Engineers in his editor's introduction to *A Week at Waterloo in 1815: Lady De Lancey's Narrative* (London: John Murray, 1906), 1–38; this passage is on page 38, citing Scott's review of *Childe Harold's Pilgrimage III* in the *Quarterly Review*, October 16, 1816, 172–208.
13. Robert F. Gleckner, ed., *The Poetical Works of Byron*, Cambridge Edition (Boston: Houghton Mifflin, 1975), 38–39; stanza 21, lines 1–4.
14. David Miller, ed., *Lady De Lancey at Waterloo: A Story of Duty and Devotion* (Staplehurst, UK: Spellmount, 2000), 116. According to Lucy Rees, "Horses are seldom afraid of fresh blood, despite the old sayings, but the reek of stale blood from an abattoir or knacker's van usually terrifies them": Rees, *The Horse's Mind* (1984; repr., London: Ebury, 1997), 143. My thanks to Susanna Forrest for recommending Rees's work; see Forrest's illuminating chapter on horses and war, including an interview with Rees, in *The Age of the Horse: An Equine Journey through Human History* (London: Atlantic Books, 2016), 311–68.
15. Philip Shaw contrasts Scott's own jingoistic Tory approach to the fallen and Byron's more capacious view, noting that in Byron "the political force" is "directed less at the collapse of republicanism and more at the loss of life itself," because "the commingling of rider and horse, friend and foe, signified in the exchange of clay for clay, is an erasure of difference against which the vitality of the Byronic imagination protests": Philip Shaw, *Waterloo and the Romantic Imagination* (London: Palgrave Macmillan, 2002), 188.
16. See Donna Haraway, "Cosmopolitical Critters: Preface for *Cosmopolitan Animals*," in *Cosmopolitan Animals*, ed. Kaori Nagai, Karen Jones, Donna Landry, Monica Mattfeld, Caroline Rooney, and Charlotte Sleigh (London: Palgrave Macmillan, 2015), vii-xiv; Vinciane Despret, *What Would Animals Say If We Asked the Right Questions?*, trans. Brett Buchanan (Minneapolis: University of Minnesota Press, 2016). Despret's question for horses, "Can Horses Consent?," targets recent court cases involving zoophilia, a concept ironically if tangentially related to my investigation here (203–11).
17. Despret, "Body We Care For," 133n21.
18. David A. Nibert, *Animal Oppression and Human Violence: Domesecration, Capitalism, and Global Conflict* (New York: Columbia University Press, 2013), 16, citing Marija Gimbutas, "The First Wave of Eurasian Steppe Pastoralists into Copper Age Europe," *Journal of Indo-European Studies* 5, no. 4 (1977): 277–338.
19. See Bjarke Rink, *The Centaur Legacy: How Equine Speed and Human Intelligence Shaped*

the Course of History (n.p.: Long Riders' Guild Press, 2004), and David W. Anthony, *The Horse, the Wheel, and Language: How Bronze-Age Riders from the Eurasian Steppes Shaped the Modern World* (Princeton, NJ: Princeton University Press, 2007).

20. "Situated histories, situated naturecultures" is Haraway's formulation: *When Species Meet*, 25. On horse-human bodies and identities, see Ann Game, "Riding: Embodying the Centaur," *Body and Society* 70, no. 4 (2001): 1–12, and Lisa Blackman, *The Body: The Key Concepts* (Oxford: Berg, 2008), 119–20, 132.

21. Jacques Derrida, "The Animal That Therefore I Am (More to Follow)" [1997], in *The Animal That Therefore I Am*, ed. Marie-Louise Mallet, trans. David Wills (New York: Fordham University Press, 2008), 1–51, 42. The English translation first appeared in *Critical Inquiry* 28, no. 2 (2002): 369–418. The "bit" is only a small part of the story of horsemanship; bitless bridles are common. Yet in French as in English, there is a concatenation of bits, winged horses, and writing; the word for the piece of metal in a bridled horse's mouth—in English bit, in French *mors*—is the same as the word for a small piece of anything, including writing; Sarah Wood, "Commentary," Kent Animal Humanities Research Day, September 16, 2016. Even in criticizing Derrida for failing to follow through in his response to species difference, Haraway concedes the excellence of such Derridian questions; her criticism centers on the fact that despite his insistence that the cat he writes about is a "real cat," Derrida failed to consider "seriously" "an alternative form of engagement" with his cat, "one that risked knowing something more about cats and *how to look back*, perhaps even scientifically, biologically, and *therefore* also philosophically": Haraway, *When Species Meet*, 20. For Derrida Pegasus is at once "the archetypal horse," "an allegory for all the horses on earth," and a figure for writing and the literary, but Derrida's philosophical question in this case, because species-specific, also has scientific purchase.

22. Rees, *Horse's Mind*, 53–61, 56, 169.

23. Hay has been voted the most important invention of the past two millennia: "Without grass in winter, you could not have horses, and, without horses, you could not have urban civilisation. Some time during the so-called Dark Ages, some unknown genius invented hay. Forests were turned into meadows and hay was reaped, allowing civilisation to move north over the Alps giving birth to Paris, Vienna and London": Freeman Dyson, Institute for Advanced Study, Princeton University, quoted by Hilary Bracegirdle, "The Essential Horse," in *The Essential Horse*, ed. Hilary Bracegirdle and Patricia Connor (London: Philip Wilson, 2000), 9.

24. Thomas Creevey, *The Creevey Papers: A Selection from the Correspondence and Diaries of the late Thomas Creevey, M.P. (Born 1768—Died 1838)*, ed. Sir Herbert Maxwell, 3rd ed. (London: John Murray, 1923), 236.

25. General Alexander Cavalié Mercer, *Journal of the Waterloo Campaign*, ed. Andrew Uffindell, new, unabridged, illustrated edition (Barnsley, UK: Pen and Sword Military, 2012), 156, 249.

26. Gronow, *Reminiscences*, 28.

27. Mercer, *Journal*, 285.

28. By Meteor, out of Lady Catherine by John Bull, Copenhagen was a grandson of Eclipse on his sire's side, with Eclipse also in the fourth generation on his dam's side of the pedigree. See http://www.pedigreequery.com/copenhagen4. Copenhagen raced for three seasons, and as a three-year-old in 1811 he won a £50 match at Newmarket and a sweepstakes at Huntingdon: Peter Willett, *An Introduction to the Thoroughbred* (London: Stanley Paul, 1969), 95, and Archibald Forbes, "Copenha-

gen and Other Famous Battle-Horses," *Pall Mall Magazine* 3, no. 16 (May-August 1894): 625–38.

29. Willett, *Introduction to the Thoroughbred*, 131, quoting the *General Stud Book*, vol. 2 (1821).
30. De Lacy Evans, letter of 1839, in Siborne, *Waterloo Letters*, 62.
31. De Lacy Evans, letter of 1842, in Siborne, *Waterloo Letters*, 65.
32. See Donna Landry, *Noble Brutes: How Eastern Horses Transformed English Culture* (Baltimore: Johns Hopkins University Press, 2008).
33. Sanjay Subrahmanyam, *Explorations in Connected History: From the Tagus to the Ganges* (Delhi: Oxford University Press, 2005), 2.
34. John Tolan, Gilles Veinstein, and Henry Laurens, *Europe and the Islamic World: A History*, trans. Jane Marie Todd (Princeton, NJ: Princeton University Press, 2013), 273.
35. The Eastern, principally Ottoman, influence on cavalry forms part of the larger study initiated in my "History from the Horse's Back: Comparative Empires and Connected Histories at Waterloo, 1815," a keynote address delivered at the conference on "Relational Forms III: Imagining Europe; Wars, Territories, Identities—Representations in Literature and Art," University of Porto, November 19–21, 2015.
36. Geoffrey Tylden, *Horses and Saddlery: An Account of the Animals Used by the British and Commonwealth Armies from the Seventeenth Century to the Present Day with a description of Their Equipment* (London: J. A. Allen, 1965), 16.
37. Ibid., 18.
38. Ibid., 19.
39. Ibid., 15.
40. Gronow, *Reminiscences*, 56.
41. Tylden, *Horses and Saddlery*, 15.
42. Gronow, *Reminiscences*, 75.
43. Jill Hamilton, *Marengo: The Myth of Napoleon's Horse* (London: Fourth Estate, 2001), 137–38; Hamilton acknowledges the work of Phillipe Osché and the thesis of Dr. Godefroy de la Roche, "Les chevaux de Napoléon I et les écuries impériales" (1992).
44. Excellmann observed that the fault lay with British officers, who had "nothing to recommend them but their dash and sitting well in their saddles"; Gronow, *Reminiscences*, 75. The most recent assessment by modern historians is that while "the finest equipped cavalry was certainly the British," "the finest in terms of both tactics and control and experience was undoubtedly the French, although the quality of the French horses was generally poorer than in previous campaigns": Gareth Glover, *Waterloo: Myth and Reality* (Barnsley, UK: Pen and Sword Military, 2014), 155n9.
45. Landry, *Noble Brutes*, 42–43, 131–42, 150–52.
46. Landry, *Noble Brutes*, 8–10, 97–98, 132–36; Landry, "English Brutes, Eastern Enlightenment," in "Animal, All Too Animal," ed. Lucinda Cole, a special issue of *Eighteenth Century: Theory and Interpretation* 52, no. 1 (Spring 2011): 11–30; Donna Landry, "Horse-Human Companionship: Creaturely Cosmopolitanism across Eurasia," in *Cosmopolitan Animals*, ed. Nagai et al., 181–93.
47. Rees, *Horse's Mind*, 169.
48. Ibid.
49. August Ludolf Friedrich Schaumann, *On the Road with Wellington: The Diary of a War Commissary*, trans. Anthony Ludovici (London: Greenhill Books, 1999), 219.
50. Comte Maximilien-Sébastien Foy, *Histoire de la guerre de la Péninsule sous Napoléon*, 4 vols. (Paris: Badouin Frères, 1827), 1:287; quoted in Mercer, *Journal*, 59.

51. According to Peter Edwards, "far more damning" evidence exists regarding "abuse" of horses by "servants, carriers, coachmen and the like" than exists for the seventeenth- and eighteenth-century English upper classes, who were to some extent influenced by equestrian manuals that "displayed a softening of attitudes towards horses"; yet the upper classes too "in certain circumstances" "continued to abuse their animals": Peter Edwards, *Horse and Man in Early Modern England* (London: Hambledon Continuum, 2007), 242.
52. Most famously, the Allied cavalry commander Lord Uxbridge led the charge of the heavy cavalry himself, which, though brilliant and devastating in its effects, resulted in heavy losses because it was impossible for him to stop, rally, and retreat in a timely fashion, and no units remained in reserve to cover the retreat. As he himself put it, "The *carrière* once begun, the leader is no better than any other man": Henry Paget, later first Marquess of Anglesey, letter of 1839, in Siborne, *Waterloo Letters*, 9–10. Excellmann's observation mentioned above, that British officers had "nothing to recommend them but their dash and sitting well in their saddles," was offered in contrast to the French cavalry's control, a result of the discipline of the manège; Gronow, *Reminiscences*, 75. David Hamilton-Williams describes the dilemma succinctly: "Uxbridge, who had done so much to win the day at Waterloo, brooded for years afterwards over the terrible losses his men had suffered and was haunted by the regret that if he had not led that charge he might have been able to restrain the supports from joining in the melee, thus avoiding their losses from the French cavalry's counter-attack": David Hamilton-Williams, *Waterloo New Perspectives: The Great Battle Reappraised* (London: Arms and Armour, 1993), 311.
53. Mercer, *Journal*, 151.
54. Ibid., 176. One bullet, missing Mercer, killed Miller, one of the artillery drivers.
55. Ibid., 176.
56. Ibid., 177.
57. Ibid., 178.
58. Ibid., 188.
59. Ibid., 169–70. Dispatching a horse with a saber to the heart would have been no easy feat, though just about feasible with a good knowledge of equine anatomy.
60. Ibid., 182.
61. Ibid.
62. Ellen B. Wells and Anne Grimshaw, eds., Introduction to Anna Sewell, *The Annotated Black Beauty* (1877; repr., London: J. A. Allen, 1989), xv–xvii, xvi. All further quotations are from this edition.
63. Alfred Tennyson, "The Charge of the Light Brigade" (first published December 9, 1854, in the *Examiner*), in *The Poems of Tennyson*, ed. Christopher Ricks (London: Longman, 1972), 1034–36. Jerome J. McGann reads the historicity of Tennyson's poem in the light of Waterloo (199–201), mapping the battle's legacy in the cavalry's reputation on both sides: "Wellington had won the battle of Waterloo, but England had lost to France the ideological struggle which followed": Jerome J. McGann, *The Beauty of Inflections: Literary Investigations in Historical Method and Theory* (Oxford: Clarendon, 1988), 191–203, 200.
64. Sewell, "An Old War Horse," in *Black Beauty*, 298–308, 304–6.
65. Ibid., 308.
66. Ibid.
67. Byron, *Childe Harold III*, in Gleckner, *Poetical Works*, 39, stanza 28, lines 7–9.
68. General Alava, from the *Supplement to the Madrid Gazette* of July 13, 1815, quoted in

the London *Evening Mail* of August 2 to August 4, 1815, cited by Ward, introduction to *Lady De Lancey's Narrative*, 17.

CHAPTER THREE

1. Karen Barad, *Meeting the Universe Halfway* (Durham, NC: Duke University Press, 2007), 3.
2. Margo DeMello, *Animals and Society: An Introduction to Human-Animal Studies* (New York: Columbia University Press, 2012), 326.
3. Erica Fudge, "Introduction to Special Edition: Reading Animals," *Worldviews* 4 (2000): 101–13; 101.
4. Mario Ortiz-Robles, *Literature and Animal Studies* (New York: Routledge, 2016), 1.
5. I use this term in the sense that Serpil Oppermann defines it, "as a nonlinguistic performance of matter manifesting itself often in expressive collectives" and as a denotation of the "vitality" and "agency" of nonhuman entities "in fictive or material domains": Serpil Oppermann, "From Ecological Postmodernism to Material Ecocriticism," in *Material Ecocriticism*, ed. Serenella Iovino and Serpil Oppermann (Bloomington: Indiana University Press, 2014), 30.
6. Accordingly, even though Barad's understanding of "agency" is the core of my own understanding of this concept, it needs to be expanded so it can better apply to literary animals that are the focus here and that are also depicted in relation to fictional human societies and systems in the novels of Eliot and Hardy. For this purpose, my understanding of "agency" is also informed by the work of Bob Carter and Nickie Charles, who contend that Bruno Latour's actor network theory (ANT) "attributes agency to anything that has an *effect*, whether animate or inanimate" and therefore assert that "every *thing* has agency, and agency is the ability to have an *effect*" (all italics mine): Bob Carter and Nickie Charles, "Animals, Agency and Resistance," *Journal for the Theory of Social Behaviour* 43, no. 3 (2013): 322–40, 323, 328. To illustrate how this approach has been applied to recent discussions of "animal agency," Carter and Charles refer to Richie Nimmo's work, in which "animal *agency*" and "animal *being*" are not seen as different from each other and it is maintained that "agency is no longer simply a matter of reflexive and intentional action, conceived in terms of a duality with some notion of 'structure,' but is rather about the multiple and dispersed *effects* of a certain mode of being-in-the world upon other elements in a heterogeneous *network* or *assemblage*; less about active behaviour, and more about *relational* existence" (all italics mine). See Richie Nimmo, "Bovine Mobilities and Vital Movements: Flows of Milk, Mediation and Animal Agency," in *Animal Movements, Moving Animals: Essays on Direction, Velocity and Agency in Humanimal Encounters*, ed. Jacob Bull (Uppsala: Uppsala University Press, 2011), 57–74, 72.
7. Barad, *Meeting the Universe Halfway*, 25–26.
8. Ibid., 206.
9. Karen Barad, "Posthumanist Performativity: Toward an Understanding of How Matter Comes to Matter," *Signs: Journal of Women in Culture and Society* 28, no. 3 (2003): 801–31; 828.
10. Barad, *Meeting the Universe Halfway*, 396.
11. Ibid., 90.
12. Ibid., 33.
13. "Humanimal" was coined by Pramod K. Nayar to refer to an "*interspecies* identity." See Pramod K. Nayar, *Posthumanism* (Cambridge: Polity Press, 2014), 5. I build on

this term and use "semantic humanimal" to refer to an extraordinary human animal who, in her or his conscious or unconscious entanglement, intra-acts with the world in an unusually intense way, not only gesturally (by using body parts like hands and fingers), but also agentically through a range of semiotic systems inscribed on *matter* (paper and ink).

14. Paul Shepard, *The Other: How Animals Made Us Human* (Washington, DC: Island Press, 1996), 15.
15. Ibid., 25.
16. Jeremy Bentham, *An Introduction to the Principles of Morals and Legislation*, new ed. (London: Pickering, 1823), chap. 17, n. 122. Originally published 1789.
17. Jacques Derrida, *The Animal That Therefore I Am*, ed. Marie-Louise Mallet (New York: Fordham University Press, 2008), 27.
18. George Ritzer, "Actor Network Theory," in *Encyclopedia of Social Theory*, ed. George Ritzer and Barry Smart (Thousand Oaks, CA: Sage, 2004), 1.
19. Derrida, *Animal That Therefore I Am*, 28.
20. Ibid., 160.
21. Cary Wolfe, ed., *What Is Posthumanism?* (Minneapolis: University of Minnesota Press, 2010), 84.
22. Bill Brown, "Thing Theory," *Critical Inquiry* 28, no. 1 (2001): 1–22, JSTOR, accessed November 11, 2015, 4.
23. Ibid., 4.
24. Ibid., 3.
25. Ibid., 4.
26. Shepard, *Other*, 250.
27. Ibid.
28. Ibid., 263.
29. Ibid.
30. Hannah Velten, *Beastly London: A History of Animals in the City* (London: Reaktion Books, 2013), 54–55.
31. Gina M. Dorré, *Victorian Fiction and the Cult of the Horse* (Aldershot, UK: Ashgate, 2006), 57.
32. Velten, *Beastly London*, 51.
33. Thomas Hardy, *Tess of the d'Urbervilles* (1891; repr., London: Penguin Books, 1994), 37.
34. Ibid.
35. See an extended account of this in Donna Landry, *The Invention of the Countryside: Hunting, Walking and Ecology in English Literature, 1671–1831* (London: Palgrave Macmillan, 2001).
36. D. B. D. Asker, *The Modern Bestiary: Animals in English Fiction, 1880–1945* (Lewiston, NY: Edwin Mellen Press, 1996), 74.
37. Gillian Beer, *Darwin's Plots: Evolutionary Narrative in Darwin, George Eliot and Nineteenth-Century Fiction* (London: Routledge and Kegan Paul, 1983), 157.
38. *The George Eliot Letters*, ed. G. Haight, 9 vols. (Oxford: Oxford University Press, 1954–78), 3:214; quoted in Beer, *Darwin's Plots*, 156.
39. Beer, *Darwin's Plots*, 185.
40. George Eliot, *Silas Marner* (1861; repr., London: Penguin Books, 1994), 14.
41. Ibid., 133.
42. Ibid., 150.
43. Ibid., 159.

44. Ibid., 38.
45. Ibid., 40.
46. Ibid., 38.
47. Ibid., 36.
48. Ibid., 44.
49. Ibid., 45.
50. Ibid.
51. Ibid., 46.
52. Ibid.
53. Ibid.
54. Landry, *Invention of the Countryside*, 2.
55. Eliot, *Silas Marner*, 203.
56. Beer, *Darwin's Plots*, 45.
57. Ibid., 62.
58. Asker, *Modern Bestiary*, 71.
59. Ibid.
60. Ibid, 72.
61. Elisha Cohn, "'No insignificant Creature': Thomas Hardy's Ethical Turn," *Nineteenth-Century Literature* 64, no. 4 (March 2010): 494–520, JSTOR, accessed November 4, 2015, 495–96.
62. Asker, *Modern Bestiary*, 73.
63. Ibid., 76. As Asker points out, Hardy's biography by his second wife, Florence Emily Hardy, notes that he was an admirer of Darwin's *Origin of Species* (1859).
64. Ibid., 77.
65. Ibid., 83.
66. Hardy, *Tess of the d'Urbervilles*, 32.
67. Ibid.
68. Ibid., 35.
69. Ibid.
70. Ibid.
71. Ibid.
72. Ibid., 37.
73. Dorré, *Victorian Fiction*, 15.
74. Cohn, "'No Insignificant Creature,'" 510.
75. Quoted in ibid., 497.
76. Hardy, *Tess of the d'Urbervilles*, 38.
77. Ibid., 40.
78. Cohn, "'No Insignificant Creature,'" 495–96.
79. Ibid., 496.
80. Hardy, *Tess of the d'Urbervilles*, 4.
81. Ibid., 43–44.
82. Beer, *Darwin's Plots*, 62–63.
83. Carter and Charles, "Animals, Agency and Resistance," 331.

CHAPTER FOUR

1. Charlotte Dumas, *Anima* (Amsterdam, 2012).
2. Karen Raber, *Animal Bodies, Renaissance Culture* (Philadelphia: University of Pennsylvania Press, 2013), 179.

3. Donna Haraway, *When Species Meet* (Minneapolis: University of Minnesota Press, 2008), 36.
4. Nicholas Ridout, *Stage Fright, Animals, and Other Theatrical Problems* (Cambridge: Cambridge University Press, 2006), 127.
5. Joyce E. Bedi, "In the Days before Doc: A Historical Essay," in *Seeing the Unseen: Dr. Harold Edgerton and the Wonders of the Strobe Alley*, ed. Roger R. Bruce (Rochester, NY: Publishing Trust of George Eastman House, 1994), 79.
6. François Dagognet, *Étienne-Jules Marey: A Passion for the Trace* (New York: Zone Books, 1992), 70.
7. Marta Braun, "The Expanded Present: Photographing Movement," in *Beauty of Another Order: Photography in Science*, ed. Ann Thomas (New Haven, CT: Yale University Press, 1997), 150.
8. Aaron Scharf, *Art and Photography* (1974; repr., New York: Penguin Books, 1986), 206.
9. Robert Taft, *Photography and the American Scene* (New York: Dover, 1938), 410.
10. Douglas Fordham, "The Thoroughbred in British Art," in *The Cambridge Companion to Horseracing*, ed. Rebecca Cassidy (Cambridge: Cambridge University Press, 2013), 26.
11. Charlotte Dumas, *Tiger Tiger* (Amsterdam: Galerie Paul Andriesse, 2008), 15.
12. Michel Frizot, "Model, Reference and Reflection," in *Charlotte Dumas. Companion. Polaroids 2002–2012* (Paris: Filigranes éditions, 2012), 97.
13. Roberto Dutesco, "Sable Island Story," accessed August 10, 2017, http://dutescoart.com/sable-island-story.
14. Paul Roth, "Passport," in *Charlotte Dumas. Companion. Polaroids 2002–2012* (Paris: Filigranes éditions, 2012), 17.
15. Dumas, *Anima*.
16. Roth, "Passport," 19.
17. Raber, *Animal Bodies*, 10.
18. Ibid., 30.
19. Tristan Hooper, "Charlotte Dumas" (2013), accessed August 10, 2017, http://www.faunaandflora.org/charlotte-dumas/.
20. Charlotte Dumas, *Work Horses* (Amsterdam: Ice Plant, 2015).
21. Walter Benjamin, "Little History of Photography," trans. Rodney Livingstone, et al., in *Walter Benjamin: Selected Writings*, vol. 2, *1927–1934*, ed. Michael W. Jennings, Howard Eiland, and Gary Smith (1931; repr., Cambridge, MA: Belknap Press of Harvard University Press, 1999), 510.
22. Ibid.
23. Charlotte Dumas, *The Widest Prairies* (Amsterdam: Oodee, 2013).
24. Ibid.
25. Ibid.
26. Haraway, *When Species Meet*, 19.
27. Benjamin, "Little History of Photography," 510.
28. Maurice Halbwachs, *On Collective Memory* (1941; repr., Chicago: University of Chicago Press, 1992), 119.
29. Ridout, *Stage Fright*, 101.
30. Ibid., 121.

CHAPTER FIVE

This chapter is an updated version of Christine Rüppell's master's thesis, "Ein Salett von oben bis unten mit Architectur, Figuren und Pferden: Der Stallsaal von Schloß Weißenstein in Pommersfelden," published in *Marburger Jahrbuch für Kunstwissenschaft* 31 (2004): 241–68, and chapter 8 of Magdalena Bayreuther's doctoral dissertation, "Symbolische Kommunikation: Der Marstall von Schloss Weißenstein in Pommersfelden," in *Pferde und Fürsten: Repräsentative Reitkunst und Pferdehaltung an fränkischen Höfen (1600–1800)* (Würzburg: Ergon, 2014), 387–424. For her suggestions on this chapter we thank Pia F. Cuneo.

1. Weißenstein stable and stable hall can be visited by appointment only: see www.schoenborn.de (last modified September 27, 2015). Official guide by Werner Schiedermair, *Schloss Weißenstein in Pommersfelden* (Lindenberg: Kunstverlag Josef Fink 2003); see also Erich Schneider and Dieter J. Weiß, eds., *1711–2011: 300 Jahre Schloss Weißenstein ob Pommersfelden, Wissenschaftliches Symposium der Gesellschaft für Fränkische Geschichte am 15. und 16. September 2011* (Würzburg: Gesellschaft für fränkische Geschichte, 2014).
2. Heinrich Kreisel, *Das Schloss zu Pommersfelden* (Munich: Hirmer 1953), 65–66; Wolfgang Götz, *Deutsche Marställe des Barock* (Munich: Deutscher Kunstverlag, 1964), 46–47; Wolfgang Einsingbach, "Johann Maximilian von Welsch: Neue Beiträge zu seinem Leben und zu seiner Tätigkeit für den Georg August von Nassau-Idenstein," *Nassauische Annalen* 74 (1963): 79–170; Joachim Meintzschel, *Studien zu Maximilian von Welsch* (Würzburg: Schöningh, 1963), 119; Fritz Arens, *Maximilian von Welsch (1671–1745): Ein Architekt der Schönbornbischöfe* (Munich: Schnell und Steiner, 1986).
3. See Hildegard Bauereisen-Kersting, "Die Gemäldegalerie in Schloss Weißenstein ob Pommersfelden," in *1711–2011: 300 Jahre Schloss Weißenstein ob Pommersfelden: Wissenschaftliches Symposium der Gesellschaft für fränkische Geschichte am 15. und 16. September 2011*, ed. Erich Schneider and Dieter J. Weiß (Würzburg: Gesellschaft für fränkische Geschichte, 2014), 241–66.
4. *Quellen zur Geschichte des Barock in Franken unter dem Einfluss des Hauses Schönborn*, vol. 1, *Die Zeit des Erzbischofs Lothar Franz und des Bischofs Johann Philipp Franz von Schönborn (1693–1729)*; first half-volume ed. by P. Hugo Hantsch and Andreas Scherf (Augsburg: Filser, 1931); second half-volume ed. by Max H. von Freeden (Würzburg: Schöningh, 1955); first half-volume, 312 (Lothar Franz to Friedrich Karl, Bamberg, June 13, 1714).
5. Sabine Kolck, *Bayerische und pfalz-neuburgische Prinzen auf Reisen: Kavalierstouren weltlicher und geistlicher katholischer Prinzen vom Ende des 16. bis zur Mitte des 18. Jahrhunderts im Vergleich* (Münster, 2010), 168; Bayreuther, *Pferde und Fürsten*, 276.
6. Magdalena Bayreuther, "Reitkultur und Pferdezucht in Bamberg unter den Schönborn-Bischöfen," *Bericht des historischen Vereins Bamberg* 144 (2008): 93–112; 107–9.
7. Treva Tucker, "Early Modern French Noble Identity and the Equestrian 'Airs above the Ground,'" in *The Culture of the Horse: Status, Discipline, and Identity in the Early Modern World*, ed. Karen Raber and Treva Tucker (New York: Palgrave Macmillan 2005), 273–309.
8. Pia F. Cuneo, "Visual Aids: Equestrian Iconography and the Training of Horse, Rider and Reader," in *The Horse as Cultural Icon: The Real and the Symbolic Horse in the Early Modern World*, ed. Peter Edwards, Karl A. E. Enenkel, and Elspeth Graham (Leiden: Brill, 2012), 71–96; 78.

9. Bayreuther, *Pferde und Fürsten*, 275–303.
10. Ibid., 364–66. See also Treva Tucker, "From Destrier to Danseur: The Role of the Horse in Early Modern French Noble Identity," PhD diss. (University of Southern California at Los Angeles, 2007), 159–61.
11. Bayreuther, *Pferde und Fürsten*, 356–57.
12. See, for example, Pia F. Cuneo, "Just a Bit of Control: The Historical Significance of Sixteenth- and Seventeenth-Century German Bit Books," in *The Culture of the Horse: Status, Discipline, and Identity in the Early Modern World*, ed. Karen Raber and Treva Tucker (London: Palgrave Macmillan, 2005), 141–73; Walter Liedtke, *The Royal Horse and Rider: Painting, Sculpture, and Horsemanship, 1500–1800* (New York: Abaris Books, 1989).
13. For example, the walls of the *sala di cavalli* in the Palazzo Te in Mantua: see Giulio Romano, *"Une manière extravagante et moderne"* (Paris: Lagune 1994), 106; a series of portraits for Louis XIV of France: see Daniel Roche, ed., *Les écuries royales du XVIe au XVIIIe siècle* (Paris: Association pour l'Académie d'art équestre de Versailles 1998), 86–95; a series by Johann Georg von Hamilton for the Prince of Liechtenstein: see Reinhold Baumstark, ed., *Joseph Wenzel von Liechtenstein: Fürst und Diplomat im Europa des 18. Jahrhunderts*, exhibition catalog (Vaduz: Sammlungen der Fürsten von Liechtenstein 1990), 162, catalog number 63; and a series of portraits at the Dresden court: Jutta Bäumel, "'So vil Dings zu sehen: Die Dresdner Rüstkammer als Festausstatter," in *Eine gute Figur machen: Kostüm und Fest am Dresdner Hof. Anläßlich der Ausstellung des Kupferstich-Kabinetts Dresden vom 10. September bis 3. Dezember 2000 im Dresdner Schloß*, ed. Claudia Schnitzer and Petra Hölscher (Dresden: Verlag der Kunst, 2000), 38–45; 40–45.
14. Bayreuther, *Pferde und Fürsten*, 88–89.
15. Ibid., 355–85. On carousels at European courts see Helen Watanabe-O'Kelly, *Triumphall Shews: Tournaments at German-Speaking Courts in Their European Context, 1560–1730* (Berlin: Gebr. Mann, 1992).
16. Bayreuther, *Pferde und Fürsten*, 438–50.
17. See anthologies by Raber and Tucker, *The Culture of the Horse*, and Edwards, Enenkel, and Graham, *The Horse as Cultural Icon*. See also Magdalena Bayreuther, "Breeding Nobility: Raising Horses at Early Modern German Courts," 109–29, and Peter Edwards, "Horses and Elite Identity in Early Modern England: The Case of Sir Richard Newdigate II of Arbury Hall, Warwickshire (1644–1710)," 131–48, both in *Animals and Early Modern Identity*, ed. Pia F. Cuneo (Burlington, VT: Ashgate, 2014).
18. Giles Worsley, *The British Stable* (New Haven, CT: Yale University Press, 2004), 2.
19. For the growing wealth and political influence of the Schönborn family see Sylvia Schraut, *Das Haus Schönborn: Eine Familienbiographie; Katholischer Reichsadel, 1640–1840* (Paderborn: Schöningh, 2005), 139–226.
20. Kreisel, *Schloss zu Pommersfelden*, 18–24.
21. Walter Jürgen Hofmann, *Schloss Pommersfelden: Geschichte seiner Entstehung* (Nuremberg: Carl, 1968), 26, 153; Franz Matsche, "Kurfürst Lothar Franz von Schönborn huldigt Kaiserin Elisabeth Christine im Festsaal seines Schlosses Weissenstein in Pommersfelden: Die Bedeutung der Deckenbilder Johann Michael Rottmayrs," in *Musis et Litteris: Festschrift für Bernhard Rupprecht zum 65. Geburtstag*, ed. Silvia Glaser and Andrea M. Kluxen (Munich: Fink 1993), 231–62; 231, 232.
22. The stables of Chantilly, France, built 1719–25 represent the culmination of baroque equine architecture: Worsley, *British Stable*, 143.
23. Bayreuther, *Pferde und Fürsten*, 412.

24. Hantsch and Scherf, *Quellen zur Geschichte des Barock*, 480–81; Götz, *Deutsche Marställe des Barock*, 47.
25. Michael Krapf, "Der Marstall des Prinzen Eugen aus architektonischer Sicht," in *Prinz Eugen der edle Reiter: Der Prunkstall des Türkensiegers*, exhibition catalog, ed. Michael Krapf (Vienna: Österreichische Galerie, 1986), 13–34; 15–16.
26. Hantsch and Scherf, *Quellen zur Geschichte des Barock*, 364 (castle inventory of 1752: "Wohl ausgeziehrte Stallung worinnen 50 Pferd in allen wohl verpflegt werden können").
27. Ibid., 301; von Freeden, 478; Rüppell, "Salett von oben bis unten mit Architectur, Figuren und Pferden," 242.
28. For example Kreisel, *Schloss zu Pommersfelden*, 67; Götz, *Deutsche Marställe des Barock*, 48; Leo Broder, "Studien zu Johann Rudolf Bys (1660–1738)," *Jahrbuch für Solothurnische Geschichte* 38 (1965): 13; Georg Dehio, *Handbuch der deutschen Kunstdenkmäler, Bayern I: Franken*, ed. Tilman Breuer (Darmstadt: Wissenschaftliche Buchgesellschaft, 1979), 859–60; Max H. von Freeden, *Pommersfelden: Schloß Weißenstein* (Königstein im Taunus: Langewiesche, 1987), 10; Bernd M. Mayer, *Johann Rudolf Bys (1662–1738): Studien zu Leben und Werk* (Munich: Scaneg, 1994), 288.
29. Johann Rudolf Bys, *Fürtrefflicher Gemähld- und Bilderschatz, so in denen Gallerie und Zimmern des Churfürstl: Pommersfeldischen . . . Privat-Schlos zu finden ist*, ed. Katharina Bott (1719; repr., Weimar: VDG, 1997), 136; Mayer, *Johann Rudolf Bys*, 36–37.
30. They are based on the Dioscuri twin Castor as horse tamer on the stairs of the Capitol in Rome.
31. Contemporary French riding equipment can be seen in the Musée de l'armée, Paris. In Germany several state-run museums and institutions possess important collections: Coburg (Kunstsammlungen der Veste Coburg), Dresden (Staatliche Kunstsammlungen), Karlsruhe (Badisches Landesmuseum), and Munich (Bayerische Schlösserverwaltung). See also Henri-Christian Tavard, *Sattel und Zaumzeug: Das Pferdegeschirr in Vergangenheit und Gegenwart* (Cologne: DuMont, 1975); Lauren Gilmour, ed., *In the Saddle: An Exploration of the Saddle through History* (London: Archtype, 2004).
32. While comparable saddles can be found in antique portraits, they seem to have no saddle tree. Apart from that, only saddle cloths made of animal hide are known. See also equestrian portraits by Pierre Mignard of Louis XIV of France (*Louis XIV à cheval devant Maastricht*, 1647) or Philippe I, Duke of Orléans (*Portrait équestre de Philippe de France, duc d'Orléans, alors duc de Chartres, vêtu à la romaine et dirigeant une charge de cavalerie*, 1693); see also Jean-Claude Boyer, "Portrait équestre, archéologie et querelle des anciens et des modernes: Le Louis XIV de Mignard jugé par Solleysel," in *Le cheval et la guerre du XVe au XXe siècle*, ed. Daniel Roche (Paris: Association pour l'académie de l'art équestre de Versailles, 2002), 333–45; 332, 337.
33. A similar item is depicted in Peter Thein, *Handbuch Pferd. Zucht, Haltung, Ausbildung, Sport, Medizin, Recht* (Munich: BLV, 1992), 207.
34. Bamberg Stable Inventory, June 4, 1714 (State Archive Bamberg, Geheime Kanzlei, no. 1305, prod. 113, pp. 676–85).
35. Besides the games on horseback, there were jousts on foot (Bäumel, "'So vil Dings zu sehen,'" 43; Rüppell, *"Salett von oben bis unten mit Architectur, Figuren und Pferden,"* 256–57).
36. Bäumel, "'So vil Dings zu sehen,'" 44.
37. Ibid.; Schnitzer, *Höfische Maskeraden: Funktion und Ausstattung von Verkleidungsdivertissements an deutschen Höfen der Frühen Neuzeit* (Tübingen: Niemeyer, 1999), 115.

38. Watanabe-O'Kelly, *Triumphall Shews*, 45–48.
39. Marcel Benoit and André Philidor, *Marches, fêtes et chasses*, booklet accompanying the CD André Philidor, *Marches, fêtes et chasses pour Louis XIV*, by Hugo Reyne, Virgin Classics 2000. For illustrations see, for example, Schnitzer, *Höfische Maskeraden*, ills. 77–78.
40. William Smith, ed., *A Dictionary of Greek and Roman Biography and Mythology*, 3 vols. (London: Murray, 1872), 1:173, 397–400 (Andromeda, Athena), 3:165–66, 205–6, 306 (Pegasus, Perseus, Poseidon).
41. See Pierre Bourdieu, *Die feinen Unterschiede: Kritik der gesellschaftlichen Urteilskraft* (Frankfurt am Main: Suhrkamp, 1982).
42. See Barbara Stollberg-Rilinger, "Symbolische Kommunikation in der Vormoderne: Begriffe—Thesen—Forschungsperspektiven," *Zeitschrift für historische Forschung* 31 (2004): 489–527.
43. Copperplate engraving by Salomon Kleiner in *Wunder würdiges Kriegs- und Siegs-Lager deß unvergleichlichen Heldens unserer Zeiten*, part 9, 1738. Available at the Herzogin Anna Amalia Bibliothek web page, Weimar (sign.: Aa 1 : 127): http://ora-web.swkk.de/digimo_online/digimo.entry?source=digimo.Digitalisat_anzeigen&a_id=4661 (last modified October 29, 2015). See also Krapf. "Der Marstall des Prinzen Eugen aus architektonischer Sicht," in *Prinz Eugen der edle Reiter: Der Prunkstall des Türkensiegers*, exhibition catalog, ed. Michael Krapf (Vienna: Österreichische Galerie, 1986). For the history of the Belvedere palace see Ulrike Seeger, *Stadtpalais und Belvedere des Prinzen Eugen: Entstehung, Gestalt, Funktion und Bedeutung* (Vienna: Böhlau, 2004).
44. Von Freeden, *Pommersfelden*, 480–81.
45. Friedrich Karl was a close friend of Prince Eugene, with whom he shared interest in art and architecture. Their exchange about the sketches for the stables' interior fittings was followed by communication about other architectural projects. See Max Braubach, "Friedrich Karl von Schönborn und Prinz Eugen," in *Diplomatie und geistiges Leben im 17. und 18. Jahrhundert: Gesammelte Abhandlungen*, ed. Max Braubach (Bonn: Ludwig Röhrscheid, 1969), 301–20; Bayreuther, *Pferde und Fürsten*, 394–99.
46. Claudia Brink, "Pegasus und die Künste: Eine Einführung," in *Pegasus und die Künste: Katalog zur Ausstellung im Museum für Kunst und Gewerbe in Hamburg, 08. April-21. Mai 1993*, ed. Claudia Brink and Wilhelm Hornborstel (Munich: Deutscher Kunstverlag, 1993), 10–25; 16–17.
47. For images of Prince Eugene see Elisabeth Großegger, *Mythos Prinz Eugen: Inszenierung und Gedächtnis* (Vienna: Böhlau, 2014). On his success in the Ottoman Wars see Ilber Ortayli, "Prince Eugene and the Ottomans: Cultural Exchange in War and Victory Encampments from 1683 to 1717," in Agnes Husslein-Arco and Marie-Louise Plessen, eds., *Prince Eugene: General, Philosopher and Art Lover; Belvedere Vienna, 11 February—6 June 2010* (Munich: Hirmer, 2010), 49–115.
48. David Klemm, "Pegasus am Tegernsee: Anmerkungen zur Darstellung des geflügelten Pferdes in der Freskomalerei Süddeutschlands und Österreichs im 17. und 18. Jahrhundert," in Brink and Hornborstel, *Pegasus und die Künste*, 102–10; 103. For other examples see Franz Matsche, *Die Kunst im Dienst der Staatsidee Kaiser Karls VI: Ikonographie und Programmatik des "Kaiserstils"* (Berlin: de Gruyter, 1981), 370; Brink and Hornborstel, *Pegasus und die Künste*, 178, 187.
49. Rüppell, *"Salett von oben bis unten mit Architectur, Figuren und Pferden,"* 259–60.
50. Ibid., 260–61. Worsley, too, sees the physical relation between the stable and the country house as "a key determinant in understanding attitudes towards the house

and its landscape" but noted that it "goes unmentioned" in scientific architectural research: Worsley, *British Stable*, 2.

51. Hofmann, *Schloss Pommersfelden*, 39–40.
52. Helmut-Eberhard Paulus, "Zur Ikonologie von Schloß Weißenstein zu Pommersfelden," *Ars Bavaria* 25–26 (1982): 73–100; 76–77; see also Franz Matsche, "Das sog. Vestibül in Schloß Weißenstein zu Pommersfelden: Ein 'Ehrentempel' für Kurfürst und Reichserzkanzler Lother Franz von Schönborn," in Thüringer Landesmuseum Heidecksburg, ed., *Bildnis, Fürst und Territorium* (Munich: Deutscher Kunstverlag, 2000), 219–48.
53. Paulus, "Zur Ikonologie von Schloß Weißenstein zu Pommersfelden," 95–96.
54. Matsche, "Das sog. Vestibül in Schloß Weißenstein zu Pommersfelden," 231.
55. Schnitzer, *Höfische Maskeraden*, 115–16; Schnitzer and Hölscher, *Eine gute Figur machen*, 44.
56. Schnitzer, *Höfische Maskeraden*, 114–16; Bäumel, "'So vil Dings zu sehen,'" 44.
57. Kreisel, *Schloss zu Pommersfelden*, 68 (translation by the authors).
58. Christoph Pinter von der Au, *Neuer vollkommener verbesserter und ergänzter Pferdt-Schatz* (Frankfurt am Main: Oehrling, 1688), 65–68.
59. Stephan Hiller, "Triumph des Pferdes: Zur Ikonographie der Salzburger Pferdeschwemme," in *Barock in Salzburg: Festschrift für Hans Sedlmayr*, ed. Johannes Graf von Moy (Salzburg: Universitätsverlag Pustet, 1977), 57–97; 74.
60. Monique Dossenbach and Hans D. Dossenbach, *König Pferd* (Bern: Hallwag, 1985), 156–57; Holger Schuckelt, "'Folget das Türckische Serail': Das Wachsfigurenkabinett Augusts des Starken; Kammertürken und Türkenkammer am Dresdner Hof," in Schnitzer and Hölscher, *Eine gute Figur machen*, 68–83, 69. Louis XIV of France, for example, acquired thirty-eight purebred Arab horses in 1668: Chantal Humbert, "Die königlichen Marställe in Frankreich während der zweiten Hälfte des 17. Jahrhunderts," in Krapf, *Prinz Eugen der edle Reiter*, 7–11. For the influence of Arabian and Turkish horses on early modern equine culture in England, see Donna Laundry, *Noble Brutes: How Eastern Horses Transformed English Culture* (Baltimore: Johns Hopkins University Press, 2009).
61. *Im Lichte des Halbmonds (Exhibition Staatliche Kunstsammlungen Dresden)* (Leipzig: Ed. Leipzig, 1995), 263–346; Ernst Petrasch et al., *Die Karlsruher Türkenbeute: Die "Türckische Kammer" des Markgrafen Ludwig Wilhelm von Baden-Baden. Die "Türckischen Curiositaeten" der Markgrafen von Baden-Durlach* (Munich, 1991). Schuckelt, "'Folget das Türckische Serail,'" 69–83. Representations of Ottoman objects, persons, and animals in the Pommersfelden stable hall can be viewed in this context: Schnitzer and Hölscher, *Eine gute Figur machen*, 249.
62. Bamberg Stable Inventory, March 9, 1729 (State Archive Bamberg, Geheime Kanzlei, no. 1623, prod. 53, pp. 346–47).
63. Bamberg Stable Inventory, January 22, 1730 (State Archive Bamberg, Geheime Kanzlei, no. 1305, prod. 60, pp. 420–21).
64. Schnitzer, *Höfische Maskeraden*, 112–21.
65. Ibid., 114–16; Bäumel, "'So vil Dings zu sehen,'" 44.
66. Cesare Ripa, *Iconologie, où Les principales choses qui peuvent tomber dans la pensée touchant les Vices et les Vertus, sont représentées sous divers figures* (1643; repr., Lille: Aux amateurs de livre, 1989); Mayer, *Johann Rudolf Bys*, 55.
67. Schnitzer, *Höfische Maskeraden*, 115; *Im Lichte des Halbmonds*, 256.
68. Bäumel, "'So vil Dings zu sehen," 44; Schnitzer, *Höfische Maskeraden*, 115.
69. Watanabe-O'Kelly describes this in detail: *Triumphall Shews*, 45–48. On the origin

of this game see Carl Diem, *Asiatische Reiterspiele: Ein Beitrag zur Kulturgeschichte der Völker* (Berlin: Deutscher Archiv-Verlag, 1941), 86–99.

70. Watanabe-O'Kelly, *Triumphall Shews*, 47–48; Lucien Clare, "Un jeu de L'Espagne classique: Le jeu des 'cannes,'" in Roche, *Cheval et la guerre*, 317–31; Schnitzer, *Höfische Maskeraden*, 116; Schnitzer and Hölscher, *Eine gute Figur machen*, 164, catalog number 71, and 158, catalog number 64a.

71. Kreisel, *Schloss zu Pommersfelden*, 68; Götz, *Deutsche Marställe des Barock*, 48; Mayer, *Johann Rudolf Bys*, 289.

72. Painted in 1697–98 (Mayer, *Johann Rudolf Bys*, 290). See also Liliane Skalecki, *Das Reithaus: Untersuchungen zu einer Bauaufgabe im 17. und 19. Jahrhundert* (Hildesheim: Olms, 1992), 281, ill. 44.

73. Mayer, *Johann Rudolf Bys*, 289. Representations of Pegasus in combination with the rescue of Andromeda are relatively rare. Pegasus more typically appears in decorations in south German border regions, infrequently in connection with Perseus. Johann Michael Rottmayr created a fresco of the liberation of Andromeda in the Liechtenstein Palace in Vienna in 1706–8, and he painted a fresco with this theme in Vranov castle. Martino Altomonte represented the same theme in the Lower Belvedere of Prince Eugene of Savoy in 1716 (Klemm, "Pegasus am Tegernsee," 102–10).

74. Hantsch and Scherf, *Quellen zur Geschichte des Barock*, 478.

75. Elspeth Graham, "The Duke of Newcastle's 'Love . . . for Good Horses': An Exploration of Meanings," in *The Horse as Cultural Icon: The Real and the Symbolic Horse in the Early Modern World*, ed. Peter Edwards, Karl Enenkel, and Elspeth Graham (Leiden: Brill, 2011), 37–70; 38, 61–63.

76. Peter Stephan describes Pommersfelden architecture and iconography as Schönborn imperial style ("Schönbornscher Reichsstil"), a reference to its self-conscious relation to the visual schemes of castles in Prussia, Saxony, Prince Eugene's city palace in Vienna, and even the Holy See in Rome: "'Pommersfelden und der Schönbornsche Reichsstil': Das Schloss des Kurfürsten Lothar Franz im Wettstreit mit anderen Fürstenhöfen," in *1711–2011: 300 Jahre Schloss Weißenstein ob Pommersfelden, Wissenschaftliches Symposium der Gesellschaft für Fränkische Geschichte am 15. und 16. September 2011*, ed. Erich Schneider and Dieter J. Weiß (Würzburg: Gesellschaft für fränkische Geschichte, 2014), 267–299. The self-confidence of his social position is also evident in the exchange of letters between Lothar Franz and his nephew Friedrich Karl during the planning and construction of the castle. Karl tried to highlight the imperial sphere but was modestly restricted by Lothar Franz, who acted as an independent prince (Erich Schneider, "'Dass man auch hier zu landt was hübsch machen kann': Pommersfelden in der Korrespondenz zwischen Lothar Franz und Friedrich Karl von Schönborn zwischen 1710 und 1714," in Schneider and Weiß, *300 Jahre Schloss Weißenstein*, 171–72).

77. For example, in the stables of the eighteenth-century monastery and castle in Salem (South Germany) and the riding schools in Salzburg (1690) and in Dessau (1790/91, destroyed). See Bayreuther, *Pferde und Fürsten*, 83–84, 411.

78. Christ rode into Jerusalem on a donkey, a beast of burden, not on a finely bred warhorse. We thank Pia F. Cuneo for drawing our attention to this shift.

CHAPTER SIX

1. *Weekly Rehearsal* (Boston), October 8, 1733.
2. "The Early History of Narragansett," in *Collections of the Rhode-Island Historical Society*, vol. 3, ed. Elisha R. Potter Jr. (Providence, RI: Marshall, Brown, 1835), 67.
3. Robert K. Fitts, *Inventing New England's Slave Paradise: Master/Slave Relations in Eighteenth Century Narragansett, Rhode Island* (London: Taylor and Francis, 1998), 73, 85, 92. For a further discussion of plantation life in Narragansett see Joanne Pope Melish, *Disowning Slavery: Gradual Emancipation and "Race" in New England, 1780–1860* (Ithaca, NY: Cornell University Press, 1998), chap. 1.
4. John Winthrop, *History of New England, 1630–1649*, ed. James Kendall Hosmer (New York: Charles Scribner's Sons, 1908), 1:368. The record of William Coddington's shipping horses to the West Indies in 1656 is not definite proof that they were from Rhode Island, since his transactions are clouded by accusations of theft. John Russell Bartlett, ed., *Records of the Colony of Rhode Island and Providence Plantations in New England* (Providence, RI: A. Crawford Greene and Brother, State Printers, 1856), 1:337–38.
5. Sanford was governor of the colony from 1680 to 1683: *Letter Book of Peleg Sanford* (Providence, RI: Rhode Island Historical Society, 1928), 7–8.
6. Letter to Benedict Arnold, dated September 8, 1672, in "John Hull Letter Book," vol. 1, transcribed by Florence Berlin for the American Antiquarian Society (1930) 132–33, 337–38.
7. "The Horse in Colonial New England," International Museum of the Horse website, http://www.imh.org/imh/kyhpl3a.html, accessed May 14, 2015.
8. Published in 1737, John Chamberlayne's *Magnae Britanniae Notitia, or The Present State of Great Britain* (London, 1737), 333, argues that New England horses "are esteemed as the swiftest Pacers; also for Plough and Pack-Carriage; insomuch as Mules and Asses, so generally made use of in France, Italy and Spain, are utterly despised in England." Chamberlayne also discusses how Scottish Galloway ponies, "little Horses" known for their "Hardiness in enduring Labour" and their "Compactness of their Bodies," were rumored to have influenced the Pacers. These horses were "frequently brought up in England" and may have been among those shipped to New England. See also Esther Forbes, *Paul Revere and the World He Lived In* (Boston: Houghton Mifflin, 1942), 191–95.
9. Alice Morse Earle, *Customs and Fashions in Old New England* (New York: Charles Scribner's Sons, 1894), 187.
10. Ibid., 189.
11. Rip Van Dam commented that the horse was "no beauty though so high priced, save in his legs": *Farmers' Cabinet* (Amherst, NH), April 1, 1847. Alice Morse Earle describes "a Narragansett Pacer that was nearly full blooded. She was a villainously ugly animal": Earle, *Customs and Fashions*, 189.
12. James McSparren, "America Dissected, Being a Full and True Account of the American Colonies" (1752), published as an appendix in Wilkins Updike, *A History of the Episcopal Church in Narragansett Rhode Island, Including a History of Other Episcopal Churches in the State* (Boston: Merrymount Press, 1907).
13. *Farmers' Cabinet* (Amherst, NH), April 1, 1847.
14. South Kingstown Probate Records, 3:103.
15. Ibid., vols. 2, 4, 5:107.
16. Ibid., 3:70, 103, 1:86, 4:14.

17. See, for example, *Providence Gazette and Country Journal*, January 3, 1781, *and* November 22, 1783.
18. *Newport Mercury*, May 2 to May 9, 1768.
19. The advertisement ran in the *Newport Mercury* on May 9 and May 16, 1774.
20. *Connecticut Gazette*, May 12, 1775.
21. *American Mercury* (Hartford, CT), May 30, 1795; *Connecticut Journal*, May 3, 1786.
22. The advertisement ran in *Connecticut Gazette*, May 24, 1792, June 7, 1792, and June 21, 1792.
23. South Kingston Probate Records, 4:335.
24. "Early History of Narragansett," 114.
25. Updike, *History of the Episcopal Church in Narragansett*, 1:207–8. See also William Douglass, *A Summary, Historical and Political, of the First Planting, Progressive Improvements, and Present State of the British Settlement in North-America* (Boston, 1755), 89, for census figures.
26. *Newport Mercury*, January 2, 1764.
27. *Boston Post-Boy*, June 3, 1751.
28. *Newport Mercury*, March 10, 1776.
29. *Calendar of British State Papers* (1714/15), 654; (1720/21), 197.
30. From 1649 to 1658 the import of English horses was high. The British Colonial Papers note forty-eight permits for such shipments, for a total of more than 1,900 horses. By the 1660s New England had begun to take over this trade: *Calendar of British State Papers, Colonial Series*, 1574–1660 (London, 1860–1916), 329, 379, 382, 385, 390, 392, 393, 395, 401, 402, 404, 409, 411, 417, 420–26, 428, 431, 432, 436, 438, 451, 461.
31. Updike, *History of the Episcopal Church in Narragansett*, 515.
32. Hazard's work reveals that the Rhode Island Pacer had depreciated greatly in value and notes that £7 = 1 Spanish milled dollar: Caroline Hazard, *Thomas Hazard, son of Robt. Call'd College Tom: A Study of Life in the Narragansett in the XVIIIth Century* (Boston: Houghton, Mifflin, 1893), 63.
33. Richard Ligon's map of Barbados in his *True and Exact History of the Island of Barbados*, first published in 1657, illustrates horses being used in the militia, to chase runaway slaves, and for travel and hunting: Richard Ligon, *True and Exact History of the Island of Barbados*, ed. Karen Kupperman (1673; repr., Indianapolis: Hackett, 2011), 38–39.
34. *The British Empire in America, Consider'd, in a Second Letter, from a Gentleman of Barbadoes, to His Friend in London* (London, 1732), 19–20.
35. Deane Phillips, *Horse Raising in Colonial America* (Ithaca, NY: Cornell University Press, 1922), 889, 900.
36. Quoted by James Arnold, *The History of the State of Rhode Island and Providence Plantations, 1636–1790* (New York, 1859–78), 2 vols., 1:488, from the original in British State Papers Office, *New England Papers*, vol. 3, no. 21.
37. Phillips, *Horse Raising*, 908.
38. *Records of the Colony of Rhode Island*, 4:59, 60.
39. Governor Joseph Jencks to the Lords of Trade, cited by Arnold, *History of the State of Rhode Island*, 2:106.
40. *Records of the Colony of Rhode Island*, 5:13.
41. William Douglass, *A Summary, Historical and Political, of the First Planting, Progressive Improvements, and Present State of the British Settlements in North America*, 2 vols.

(Boston, 1755), 2:99; MacSparren, "America Dissected," quoted in Updike, *History of the Episcopal Church in Narragansett*, 514.

42. "A Swiss Medical Doctor's Description of Barbados in 1661: The Account of Felix Christian Spoeri," ed. and trans. Alexander Gunkel and Jerome S. Handler, *Journal of the Barbados Museum and Historical Society*, May 1969, 3, 10.
43. Henry Whistler, "An Account of Barbados in 1654," in N. C. Connell, "An Extract from Henry Whistler's Journal of the West Indian Expedition under the Date 1654," *Journal of the Barbados Historical Society*, 1938, 146–47.
44. James Brandow, ed., *Genealogies of Barbados Families* (Baltimore: Clearfield, 2009), 341–42; Larry Dale Gragg, *Englishmen Transplanted: The English Colonization of Barbados, 1627–1660* (Oxford: Oxford University Press, 2003), 103–4.
45. *British Empire in America*, 19–20.
46. Ibid., 3, 7–8, 19.
47. Nicholas Brown Papers, John Carter Brown Library, Providence, Rhode Island, manuscripts—BFBR B. 357, ML 1764–67; BFRB, 1765 B. 357, folders 1–10. Hereafter Nicholas Brown Papers.
48. *The Letter Book of James Brown of Providence, Merchant, 1735–1738* (Providence: Rhode Island Historical Society, 1929), 19, 60.
49. Ibid., 19.
50. Nicholas stipulates "none of wich to be under two years old & all to have good teath two eyes, to be free from lameness and to be in good shipping care": Nicholas Brown Papers, folder 3, fol. 11.
51. *Letter Book of James Brown*, 49.
52. *Providence Gazette and Country Journal*, January 3, 1781.
53. Nicholas Brown Papers, folder 3, fol. 14.
54. Ibid., folder 7, fol. 2.
55. Ibid., folder 3, fol. 1.
56. Ibid., folder 4, fol. 16.
57. See, for example, *Providence Gazette and Country Journal*, January 29, 1763, and January 14, 1764.
58. Nicholas Brown Papers, folder 4, fol. 19.
59. *Letter Book of James Brown*, 36.
60. Nicholas Brown Papers, folder 5, fols. 3 and 5.
61. Ibid., folder 5, fol. 2.
62. Nicholas wrote to Matthew Manchester in December 1765 that he was willing to let the horses stay in Narragansett "to work on the . . . farms" and to send the rest to Rowland Robinson to keep for thirty shillings a week. Ibid., folder 5, fols. 2 and 3.
63. Ibid., folder 5, fol. 14.
64. Ibid., folder 5, fol. 15.
65. *The Smithfield Jockey, or The Character and Original of a Horse-Courser, with the Tricks and Rogueries of an Ostler; Published for the Benefit of Gentlemen and Others* (W. D., 1675).
66. Philip Astley, *The Modern Riding Master, or A Key to the Knowledge of the Horse, and Horsemanship; with Several Necessary Rules for Young Horsemen* (Philadelphia: Robert Aitken, 1776), copy held at the John Carter Brown Library, Providence, RI, JCB D776 A855M, 11–12.
67. A. S., *The Gentlemans Complete Jockey* (London, 1700), 18.
68. On March 29, 1720, he paid a total of £369 for twenty-four horses to be shipped to St. Christopher (approximately £15 per horse on average). In practice, Malbone

paid anywhere from £17 to £57, with most of the horses costing £20 to £25. On March 27, 1733, Malbone recorded that twenty-one horses bound for Antigua cost him £592: however, he went on to break down the cost per horse, which ranged from £18 to £55. The most expensive horse, at £65, was most likely a saddle horse, and it was the only horse he sent to Antigua in 1735: 105 reel 11 of 30 Papers of the American Slave Trade, ser. A, pt. 2, E445.R4; pt. 2, reel 11. Mss549, Malbone Family Collections, 1728–1825, 0694 vol. 1. Godfrey Malbone Sr. account book, 1728–38. #1951.2, Rhode Island Historical Society, Providence, Rhode Island. Hereafter Malbone Papers.

69. Ibid., fol. 114.
70. Ibid., fol. 105.
71. John Banister Journal [Account Book], 1746–49, MS.2003.18, Newport Historical Society, Newport RI. fol. 244. Hereafter Banister Account Book.
72. The total cost including board before shipping was £1,187: Ibid., fol. 319.
73. Banister Account Book, fol. 523.
74. Isaac Pereira Mendes to Aaron Lopez, Kingston, Jamaica, February 15, 1767, "Commerce of Rhode Island, 1726–1800," vol. 1, "1726–1774," in *Collections of the Massachusetts Historical Society*, 7th ser., vol. 9 (Boston: Massachusetts Historical Society, 1864), 183.
75. *Boston News-Letter*, March 19, 1716.
76. Ligon, *True and Exact History*, 89–90; Ward Barrett, "Caribbean Sugar-Production Standards in the Seventeenth and Eighteenth Centuries," in *Merchants and Scholars: Essays in the History of Exploration and Trade*, ed. John Parker (Minneapolis: University of Minnesota Press, 1965), 154, 155, 158; Larry Gragg, *Englishmen Transplanted; Journals of the House of Commons From June the 15th, 1727 to December the 5th, 1732* (London: House of Commons, 1803), 21 (1730): 686.
77. Dean Phillips erroneously suggests that horses were widely used "to transport sugar and supplies." Phillips, *Horse Raising*, 889.
78. "Slavery in Suriname," http://surinamslavery.blogspot.com, accessed May 27, 2015.
79. John Gabriel Stedman, *Narrative of a Five Years Expedition against the Revolted Negroes of Surinam* (London: Johnson and Payne, 1796), 104.
80. Whistler, "Account of Barbados in 1654," 146–47.
81. Stedman, *Narrative of a Five Years Expedition*, 51.
82. Ibid., 366.
83. Ligon, *True and Exact History*, 86.
84. Ibid., 86, 58–59; Gragg, *Englishmen Transplanted*, 24.
85. *Journals of the House of Commons* 21 (1730): 685.
86. Ibid., 686.
87. "Debate in the Commons on the Sugar Colony Bill February 23, 1732," in *Cobbett's Parliamentary History of England from the Norman Conquest in 1066, to the Year 1803*, vol. 8, *1722–1733* (London, 1811), 995–97.
88. *The British Empire in America, Consider'd*, 3, 7–8. Other pamphlets concurred. See, for example, William Cleland, a Barbadian merchant, *The Present State of the Sugar Plantations Consider'd; but More Especially That of the Island of Barbadoes* (London, 1714). Almost twenty years before things came to a head with the Molasses Act of 1733, Barbadians felt it was "indispensibly necessary for the Government, to cherish and support this valuable Trade, and to discourage all Attempts to wrest it out of our Hands; in order to do this, some Inspections may be necessary into the Trade from New England, and the Northern Colonies to St. Thomas's Curasoa and Suri-

nam, to the last they send Horses, by which they carry on their Sugar making, which promotes that Dutch Colony in that Manufacture; there is a Law or Order in Surinam, that these Northern Vessels shall not be admitted to Trade with them, unless they bring such a number of Horses."

89. *British Empire in America, Consider'd*, 20–28.
90. Ibid., 19.
91. Phillips, *Horse Raising*, 912–13.
92. *Providence Gazette and Country Journal*, October 20, 1764. This report was picked up and republished by the *New-York Mercury* on November 12, 1764.
93. Ibid.
94. Isaac Pereira Mendes to Aaron Lopez, Kingston, Jamaica, February 15, 1767, "Commerce of Rhode Island, 1726–1800," vol. 1, "1726–1774," 183.
95. However, Wright was able to sell all the horses he had transported on board the *Charlotte*, "one at Thirty-Two Pounds, Two at Twenty-Six Pounds each, one at Twenty-Eight Pounds. They turned out on average Twenty-Eight Pounds per Horse." Benjamin Wright to Aaron Lopez, Savanna La Marr, Jamaica, April 8, 1769, ibid., 271.
96. The *Providence Gazette* (reprinted in the *New-York Gazette or* the *Weekly Post-Boy*, November 26, 1767).
97. *Newport Mercury*, March 28, 1763. To maximize publicity and gather as many entries as possible, the advertisement ran again on April 4, April 11, April 18, and April 25, and finally on May 2.
98. *Newport Mercury*, May 9, 1763.
99. Letter of I. P. Hazard, in Updike, *History of the Narragansett Church*.
100. Bryan Edwards, *The History, Civil and Commercial, of the British Colonies in the West Indies*, 4 vols. (Philadelphia, 1806), 3:285.
101. Louis George Beer, *British Colonial Policy, 1754–1765* (New York: P. Smith, 1907), chap. 13.
102. Benjamin Ladd Cook, "The Narragansett Pacer," in *Rhode Island Yearbook* (Providence: Rhode Island Yearbook Foundation, 1956–66), 56–58.
103. Leading Newport merchants Abraham Redwood and Godfrey Malbone both sought to keep up with the latest travel innovations from England. Redwood sought coach horses from London in 1732, and in 1742 Malbone ordered an elaborate coach from London. Rowland and Samuel Frye to Abraham Redwood, April 26, 1732, in "Commerce of Rhode Island, 1726–1800," vol. 1, "1726–1774": copy of bill for a coach ordered from England by Godfrey Malbone, London 1742. Original owned by Miss Mary Fogg of Brooklyn CT. Lost after her death. Malbone Papers, folder 1 (typescript copy).
104. *Providence Gazette and Country Journal*, June 11, 1763.
105. See, for example, *Providence Gazette and Country Journal*, January 3, 1781; November 22, 1783; January 29, 1785. There were still Narragansett Pacers in Rhode Island in the 1780s; Griffin Green advertised in the *Providence Journal* in 1718 seeking "natural Pacers" to ship "for a particular Market." In 1783 Alexander Sampson offered "good pay" for "natural Pacers": *Providence Gazette and Country Journal*, November 22, 1783.
106. *Providence Journal, and Town and Country Advertiser*, May 27, 1801. Also, in July 1801 Joseph Tillinghast appealed in the *Providence Gazette* for "Good SHIPPING HORSES: *Providence Gazette*, July 11, 1801.
107. *Connecticut Journal*, March 28, 1820; *The Common Place Book of a Gentleman: Horses and Neat Cattle* concurred, blaming crossbreeding with Arabians as New Englanders

sought more "elegant saddle horses" that were a "mixture of the Narraganset and Arabian": "Extracts from *The Common Place Book of a Gentleman: Horses and Neat Cattle,*" *Connecticut Mirror*, August 11, 1823.

108. *Connecticut Courant*, November 4, 1823.
109. "Extracts from *The Common Place Book of a Gentleman: Horses and Neat Cattle,*" *Connecticut Mirror*, August 11, 1823.
110. The breeders were willing to incur a loss, with a cover fee of only "three dollars . . . being barely sufficient to pay for the keeping of the Horse": *Connecticut Courant*, May 29, 1826.

CHAPTER SEVEN

1. Charles Stewart, "My Life as a Slave," ed. Annie Porter, *Harper's New Monthly Magazine*, October 1884, 732.
2. Ibid., 730–38.
3. Falling lame in an 1828 race, Medley (foaled in 1824) now made his career as a breeding stallion. "Medley," *American Turf Register and Sporting Magazine*, May 1833, 438; Genevieve Baird Lacer, *Edward Troye: Painter of Thoroughbred Stories* (Prospect, KY: Harmony House, 2006), 42; Alexander Mackay-Smith, *The Race Horses of America, 1832–1872: Portraits and Other Paintings by Edward Troye* (Saratoga Springs, NY: National Museum of Racing, 1981), 10–13.
4. Mackay-Smith's *Race Horses of America* remains the most comprehensive account of Troye's life and work. On Troye, see also "Death of Edward Troye," *Turf, Field, and Farm*, August 7, 1874, 100; "Sketch of Edward Troye and His Works," unpublished manuscript from Van Shipp family, Harry Worcester Smith Papers, National Sporting Library, Middleburg, VA; Harry Worcester Smith, "Edward Troye (1808–1874), Painter of American Blood Horses," *Field*, January 21, 1926, 96–98; J. Winston Coleman Jr., *Edward Troye, Animal and Portrait Painter* (Lexington, KY: Winburn Press, 1958); Lacer, *Edward Troye*; Malcolm Cormack, "Sport and Sporting Art in America," in *Country Pursuits: British, American, and French Sporting Art from the Mellon Collection in the Virginia Museum of Fine Arts* (Richmond: Virginia Museum of Fine Arts, 2007), 295–302; and Martha Wolfe and Claudia Pfeiffer, *Coming Home Series: Edward Troye (1808–1874)* (Middleburg, VA: National Sporting Library and Museum, 2014).
5. Pellom McDaniels III, *The Prince of Jockeys: The Life of Isaac Burns Murphy* (Lexington: University Press of Kentucky, 2013).
6. Katherine C. Mooney, *Race Horse Men: How Slavery and Freedom Were Made at the Racetrack* (Cambridge, MA: Harvard University Press, 2014), 6.
7. Edward Hotaling, *The Great Black Jockeys: The Lives and Times of the Men Who Dominated America's First National Sport* (New York: Prima, 1999), 104–5, 178.
8. Mooney, *Race Horse Men*, 48, 79.
9. Jessica Dallow, "Antebellum Sports Illustrated: Representing African Americans in Edward Troye's Equine Paintings," *Nineteenth-Century Art Worldwide* 12, no. 2 (Autumn 2013); http://www.19thc-artworldwide.org/autumn13/dallow-on-edward-troye-s-equine-paintings.
10. Mackay-Smith's inventory of paintings in *Race Horses of America*, 411–36, lists twelve paintings that contain a single figure—groom or jockey—and horse, and five with two or three figures—groom, jockey or trainer or both—and horse. The whereabouts of many of these are unknown, in private collections, or no reproductions exist.
11. Mackay-Smith, *Race Horses of America*, 9.

12. Hotaling, *Great Black Jockeys*, 104–6. For a discussion of the Irish as a racial and ethnic minority, see Elizabeth L. O'Leary, *At Beck and Call: The Representation of Domestic Servants in Nineteenth-Century American Painting* (Washington, DC: Smithsonian Institution Press, 1996), 111–15.
13. Mackay-Smith, *Race Horses of America*, 13–14, 61. For a record of Trifle's races, see "Memoir of Trifle," *American Turf Register*, December 1835, 145–50.
14. Mackay-Smith, *Race Horses of America*, 31.
15. Richmond Jockey Club, Records, 1824–38, Mss4 R4153 a 1, Manuscript Collection, Virginia Historical Society, Richmond, VA.
16. Mackay-Smith, *Race Horses of America*, 247; Mooney, *Race Horse Men*, 117–19; Hotaling, *Great Black Jockeys*, 143.
17. William Preston Mangum II, *A Kingdom for the Horse: The Legacy of R. A. Alexander and Woodburn Farm* (Prospect, KY: Harmony House, 1999), 54–57.
18. Alex Potts, "Natural Order and the Call of the Wild: The Politics of Picturing," *Oxford Art Journal* 13, no. 1 (1990): 13.
19. Robin Blake, "Fieldwork: Stubbs and the Humbler Sort," in Malcolm Warner and Robin Blake, *Stubbs and the Horse*, ed. Malcolm Warner and Robin Blake, exhibition catalog (New Haven, CT: Yale University Press, 2004), 82.
20. Dallow, "Antebellum Sports Illustrated."
21. Matthew Craske, "In the Realm of Nature and Beasts," in *Below Stairs: 400 Years of Servants' Portraits*, ed. Giles Waterfield and Anne French, exhibition catalog (London: National Portrait Gallery, 2003), 158.
22. John Davis and Mackay-Smith interpret differently the phrase used in Troye's obituary that states he "had charge of" a sugar estate. For Davis that means overseer; for Mackay-Smith it means bookkeeper: Mackay-Smith, "Death of Edward Troye," 100; John Davis, *The Landscape of Belief: Encountering the Holy Land in Nineteenth-Century American Art and Culture* (Princeton, NJ: Princeton University Press, 1996), 134; Mackay-Smith, handwritten notes, Mackay-Smith Papers, National Sporting Library, Middleburg, Virginia.
23. Troye's best friends were southern plantation owners, farmers, and turfmen such as Keene Richards and Robert Aitcheson Alexander. He married a woman from Kentucky and made his home in Alabama. He was reputedly an opponent of secession and a supporter of the federal cause. For a further discussion of Troye's sympathies, politics, and religion see Dallow, "Antebellum Sports Illustrated."
24. Mooney, *Race Horse Men*, 79.
25. John Campbell, *Negro-Mania: Being an Examination of the Falsely Assumed Equality of the Various Races of Man* (Philadelphia: Campbell and Power, 1851).
26. Peter A. Browne, *Trichologia Mammalium, or A Treatise on the Organization, Properties and Uses of Hair and Wool; Together with an Essay upon the Raising and Breeding of Sheep* (Philadelphia: J. H. Jones, 1853), 158. For a discussion of Campbell, Browne's taxonomy, and race, see Eric C. Stoykovich, "The Culture of Improvement in the Early Republic: Domestic Livestock, Animal Breeding, and Philadelphia's Urban Gentlemen, 1820–1860," *Pennsylvania Magazine of History and Biography* 134, no. 1 (January 2010): 52, 55–56.
27. Melissa Stein, *Measuring Manhood: Race and the Science of Masculinity* (Minneapolis: University of Minnesota Press, 2015), 50.
28. J. T., Review of *Negro-Mania*, *Southern Quarterly Review* 5, no. 9 (1852): 174–75.
29. Ian Frederick Finseth, *Shades of Green: Visions of Nature in the Literature of American Slavery, 1770–1860* (Athens: University of Georgia Press, 2009), 208–9.

30. Kirk Savage, *Standing Soldiers, Kneeling Slaves: Race, War, and Monument in Nineteenth-Century America* (Princeton, NJ: Princeton University Press), 43.
31. Finseth, *Shades of Green*, 237.
32. Ibid., 237–38.
33. Ibid., 235; Harriet Ritvo, *The Animal Estate: The English and Other Creatures in the Victorian Age* (Cambridge, MA: Harvard University Press, 1987), 17–19.
34. Karl Jacoby, "Slave by Nature? Domestic Animals and Human Slaves," *Slavery and Abolition* 15, no. 1 (1994): 89–90.
35. Philip D. Morgan, "Slaves and Livestock in Eighteenth-Century Jamaica: Vineyard Pen, 1750–1751," *William and Mary Quarterly* 52, no. 1 (January 1995): 76.
36. Ibid.
37. Mia Bay, *The White Image in the Black Mind: African American Ideas about White People, 1830–1925* (New York: Oxford University Press, 2000), 118–19.
38. Ibid., 127–33.
39. Walter Johnson, *River of Dark Dreams: Slavery and Empire in the Cotton Kingdom* (Cambridge, MA: Harvard University Press, 2013), 190.
40. Bay, *White Image in the Black Mind*, 132.
41. Charles Ball, *Fifty Years in Chains, or The Life of an American Slave* (New York: H. Dayton, 1859), 89; http://docsouth.unc.edu/fpn/ball/ball.html; Johnson, *River of Dark Dreams*, 190–91.
42. Johnson, *River of Dark Dreams*, 190–91.
43. Bay, *White Image in the Black Mind*, 136.
44. Johnson, *River of Dark Dreams*, 222. Rhys Isaac discusses the iconography of the slaveholder on horseback in *The Transformation of Virginia, 1740–1790* (Chapel Hill: University of North Carolina Press, 1982), 52–57.
45. "Medley," *American Turf Register and Sporting Magazine*, May 1833, 437–38.
46. Randy J. Sparks, "Gentleman's Sport: Horse Racing in Antebellum Charleston," *South Carolina Historical Magazine* 93, no. 1 (1992): 27.
47. "Worthy of Regard," *American Turf Register and Sporting Magazine*, March 1832, 358.
48. Mackay-Smith, *Race Horses of America*, 222–24; Hotaling, *Great Black Jockeys*, 187.
49. Jacob Stroyer, *My Life in the South* (Salem, NC: Salem Observer Book and Job Print, 1885), 19.
50. Ibid., 24–25.
51. Mackay-Smith, *Race Horses of America*, 31; Mooney, *Race Horse Men*, 43.
52. Mackay-Smith, *Race Horses of America*, 13–14; "Union Course (N.Y.) Races," *American Turf Register*, December 1832, 201–5.
53. Curtis Parker Flowers, *Thoroughbred Horses at the Muscle Shoals* (Florence, AL: printed by author, 2009), 12n26; Dallow, "Antebellum Sports Illustrated."
54. Stewart, "My Life as a Slave," 735.
55. In 1843, Wade Hampton brought his best slave jockey Sandy to Nashville to ride in the Peyton Stakes: Hotaling, *Great Black Jockeys*, 139.
56. Stewart, "My Life as a Slave," 734–37; Mooney, *Race Horse Men*, 40–42, 45.
57. Ann Norton Greene, *Horses at Work: Harnessing Power in Industrial America* (Cambridge, MA: Harvard University Press, 2008), 85.
58. Ibid., 93, 84.
59. *Conkey's Stock Book; A Handy Reference Manual on Farm Animals* (Cleveland, OH: G. E. Conkey's, 1911), 69.
60. Mooney, *Race Horse Men*, 41.
61. "Marmaduke Johnson's Mare—Dam of Old Reality," letter to the editor, *American*

Turf Register, June 1833, 520. Curtis was a noted jockey and horseman. Starting his career as a slave of North Carolina planter Willie Jones, he was freed by Jones about 1791. Curtis found Medley for Marmaduke Johnson, William Ransom Johnson's father, during the 1790s. Allen Jones Davie was the great-nephew of Willie Jones, so he had an interest in the Medley mare's pedigree: Mooney, *Race Horse Men*, 1, 10–11.

62. Letter from Tucker R. Woodson to William Ransom Johnson, January 13, 1844, Johnson Papers, Mss1 J6398a1–4, Virginia Historical Society, Richmond, VA; Stewart, "My Life as a Slave," 736.

63. Letter from Wade Hampton to Richard Singleton, August 1, 1834, Richard Singleton Papers, South Carolina Historical Society, Charleston, SC, quoted in Sparks, "Gentlemen's Sport," 27.

64. Mackay-Smith, *Race Horses of America*, 55. Mooney notes that Lewis may have been freed by 1853, when Willa Viley became part of the syndicate that purchased the horse Darley, renamed Lexington, one of the most important sires in Thoroughbred history. Darley's previous owner, Elisha Warfield, leased him to Lewis who, as a black man, could not legally enter a horse in a race at a southern track and thus could make no decisions about the horse's sale: Mooney, *Race Horse Men*, 91. That Viley's and Lewis's interests diverged over Lexington casts doubt on Mackay-Smith's story about Viley's benevolence toward Lewis.

65. Flowers, *Thoroughbred Horses at the Muscle Shoals*, 12; Curtis Parker Flowers, "Parson Dick: Groom of the Forks," *Alabama Heritage* 80 (Spring 2006): 33.

66. William T. Porter, "Wagner and Grey Eagle's Races," *American Turf Register and Sporting Magazine*, March 1840, 116–32; Hotaling, *Great Black Jockeys*, 116–33. Porter notes that Cato "had become free at the time of the first race" (127), yet Hotaling clarifies that while legend holds that he won his freedom through his victory, freedom would have been an unusual reward, since winning made the slave more valuable. Slaves could, however, earn money by riding, and Cato may have purchased his freedom by means of his skill. Hotaling, *Great Black Jockeys*, 128.

67. Porter, quoted in Hotaling, *Great Black Jockeys*, 128; Porter, "Wagner and Grey Eagle's Races," 125.

68. Troye painted Wagner in October 1839 after his race with Grey Eagle: Hotaling, *Great Black Jockeys*, 132. For the engraving, see "Memoir of Wagner," *Spirit of the Times*, July 4, 1840, 211.

69. Mackay-Smith, *Race Horses of America*, 373–75; Hotaling, *Great Black Jockeys*, 142.

70. Mackay-Smith, *Race Horses of America*, 13.

71. "Medley," *American Turf Register and Sporting Magazine*, May 1833, 437–38.

72. Stephen F. Eisenman, *The Cry of Nature: Art and the Making of Animal Rights* (London: Reaktion Books, 2013), 110. Eisenman attributes these partly to the influence of Buffon's theory that "animal and human alike possessed the primary "passions" and "appetites": "fear, horror, anger and love" (111). See Diana Donald's discussion of Stubbs and Buffon, and Stubbs's likely debt to Charles LeBrun's treatise on the visualization of human emotion, *Expressions of the Passions* (1698), in Donald, *Picturing Animals in Britain*, 73.

73. Donald, *Picturing Animals in Britain*, 73; Eisenman, *Cry of Nature*, 111, 78.

74. Horace Walpole, "On Seeing the Celebrated Startled Horse, Painted by the Inimitable Mr Stubbs," *Public Advertiser*, November 4, 1763, quoted in Donald, *Picturing Animals in Britain*, 73, and Eisenman, *Cry of Nature*, 113.

75. Robin Blake, "Fieldwork: Stubbs and the Humbler Sort," in *Stubbs and the Horse*, ed. Malcolm Warner and Robin Blake, exhibition catalog (New Haven, CT: Yale Uni-

versity Press, 2004), 89–90; Judy Egerton, *George Stubbs, Painter: Catalogue Raisonné* (New Haven, CT: Yale University Press, 2007), 622–25.

76. He exhibited the copy after Stubbs at the Pennsylvania Academy of Art in 1832. Mackay-Smith, *Race Horses of America*, 359.
77. On Stubbs's *Comparative Anatomical Exposition* and human/animal homologies see Donald, *Picturing Animals in Britain*, 74.
78. Eisenman, *Cry of Nature*, 112.
79. Donald, *Picturing Animals in Britain*, 74.
80. Ingrid H. Tague, "Companions, Servants, or Slaves? Considering Animals in Eighteenth-Century Britain," *Studies in Eighteenth-Century Culture* 39 (2010): 112; Oliver Goldsmith, introduction to *A New and Accurate System of Natural History*, by Richard Brookes, 2nd ed., 6 vols. (London: T. Carnan and F. Newbery, 1772), 1:xviii, quoted in Tague, "Companions, Servants, or Slaves?," 113.
81. Tague, "Companions, Servants, or Slaves?," 114.
82. Marcus Wood, *Blind Memory: Visual Representations of Slavery in England and America, 1780–1865* (New York: Routledge, 2000), 114–15. For the original verses and illustrations, see *Cousin Ann's Stories for Little Children* (Philadelphia: J. M. McKim, 1849), 12–14, 24.
83. "Tom and Lucy: A Tale for Little Lizzie," in *Cousin Ann's Stories*, 17, quoted in Brigitte Nicole Fielder, "Animal Humanism: Race, Species, and Affective Kinship in Nineteenth-Century Abolitionism," *American Quarterly* 65, no. 3 (2013): 493.
84. Janet M. Davis, *The Gospel of Kindness: Animal Welfare and the Making of Modern America* (New York: Oxford University Press, 2016), 44, 52; Fielder, "Animal Humanism," 494.
85. Fielder, "Animal Humanism," 493; Davis, *Gospel of Kindness*, 52.
86. Fielder, "Animal Humanism," 501.
87. Frederick Douglass, *Narrative of the Life of Frederick Douglass, an American Slave, Written by Himself*, in *The Oxford Frederick Douglass Reader*, ed. William L. Andrews (1845; repr., New York: Oxford University Press, 1996), 39.
88. Frederick Douglass, *The Claims of the Negro, Ethnologically Considered* (Rochester, NY: Lee, Mann, 1854), 9. See Stein, *Measuring Manhood*, 61, for a discussion of these statements.
89. Stein, *Measuring Manhood*, 87.
90. David Walker, *Appeal to the Colored Citizens of the World* (1829), in *"One Continual Cry"—David Walker's Appeal to the Colored Citizens of the World: Its Settings and Meanings*, ed. Herbert Aptheker (New York: Humanities Press, 1965), 68, quoted in Stein, *Measuring Manhood*, 59.
91. James W. C. Pennington, *A Textbook of the Origin and History etc. of the Colored People* (1841; repr., Detroit: Negro History Press, 1969), 89, 46, quoted in Stein, *Measuring Manhood*, 60.
92. Stewart, "My Life as a Slave," 732.
93. Ibid., 734.
94. Ibid., 735.
95. Bay, *White Image in the Black Mind*, 72. In an 1863 speech Theodore Tilton, editor of the *New York Independent*, characterized the "negro" as the "feminine race of the world": Tilton, quoted by Bay.
96. Stein, *Measuring Manhood*, 63.
97. Stewart, "My Life as a Slave," 735.
98. Morgan, "Slaves and Livestock in Eighteenth-Century Jamaica," 74.

99. Stewart, "My Life as a Slave," 735.
100. Michael Tadman, *Speculators and Slaves: Masters, Traders, and Slaves in the Old South* (Madison: University of Wisconsin Press, 1989), 121–29; Johnson, *River of Dark Dreams*, 197; McDaniels, *Prince of Jockeys*, 39.
101. Stewart, "My Life as a Slave," 735.
102. Ibid., 737–38; Mooney, *Race Horse Men*, 53; Johnson, *River of Dark Dreams*, 214.

CHAPTER EIGHT

1. Epigraphs: Wilfrid Scawen Blust, "The Thoroughbred Horse—English and Arabian," *Nineteenth Century* 8 (September 1880): 412; Clifton P. Flynn, "Social Creatures: An Introduction," in *Social Creatures: A Human and Animal Studies Reader*, ed. Clifton P. Flynn (New York: Lantern Books, 2008), xv.
2. Muriel Lennox, *Northern Dancer: The Legend and His Legacy* (Edinburgh: Mainstream, 1999), 155.
3. Ibid., 155.
4. Ibid., 9.
5. Erica Fudge, "Animal Lives," *History Today* 54, no. 10 (2004): 21–26; 21.
6. Ibid., 23.
7. See Deirdre Lynch, *The Economy of Character: Novels, Market Culture, and the Business of Inner Meaning* (Chicago: University of Chicago Press, 1998), 6; Nancy Armstrong, *How Novels Think: The Limits of British Individualism from 1719–1900* (New York: Columbia University Press, 2005), 28; and Regina Gagnier, *Subjectivities: A History of Self-Representation in Britain, 1832–1920* (Oxford: Oxford University Press, 1991), 31.
8. Elaine Freedgood, *The Ideas in Things: Fugitive Meaning in the Victorian Novel* (Chicago: University of Chicago Press, 2006), 97–100. See also Mark Blackwell, ed., *The Secret Life of Things: Animals, Objects, and It-Narratives in Eighteenth-Century England* (Lewisburg, PA: Bucknell University Press, 2007).
9. Jacques Derrida, "The Animal That Therefore I Am (More to Follow)," trans. David Wills, *Critical Inquiry* 28, no. 2 (2002): 369–418; 394.
10. Donna Landry, *Noble Brutes: How Eastern Horses Transformed English Culture* (Baltimore: Johns Hopkins University Press, 2008), 167, 174.
11. Rebecca Cassidy, *The Sport of Kings: Kinship, Class, and Thoroughbred Breeding in Newmarket* (Cambridge: Cambridge University Press, 2002), 9.
12. Katherine Dashper and Thomas Fletcher, "'Like a Hawk among House Sparrows': Kauto Star, a Steeplechasing Legend," *Sport in History* 33, no. 4 (2013): 488–511; 493.
13. Lennox, *Northern Dancer*, 154.
14. Since the first publication of William Nack's *Secretariat* in 1975, more than one hundred racehorse biographies have been published in the United State, Great Britain, and Australia.
15. Felicity A. Nussbaum, *The Autobiographical Subject: Gender and Ideology in Eighteenth-Century England* (Baltimore: Johns Hopkins University Press, 1995), 5–6.
16. Ibid., xii.
17. Ibid., 37.
18. Ibid., xiv.
19. See, for example, Sidonie Smith and Julia Watson, *Reading Autobiography: A Guide for Interpreting Life Narratives*, 2nd ed. (Minneapolis: University of Minnesota Press, 2010), 120–21.

20. Bracy Clark, *A Short History of the Celebrated Race-Horse, Eclipse* (London: Richards, 1835); accessed June 13, 2015, http://dspace.library.uu.nl/handle/1874/30923.
21. See, for example, Newmarket, *Chapters from Turf History* (London: National Review Office, 1922).
22. John Taintor Foote, *The Look of Eagles* (1924; repr., London: J. A. Allen, 1969), 18; accessed February 20, 2016, Google Books.
23. Nack, *Secretariat*, 368.
24. Jane Schwartz, *Ruffian: Burning from the Start* (New York: Random House, 1991), 98.
25. Henrietta Knight, *Best Mate: Triple Gold* (Newbury, UK: Highdown, 2003), 33.
26. In addition to Lennox, *Northern Dancer*, see Nack, *Secretariat*, 430; Knight, *Best Mate*; and Ginger McCain, *Red Rum: A Racing Legend* (London: Weidenfeld and Nicolson, 1996).
27. Nack, *Secretariat*, 437.
28. Lennox, *Northern Dancer*, 56, 60.
29. Ibid., 97–98.
30. Quoted in Linda Hanna, *Barbaro, Smarty Jones and Ruffian: The People's Horses* (Moorestown, NJ: Middle Atlantic Press, 2008), 12.
31. Schwartz, *Ruffian*, 27.
32. Ibid., 288.
33. Ibid., 315.
34. Laura Hillenbrand, *Seabiscuit: An American Legend* (New York: Random House, 2001), 39.
35. Ibid., 105.
36. Ibid., 108, 109.
37. Quoted in Geoff Armstrong and Peter Thompson, *Phar Lap: How a Horse Became a Hero in His Time and an Icon of a Nation* (Crows Nest, New South Wales: Allen and Unwin, 2000), 160.
38. Nack, *Secretariat*, 407.
39. Ibid., 172–73, 177.
40. Ibid., 405.
41. Ibid., 444.
42. Knight, *Best Mate*, 188.
43. Ibid., 244.
44. Nack, *Secretariat*, 407.
45. Bill Lyon, quoted in Hanna, *Barbaro, Smarty Jones and Ruffian*, 119.
46. Hanna, *Barbaro, Smarty Jones and Ruffian*, 131.
47. Sally Jenkins, "A Bottomless Heart," *Washington Post*, Tuesday, January 30, 2007; accessed June 4, 2016, washingtonpost.com.
48. Nack, *Secretariat*, 367.
49. McCain, *Red Rum*, 93.
50. Ibid., 15.
51. Armstrong and Thompson, *Phar Lap*, 162.
52. Marianna Haun, "The X Factor: Heart of the Matter, part 1," *Quarter Racing Journal*, June 1998; accessed June 12, 2016, http://horsesonly.com/crossroads/xfactor/heart-1.htm. See also Haun's *The X Factor: What It Is and How to Find It: The Relationship between Inherited Heart Size and Racing Performance* (Neenah, WI: Russell Meerdink, 1997).
53. Quoted in Louise Mahr, "Phar Lap: Missing Pieces of Horse's Heart Discovered

in National Museum of Australia," September 9, 2014, ABC Canberra; accessed June 15, 2016, http://www.abc.net.au/news/2014-09-10/phar-lap-heart/5730180.

54. Quoted in Nack, *Secretariat*, 429.
55. Hanna, *Barbaro, Smarty Jones and Ruffian*, 22.
56. Jenkins, "Bottomless Heart."
57. Mike Embry, "Secretariat, Suffering from Incurable Condition, Destroyed," *LA Times*, October 5, 1989; accessed June 8, 2016, http://articles.latimes.com/1989-10-05/sports/sp-984_1_secretariat; Barbara Livingston, "Man o' War's Funeral: Remarkable Final Tribute for Majestic Champion," *Racing Form*, February 24, 2011; accessed June 20, 2016, http://www.drf.com/blogs/man-o-wars-funeral-remarkable-final-tribute-majestic-champion. See also Lucy Zeh, *Etched in Stone: Thoroughbred Memorials* (Lexington, KY: Blood-Horse, 2000).
58. Dashper and Fletcher, "'Like a Hawk,'" 491–92.
59. Leo Lowenthal, *Literature and Mass Culture* (New Brunswick, NJ: Transaction Books, 1984), 212–13.
60. Lawrence Scanlan, *The Big Red Horse: The Story of Secretariat and the Loyal Groom Who Loved Him* (Toronto: Harper Trophy Canada, 2010), 130, 131.

CHAPTER NINE

This chapter was originally presented in London at the "War Horses of the World" conference held at the School of Oriental and African Studies on May 3, 2014. I am grateful to the organizers and the participants for providing their valuable comments and criticisms. All translations from the German are my own.

1. Studies on the history of state studs in Europe have so far focused heavily on France: Nicole de Blomac, *Voyer d'Argenson et le cheval des lumières* (Paris, 2004); Eugène Gayot, *La France chevaline, 1ère partie—institutions hippiques* (Paris, 1848); Ostpreußisches Tageblatt, ed., *Zweihundert Jahre Preußische Staats-Gestütsverwaltung, 1731–1932* (Insterburg, 1932); Jacques Mulliez, *Les chevaux du royaume: Histoire de l'élevage du cheval et de la création des haras* (Paris, 1983); Joseph Vernois, "Histoire de l'administration des haras en France" (thèse vétérinaire, Lyon, 1947).
2. Vernois, "Histoire des haras," 13; Johann Christoph Justinus, *Hinterlassene Schriften über die wahren Grundsätze der Pferdezucht, über Wettrennen und Pferdehandel in England, nebst Aphorismen über das Exterieur in besonderer Beziehung auf Zuchtthiere* (Vienna, 1830), 163; J. C. Zehentner, *Kurzer und gründlicher Unterricht von der Pferdezucht, in welchem die Ursachen des heutigen Verfalls derselben, nebst dem daraus entstehenden grossen Schaden eröffnet werden, wie auch die Art und Weise, wie die Gestüte in besseren Verfassung zu bringen, daß der Landesherr sowohl, als die Einwohner grossen Nutzen davon haben können* (Berlin, 1770), introduction.
3. Hew Strachan, *European Armies and the Conduct of War* (London, 1983), 16.
4. Ibid.
5. J. J. Wörz, *Die Staats- oder Landespferdezucht-Anstalten Württembergs mit einer Einleitung über ihre geschichtliche Entwicklung aus den vormaligen fürstlichen Hofgestüten* (Ulm, 1876), 2; J. G. Prizelius, *Beschreibung des so bekannten Senner Gestüts in der Grafschaft Lippe* (Lemgo, 1771).
6. Vernois, "Histoire des haras," 15–16; Zehentner, *Kurzer und gründlicher Unterricht von der Pferdezucht*, introduction; Johann Gottlieb Wollstein, *Bruchstücke über wilde-, halbwilde-, militär- und Landgestüte* (Vienna, 1788). For how wild horses were hunted down in forests and then sold at market during the early modern period,

see Annette Krus-Bonazza, *"Auf Cranger Kirmes": Vom Pferdemarkt zum Oktoberfest des Westens* (Münster, 1992), 27–30.

7. Justinus, *Hinterlassene Schriften*, 2.
8. Vernois, "Histoire des haras," 16–17.
9. Olivier Chebrou de Lespinats, *Histoire des haras sous le premier empire: Suivi de notices biographiques et généalogiques, période 1806–1815* (Versailles, 2005).
10. Rudolf Hompertz, "Pferdezucht und Pferdehandel im deutschen Wirtschaftsleben" (dissertation, University of Cologne, 1922), 10–11.
11. Hompertz, "Pferdezucht und Pferdehandel," 27.
12. Victor Silberer, "Domink Graf Hardegg," in *Einiges über das Pferd*, ed. Dominik Graf Hardegg (Vienna, 1917), 10.
13. Hompertz, "Pferdezucht und Pferdehandel," 132.
14. It thus builds on the work of equine historians who have seen the horse as an entry point to grasp much broader social and economic forces in European history. See, for example, F. M. L. Thompson, ed., *Horses in European Economic History: A Preliminary Canter* (Reading, UK: British Agricultural History Society, 1983).
15. For biographical information on Justinus, see *Pferdezüchter* 11 (November 1909): 85.
16. Johann Christoph Justinus, *Allgemeine Grundsätze zur Vervollkommnung der Pferdezucht, Anwendbar auf die übrigen Hausthierzuchten* (Vienna, 1815); idem, *Hinterlassene Schriften*.
17. Justinus, *Hinterlassene Schriften*, 87–88.
18. Ibid., 8.
19. Ibid., 9.
20. Ibid., 25.
21. Ibid., 168–69.
22. Ibid., 106.
23. Ibid., 177.
24. Carl von Knobelsdorf, *Ueber die Pferdezucht in England* (Berlin, 1820), introduction.
25. Joseph von Hazzi, *Ueber die Pferderennen als wesentliches Beförderungs-Mittel der bessern, vielmehr edlen Pferdezucht in Deutschland und besonders in Bayern* (Munich, 1826), 23–24.
26. Carl Friedrich Wilhelm von Burgsdorf, *Versuch eines Beweises, dass die Pferderennen in England so wie sie jetzt bestehen, kein wesentliches Beförderungs-Mittel der bessern edlen Pferdezucht in Deutschland werden können* (Königsberg, 1827), 5.
27. Freiherr von den Brincken, *Bemerkungen über das Englische Pferd: Dessen verschiedene Racen, und die Pferdezucht im Allgemeinen* (Weimar, 1827), 49.
28. Karl-Wilhelm Ammon, *Bemerkungen über die Nutzen der ländlichen Hof- und Stammgestüte, und der Wettrennen nach englischer Art* (Nuremberg, 1831), 12–13.
29. Burgsdorf, *Versuch eines Beweises*, 5.
30. Ibid., 8.
31. Friedrich von Biel, *Einziges über edle Pferde* (Dresden, 1830), 129.
32. Brincken, *Bemerkungen über das Englische Pferd*, 149.
33. Ibid., 7.
34. Ibid., 8–9.
35. Ibid., 94.
36. Cf. Ammon, *Wettrennen nach englischer Art*, 61–62.
37. *Ansichten über die auf dem Continente gemachten Versuche die Pferderacen zu veredeln* (Comorn, 1854), 14.
38. Röttger von Veltheim, *Abhandlungen über die Pferdezucht Englands, noch einiger Eu-*

ropäischen Länder, des Orients u.s.w. in Beziehung auf Deutschland nebst einer Revision der seit der Mitte des 18 Jahrhunderts aufgestellten Systeme über die Pferdezucht (Braunschweig, 1833), 17.

39. Ibid., 25–28, 35–36.
40. John Lewis Burckhardt, *Travels in Arabia, Comprehending an Account of Those Territories in Hedjaz Which the Mohammedans Regard as Sacred* (London, 1829); idem, *Notes on the Bedouins and Wahabys Collected during His Travels in the East* (London, 1830).
41. Brincken, *Bemerkungen über das Englische Pferd,* 155.
42. Biel, *Einiges,* 187–88.
43. Ibid., 165.
44. Ibid., 186.
45. Ibid., 72.
46. Ibid., 196.
47. Geheimes Staatsarchiv Preußischer Kulturbesitz, I HA Rep 89: Pferdezucht- und Pferdedressurverein in Berlin, 1828–1860: Letter from Knobelsdorf, dated June 17, 1828; *Statut des Vereins für Pferdezucht und Pferdedressur* (Berlin, 1828).
48. Cf. Oskar Knispel, *Die Verbreitung der Pferdeschläge in Deutschland nach dem Stande vom Jahre 1898* (Berlin, 1900), 11.
49. Ammon, *Wettrennen nach englischer Art,* 50.
50. Heinrich von Nathusius, *Ueber die Lage der Landespferdezucht in Preußen* (Berlin, 1872), 29.
51. Franz Charles de Beaulieu, *Der klassische Sport: Ein Beitrag zur Geschichte des Rennsports und der Vollblutzucht* (Berlin, 1942), 36–37.
52. Saxon State Stud Administration, "Graditz Principal Stud—Centre of Horse Breeding," http://www.saechsische-gestuetsverwaltung.de/en/saxon-state-stud-administration/history/history-of-graditz-principal-stud/, accessed April 15, 2014.
53. Bujack-Meduni߬ten, "Die Pferdezucht in der Provinz Preußen," *Annalen der Landwirtschaft in den königlich Preußischen Staaten* 24 (1863): 228-59, 247.
54. *Promemoria über den gegenwärtigen Stand der Landespferdezucht und über die Mittel zur Hebung derselben verfasst im Februar 1870 von dem ständigen Central-Ausschuss des Congresses Deutscher Pferdezüchter* (Berlin, 1870), 24–25; *Der Sporn* 4 (January 1884): 31.
55. See Christian Eisenberg, *"English Sports" und Deutsche Bürger: Eine Gesellschaftsgeschichte, 1800–1939* (Paderborn, 1999), 162–78.
56. Heinz Reif, *Westfälischer Adel, 1770–1860: Vom Herrschaftsstand zur regionalen Elite* (Göttingen, 1979), 417.
57. *Der Sporn,* April 15, 1869, 117.
58. *Verhandlungen der Commission zur Förderung der Pferdezucht in Preußen im Auftrage des Königlich Preußischen Ministers für die landwirtschaftlichen Angelegenheiten* (Berlin, 1875).
59. *Verhandlungen der Commission zur Förderung der Pferdezucht in Preußen im Monat Juni 1876* (Berlin, 1876), 25.
60. *Verhandlungen der Commission zur Förderung der Pferdezucht in Preußen im Auftrage des Königlich Preußischen Ministers für die landwirtschaftlichen Angelegenheiten* (Berlin, 1881), 110.
61. Kurt von Tepper-Laski, *Rennreiten: Praktische Winke für Rennreiter und Manager,* 3rd ed. (Berlin, 1914), 19.
62. Karl Simons, *Die Entwicklung der rheinischen Pferdezucht (Rheinisch-belgisches Kaltblut)* (Berlin, 1912), 10–11.

63. Quoted in ibid., 11.
64. Ibid., 12–13.
65. Ibid., 12.
66. *Zeitschrift für wissenschaftliche Landwirtschaft und Archiv des Königlich Preußischen Landes Ökonomie-Kollegiums* (1878), suppl. 1, 55.
67. Waldschmidt, *Vorschläge zur Förderung der Pferdezucht mit besonderer Berücksichtigung der Rheinprovinz* (Bonn, 1865), 6.
68. Ibid.
69. Ibid., 1.
70. Simons, *Entwicklung der rheinischen Pferdezucht*, 18.
71. Ibid., 32.
72. *Deutsche Landwirtschaftliche Presse* (*DLP*) 23 (November 1894): 225.
73. *DLP* 14 (February 1894): 124.
74. *Pferdefreund* 15 (December 1898): 281.
75. By 1899, out of the 150 cooperatives that had been established after the passing of the Cooperatives Act, 75 dealt with horse breeding. See *Pferdefreund* 16 (February 1899): 45.
76. Otto Gagzow, *Der Kampf um Kalt-und Warmblut in der Pferdezucht der preußischen Remonteprovinzen* (Posen, 1902), 61.
77. Dietrich Born, "Kaltblutzucht in Ostpreußen," *Deutsche Landwirtschaftliche Tierzucht* (DLT), 12 (September 1908): 460.
78. *DLT* 12 (January 1908): 22.
79. Leonhard Hoffmann, *Spezielle Pferdezucht: Zugleich eine Lanze für die Zucht des schweren Pferdes* (Leipzig, 1902), 2.
80. Ibid.
81. Ibid., 5.
82. Ibid.
83. Ibid., v.
84. Ibid., 10.
85. Ibid., 14.
86. Reinhart Koselleck, "Das Ende des Pferdezeitalters," *Süddeutsche Zeitung*, September 25, 2003.

CHAPTER TEN

1. *Kansas City (KS) Journal*, "Horse Meat Feast," March 6, 1898, 1.
2. Ann Norton Greene, *Horses at Work: Harnessing Power in Industrial America* (Cambridge, MA: Harvard University Press, 2008).
3. Sylvain Leteux, "Is Hippophagy a Taboo in Constant Evolution?," *Menu: Journal of Food and Hospitality*, 2012, 1.
4. Pita Kelekna, *The Horse in Human History* (Cambridge: Cambridge University Press, 2009), 35.
5. Chris Otter, "Hippophagy in the UK: A Failed Dietary Revolution," *Endeavour* 35 (2011): 83.
6. Marvin Harris, *Good to Eat: Riddles of Food and Culture* (London: Allen and Unwin, 1986), 92.
7. Wilfred G. Lambert, *Babylonian Wisdom Literature* (Warsaw, IN: Eisenbrauns, 1996), 175.
8. Harold B. Barclay, *The Role of the Horse in Man's Culture* (London: J. A. Allen, 1980), 57.

9. Alain Drouard, "Horsemeat in France: A Food Item That Appeared during the War of 1870 and Disappeared after the Second World War," in *Food and War in Twentieth Century Europe*, ed. Ina Zweiniger-Bargielowska (Farnham, UK: Ashgate, 2011), 234.
10. Leteux, "Is Hippophagy a Taboo in Constant Evolution?," 4.
11. Frederick J. Simoons, *Eat Not This Flesh: Food Avoidances from Prehistory to the Present* (Madison: University of Wisconsin Press, 1994), 188. There are also instances of monks' eating horsemeat, but these seem to have involved either wild horses, which as game were still considered consumable, or circumstances exceptionable enough to be recorded.
12. Madeleine Ferrières, *Sacred Cow, Mad Cow: A History of Food Fears* (New York: Columbia University Press, 2006), 14.
13. Ramon Llull, *The Book of the Order of Chivalry*, ed. Alfred T. Byles, trans. William Caxton (London: Early English Text Society, 1926), 15.
14. Keith Thomas, *Man and the Natural World: Changing Attitudes in England, 1500–1800* (London: Penguin Books, 1991).
15. Harris, *Good to Eat*, 98.
16. Ferrières, *Sacred Cow, Mad Cow*, 14.
17. Voltaire, *Collected Works of Voltaire* (East Sussex, UK: Delphi Classics, 2015), electronic book, n.p.
18. Drouard, "Horsemeat in France," 234.
19. Mathieu Géraud, *Essai sur la suppression des fosses d'aisances, et de toute espèce de voiries, sur la manière de converter en combustibles les substances qu'on y renferme, etc.* (Amsterdam, 1786), 142.
20. Susan Freidburg, *Fresh: A Perishable History* (Cambridge, MA: Harvard University Press, 2009), 52.
21. Otter, "Hippophagy in the UK," 6.
22. Drouard, "Horsemeat in France," 235.
23. Ibid.
24. Otter, "Hippophagy in the UK," 12.
25. *Libausches Wochenblatt*, April 29, 1842.
26. C. J. F. Hoehing, *Ueber die Verwendung der thierischen Ueberreste unserer hausthiere, das Pferdefleisch-Essen und die Aufhebung der Kleemeistereien* (Stuttgart: Hoffmann'sche Verlag-Buchhandlung, 1848).
27. Drouard, "Horsemeat in France," 236.
28. Eric Pierre, "L'hippophagie au secours des classes laborieuses," *Communications* 74 (2003): 184.
29. Geoffroy Isidore Saint-Hilaire, *Lettres sur les substances alimentaires et particulièrement sur la viande de cheval* (Paris: Masson, 1856), 209.
30. Otter, "Hippophagy in the UK," 17.
31. Ghislaine Bouchet, *Le cheval à Paris de 1850 à 1914* (Paris: Broché, 1993), 221.
32. *Times* (UK), "A Horse Dinner," February 7, 1868.
33. Harvey Levenstein, *Revolution at the Table: The Transformation of the American Diet* (Oxford: Oxford University Press, 1993), 3.
34. Maureen Ogle, *In Meat We Trust: An Unexpected History of Carnivore America* (Boston: Houghton Mifflin Harcourt, 2013), 12, 11.
35. Ibid. 49.
36. Levenstein, *Revolution at the Table*, 56.
37. Ogle, *In Meat We Trust*, 81.
38. Levenstein, *Revolution at the Table*, 4.

39. Quoted in Kari Weil, "They Eat Horses, Don't They? Hippophagy and Frenchness," *Gastronomica* 7, no. 2 (2007): 46.
40. Adrienne E. Gavin, *Dark Horse: A Life of Anna Sewell* (Stroud, UK: Sutton, 2004), 188.
41. "A Fifteenth Ward Black Republican," letter to the editor, *New York Daily Tribune*, September 15, 1856.
42. Ida Tarbell, "The Meat of Paris," *Pittsburgh Dispatch*, April 10, 1892.
43. Frank G. Carpenter, "Horse Meat for Food," *National Tribune*, January 19, 1893.
44. Ogle, *In Meat We Trust*, 50.
45. *New York Sun*, December 27, 1894.
46. *Elk County (PA) Advocate*, April 24, 1879.
47. *Vermont Phoenix*, June 20, 1902.
48. *Berea (KY) Citizen*, December 28, 1905.
49. Frank G. Carpenter, *San Francisco (CA) Morning Call*, December 9, 1894, 1.
50. *Ottawa (IL) Free Trader*, "Condition of the South," June 6, 1868.
51. James Harvey Young, *Pure Food: Securing the Federal Food and Drugs Act of 1906* (Princeton, NJ: Princeton University Press, 1989), 40-65.
52. Bee Wilson, *Swindled: From Poison Sweets to Counterfeit Coffee—the Dark History of the Food Cheats* (London: John Murray, 2009), 166.
53. *Tiffin (OH) Tribune*, August 8, 1872.
54. Wilson, *Swindled*, 177.
55. *New York Times*, April 22, 1875, 2.
56. *Cincinnati Gazette*, November 24, 1870.
57. *St. Paul (MN) Daily Globe*, September 17, 1895.
58. Felix L. Oswald, "Health Hints for Old and Young," *National Tribune*, April 11, 1889.
59. *Washington (DC) National Tribune*, April 11, 1889.
60. *Fayetteville (NC) Observer*, "Getting Rid of Horses," November 17, 1870.
61. *Detroit Press*, February 28, 1883.
62. *Pike County (PA) Press*, "Arrested for Selling Horse Meat" January 17, 1896.
63. *Omaha Daily Bee*, "He Sold Horse Steaks," December 18, 1890.
64. *New York Evening World*, December 13, 1889.
65. "Horse-Meat Sausages," *Sedalia (MO) Weekly Bazoo*, February 25, 1890, 2.
66. *Anaconda (MT) Standard*, "Horseflesh for Food," January 1, 1895.
67. *Omaha Daily Bee*, March 31, 1894.
68. *Cape Girardeau (MO) Democrat*, August 10, 1895.
69. *North Platte (NE) Semi-Weekly Tribune*, September 3, 1895.
70. *Anaconda (MT) Standard*, August 15, 1895.
71. *Salem (OR) Daily Capital Journal*, October 31, 1896.
72. *Allentown (PA) Morning Call*, December 21, 1894.
73. *Kansas City Veterinary College History*, http://www.vet.k-state.edu/about/history/kcvc/, accessed October 19, 2015.
74. Kansas Historical Society, *Kansapedia*, March 2013. https://www.kshs.org/kansapedia/livestock/14196, accessed October 6, 2015.
75. *Kansas City (KS) Journal*, "Horse Meat Feast," March 6, 1898, 1.
76. *Times, DC*, April 14, 1899.
77. *Washington (DC) Weekly Post*, February 27, 1900.
78. *Indianapolis Journal*, March 24, 1902.
79. *Tacoma Times*, December 20, 1917.
80. *Chicago Eagle*, February 24, 1917.
81. *Philadelphia Evening Public Ledger*, "St Louis Likes Horse Meat," March 22, 1917.
82. *Perrysburg (OH) Journal*, June 6, 1918.

83. *Bisbee (AZ) Daily Review*, "Kansas Butchers Would Sell Horse Meat," July 31, 1917.
84. *Topeka State Journal*, "To Sell Canned Wild Horse in Kansas Soon!," April 24, 1917.
85. *Perrysburg (OH) Journal*, March 28, 1918.
86. *Bisbee (AZ) Daily Review*, June 7, 1919.

CHAPTER ELEVEN

An earlier version of this essay appeared as Kari Weil, "Men and Horses: Circus Studs, Sporting Males and the Performance of Purity In Fin-de-Siècle France," *French Cultural Studies* 17, no. 1 (February 2006): 87–105. Reprinted by permission of SAGE Publications, Ltd. Translations from French are my own.

1. As Kate Van Orden writes, for the nobility of the early modern world "horsemanship was virtually synonymous with the military calling." Kate Van Orden, "Dressage, Civility, the Ballet à Cheval," in *The Culture of the Horse: Status, Discipline and Identity in the Early Modern World*, ed. Karen Raber and Treva Tucker (London: Palgrave Macmillan, 2005), 197–222; 200. See also Treva Tucker, "Early Modern French Noble Identity and the Equestrian Airs above the Ground," in ibid., 273–309.
2. Albert Cler, La comédie à cheval, ou Manies et travers du monde équestre (Paris: Ernest Boudin, 1842), 32.
3. Robert Nye, *Crime, Madness and Politics in Modern France: The Medical Concept of National Decline* (Princeton, NJ: Princeton University Press, 1993), 8.
4. On the anxieties surrounding the woman rider, see Kari Weil, "Purebreds and Amazons: Saying Things with Horses in Late-Nineteenth-Century France," *Differences* 11, no. 1 (Spring 1999): 1-37. Guy de Maupassant's short story "À cheval," in *Contes et nouvelles*, ed. Louis Forestier (Paris: Gallimard, 1833), casts an ironic glance at the Sunday rider.
5. Eugen Weber, "Gymnastics and Sport in Fin de Siècle France," *AHR* 76, no. 1 (1971): 77–78.
6. On historical connections between horsemanship and aristocracy in France see, for instance, Treva Tucker, "Early Modern French Noble Identity and the Equestrian Airs above the Ground," in *The Culture of the Horse: Status, Discipline and Identity in the Early Modern World*, ed. Karen Raber and Treva Tucker (London: Palgrave Macmillan, 2005), 273-309.
7. Georges-Louis Leclerc Buffon, "Le cheval," in *Histoire naturelle des quadrupèdes: Oeuvres* (Paris: Gallimard, 2007), 503.
8. Cler, *Comédie à cheval*, 1.
9. On little girls and horses, see Susanna Forrest, *If Wishes Were Horses: A Memoir of Equine Obsession* (London: Atlantic Books, 2012).
10. Stendhal, *Le rouge et le noir* (Paris: Gallimard, 1972), 112. Subsequent citations in text.
11. Maya Longstaffe, "The Hero's Fall from Grace: From Lucien Leuwen on a High Horse to Hector de Gribelin *à Cheval*," *French Review* 68, no. 2 (1994): 239–50; 239.
12. Stendhal, *Le rose et le vert* (ARTFL Electronic Edition, 2009), 13. Subsequent citations in text.
13. Anne Martin-Fugier, *La vie élégante, ou La formation du Tout-Paris, 1815–1848* (Paris: Fayard, 1990), 332.
14. Charles O'Keefe, "Horses, Movement, and the Paradox of Security in *La chartreuse de Parme*," *French Review* 63, no. 2 (1989): 250–59.
15. D. A. Miller, "Body Building and Textual Liberation," in *A New History of French Literature*, ed. Denis Holier (Cambridge, MA: Harvard University Press, 1989), 681–87; 683.

16. J. C. Flugel, *The Psychology of Clothes* (London: Hogarth Press, 1930), 118.
17. Cler, *Comédie à cheval*, 56. On the rise of the *amazone*, see also Weil, "Men and Horses."
18. Charles Baudelaire, *Petits poèmes en prose* (Paris: Garnier-Flammarion, 1967), 136.
19. Martin-Fugier, *Vie élégante*, 340.
20. On female performers in the French circus see Baron de Vaux, *Écuyers et écuyères: Histoire des cirques d'Europe, 1690–1891* (Paris: Rothschild, 1893), and more recently Hilda Nelson, *Great Horsewomen of the Nineteenth Century in the Circus* (Franktown, VA: Xenophon Press, 2015).
21. Henri Thétard, *La merveilleuse histoire du cirque* (Paris: Prisma, 1947), 2:165.
22. On the origins and institutions of the circuses and hippodromes in nineteenth-century Paris see Thétard, *Merveilleuse histoire*, and Baron de Vaux, *Écuyers et écuyères*, esp. 293–339.
23. Thétard, *Merveilleuse histoire*, 14.
24. Ibid., 184.
25. Ibid.
26. On Lulu see Andrea Oberhuber, "Secrets de Lulu: Félicien Champsaur et la conception du roman 'moderniste,'" *Lettres romanes* 69 (2015): 1–33; 3–4.
27. Ernest Molier, *Cirque Molier, 1880–1904* (Paris: Dupont, 1905), 18.
28. Tamar Garb, *Bodies of Modernity* (London: Thames and Hudson, 1998), 101.
29. Molier, *Cirque Molier*, 185–92. The following excerpts from the press are taken from these pages in Molier.
30. Ibid., 190.
31. Ibid., 191.
32. Ibid., 186.
33. Ibid.
34. Ibid., 186; 189–90; 7.
35. Ibid., 18.
36. For more on Tissot's painting see Garb, *Bodies of Modernity*, and David Brooke, "James Tissot's Amateur Circus," *Boston Museum Bulletin* 67 (1969): 1–17.
37. Garb, *Bodies of Modernity*, 100.
38. Lee Edelman, "Seeing Things: Representation, the Scene of Surveillance, and the Spectacle of Gay Male Sex," in *Inside/Out: Lesbian Theories, Gay Theories*, ed. Diana Fuss (New York: Routledge, 1991), 103.
39. Baron de Vaux, *L'équitation en France: Les écoles de cavalerie* (Paris: Jules Rothschild, 1896).
40. Peter Stallybrass and Allon White, *The Politics and Poetics of Transgression* (Ithaca, NY: Cornell University Press, 1986), 5.
41. Marcus Verhagen, "The Poster in Fin-de-Siècle Paris: That Mobile and Degenerate Art," in *Cinema and the Invention of Modern Life*, ed. Leo Charney and Vanessa Schwartz (Berkeley: University of California Press, 1995), 103–29.
42. Daniel Lesueur, *Névrosée* (Paris: Alphonse Lemerre, 1892), 204. Subsequent citations in text.
43. Ibid., 53.
44. According to sports enthusiast Pierre de Coubertin, "a man who likes to put on breeches, boots, and spurs only to look at himself in the mirror would be a sick man, and that's all." See his "La psychologie du costume sportif," in *Essais de psychologie sportive* (Lausanne: Librairie Payot, 1913), 81.
45. Stallybrass and White, *Politics and Poetics of Transgression*, 182–83.

46. Le Bon, *L'équitation actuelle et ses principes* (Paris: Éditions Jean-Michel Place, 1990), xvi.
47. Cited in Robert Nye, *Masculinity and Male Codes of Honor in Modern France: Studies in the History of Sexuality* (Oxford: Oxford University Press, 1984), 324.
48. Baron de Vaux, *Équitation en France*, 6–7, 8.
49. Coubertin, *Essais*, 87.
50. Georges Rouhet and Professeur Desbonnet, *L'art de créer le pur-sang humain* (Paris: Berger-Levrault, 1908), lxvii. Subsequent citations in text.
51. See Weil, "Purebreds and Amazons."
52. Anson Rabinbach, *The Human Motor: Energy, Fatigue and the Origins of Modernity* (Berkeley: University of California Press, 1990), chap. 4.
53. On the use of classical statuary in the photography of *La culture physique*, see Garb, *Bodies*, chap. 2.
54. Coubertin, *Essais*, 89.
55. Ibid., 164.
56. Ibid., 22.
57. Ibid., 245.
58. Le Bon, *Équitation*, 127.
59. Gustave Le Bon, *The Crowd* (London: Ernest Benn, 1952), 6.
60. On Le Bon's notion of the "race historique," see Catherine Rouvier, *Les idées politiques de Gustave Le Bon* (Paris: Presses universitaires de France, 1986), 68–69.
61. Le Bon, *Équitation*, 121.
62. Rouvier, *Les idées politiques de Gustave Le Bon*, 228.
63. Le Bon, *Équitation*, 123.
64. "Women are also like children in being highly impressionable," he writes in *The Crowd* (46). And, not surprisingly, they are more like *les peuples* and like animals. Just as individuals in crowds are said to become more like animals, they also become more like women. "Crowds are everywhere distinguished by feminine characteristics," he writes, adding moreover that "Latin crowds are the most feminine of all" (39).
65. Le Bon, *Équitation*, 452.
66. Gustave Le Bon, "La psychologie des femmes et les effets de leur éducation actuelle," *Revue Scientifique* 46, no. 15 (1890): 449–60; 460.
67. Cited in Françoise Labridy-Poncelet, "Imaginaries féminins et pratiques sportives," in *Les athelètes de la république*, ed. Pierre Arnaud (Paris: L'Harmatton, 1997), 317.
68. Pierre de Coubertin, *Olympisme: Selected Writings*, ed. Norbert Muller (Lausanne: International Olympic Committee, 2000), 711–13.
69. John Berger, *Ways of Seeing* (New York: Penguin Books, 1972), 47.

CHAPTER TWELVE

1. Australian Brumby Alliance, "The Burra Charter," posted May 12 2015, accessed August 25, 2015. http://australianbrumbyalliance.org.au/the-burra-charter/.
2. Ibid.
3. Laurajane Smith, *Uses of Heritage* (Abington, UK: Routledge, 2006), 1.
4. Ibid., 3.
5. Karen Welberry, "Wild Horses and Wild Mountains in the Australian Cultural Imaginary," *PAN: Philosophy, Activism, Nature* 3 (2005): 23–32.
6. New South Wales National Parks and Wildlife Service, "Guy Fawkes River National

Park: Horse Management Plan" (Sydney South: Department of Environment and Conservation, New South Wales, 2006), i.

7. Pallavi Singhal and Tim Elliot, "Aerial Culling of Brumbies in Snowy Mountains: Controversial Ban to Remain," *Sydney Morning Herald*, January 3, 2015, accessed March 3, 2016, http://www.smh.com.au/world/australia/aerial-culling-of-brumbies-in-snowy-mountains-controversial-ban-to-remain-20150102–12h144.html/.
8. New South Wales Office of Environment and Heritage, "Point of View: Alexandra Brown on Rehoming the Wild Horses," video, "Protect the Snowies" web page, accessed October 29, 2015, http://protectsnowies.environment.nsw.gov.au/; also available via YouTube, https://www.youtube.com/watch?v=bnDgzZzza6I.
9. Madison Young, "Protect the Snowies: Videos," web page, accessed October 15, 2015, https://engage.environment.nsw.gov.au/protectsnowies/videos/1339.
10. Dale Graeme Nimmo and Kelly K. Miller, "Ecological and Human Dimensions of Management of Feral Horses in Australia: A Review," *Wildlife Research* 34 (2007): 409.
11. Amanda Burdon, "Where the Wild Horses Are," *Australian Geographic*, January/February 2016, 76.
12. New South Wales Office of Environment and Heritage, "Explore the History of Kosciuszko National Park," accessed October 29, 2015, http://protectsnowies.environment.nsw.gov.au/.
13. Isa Menzies, "A Great Hue and Cry," *Horses for Discourses* blog post, July 23, 2014, https://horsesfordiscourses.wordpress.com/2014/07/23/a-great-hue-and-cry/.
14. Susan Chenery, "A Horse with No Name," *Good Weekend*, January 24, 2015, 26–31. Published online under the more emotive title "The Brumbies' Fight for Survival," *Sydney Morning Herald Good Weekend* online, January 16, 2015, accessed October 30, 2015, http://www.smh.com.au/good-weekend/the-brumbies-fight-for-survival-20141030–11eix8.html.
15. New South Wales National Parks and Wildlife Service, "Kosciuszko National Park Wild Horse Management Plan Review Update for Stakeholders," September 3, 2015.
16. Not all states or territories are opposed to shooting feral horses: currently only Queensland, the Northern Territory, Western Australia, and the Australian Capital Territory implement lethal control strategies.
17. Nimmo and Miller, "Ecological and Human Dimensions," 413.
18. New South Wales Office of Environment and Heritage, "Point of View: Alexandra Brown"; Leisa Caldwell, "Protect the Snowies: videos" webpage, accessed October 15, 2015, https://engage.environment.nsw.gov.au/protectsnowies/videos/1338.
19. Nicholas Smith, "The Howl and the Pussy: Feral Cats and Wild Dogs in the Australian Imagination," *Australian Journal of Anthropology* 10 (1999): 294.
20. Young, "Protect the Snowies: Videos."
21. Robyn MacDougall, *The History of the Guy Fawkes River Australian Brumbies and the Brumbies of the Northern Tablelands* (Sydney: New South Wales Department of Environment, 2001), 9.
22. Nimmo and Miller, "Ecological and Human Dimensions," 413.
23. Ibid.
24. Smith, *Uses of Heritage*.
25. Simon Cubit, "Tournaments of Value: Horses, Wilderness, and the Tasmanian Central Plateau," *Environmental History* 6 (2003): 398.
26. Ibid., 395; Smith, *Uses of Heritage*, 166–67; David Lowenthal, "Nature and Cultural Heritage," *International Journal of Heritage Studies* 11 (2005): 81–92.

27. Smith, *Uses of Heritage*, 166–67.
28. Ibid., 168.
29. Lowenthal, "Nature and Cultural Heritage," 82.
30. Laurajane Smith, "Affective Experiences: The Embodied Performances of Heritage Making," seminar presented at the Centre of Heritage and Museum Studies Seminar Series, Australian National University, Canberra, September 4, 2015.
31. Smith, "Affective Experiences."
32. William S. Logan and Laurajane Smith, foreword to *Intangible Heritage*, edited by Laurajane Smith and Natsuko Akagawa (Abington, UK: Routledge, 2009), xii.
33. Smith, *Uses of Heritage*.
34. Ibid., 175.
35. Caldwell, "Protect the Snowies: Videos."
36. Nanette Mantle, *Horse and Rider in Australian Legend* (Carlton, AU: Miegunyah Press, 2004); Cameron Forbes, *Australia on Horseback: The Story of the Horse and the Making of Australia* (Sydney: Pan Macmillan, 2014); Nicholas Brasch, *Horses in Australia: An Illustrated History* (Sydney: Newsouth, 2014); Maree Bentley, Susan Hall, and Tina Mattei, comps., *The Little Book of Horses* (Canberra: National Library of Australia, 2010), verso.
37. See Forbes, *Australia on Horseback*.
38. Nimmo and Miller, "Ecological and Human Dimensions," 408.
39. Ibid.
40. Forbes, *Australia on Horseback*, 8–9, 12; Mantle, *Horse and Rider*, 3.
41. Forbes, *Australia on Horseback*, 18–19.
42. Ibid., 19.
43. See Phil McManus, Glenn Albrecht, and Raewyn Graham, *The Global Horseracing Industry: Social, Economic, Environmental and Ethical Perspectives* (Abingdon, UK: Routledge, 2013).
44. Mantle, *Horse and Rider*, 6.
45. Ibid., from "Introduction," 3.
46. When explaining the gist of my thesis topic I was asked, "But horses are native to Australia, aren't they?" November 11, 2015.
47. National Museum of Australia, "Turning Hay into Chaff," *Spirited: Australia's Horse Story* exhibition website, accessed November 17, 2015, http://www.nma.gov.au/exhibitions/spirited/stories_and_objects/farm/chaffcutter.
48. Kirsten Wehner, Martha Sear, Laura Breen, Carol Cooper, Cheryl Crilly, Nicole McLennan, and Jennifer Wilson, curators, *Spirited: Australia's Horse Story*, National Museum of Australia, September 11, 2014, to March 9, 2015.
49. National Museum of Australia, "Through the City," *Spirited: Australia's Horse Story* exhibition website, accessed 17 November 2015, http://www.nma.gov.au/exhibitions/spirited/stories_and_objects/city.
50. Caldwell, "Protect the Snowies: Videos"; Guy Fawkes Heritage Horse Association, "History," website accessed October 30, 2015, http://guyfawkesheritagehorse.com/history/.
51. Waler Horse Society of Australia, Inc., website accessed March 8, 2016, http://www.walerhorse.com/?page_id=62.
52. Guy Fawkes Heritage Horse Association, "About Us," website accessed April 22, 2016, http://guyfawkesheritagehorse.com.
53. Invasive Animals Cooperative Research Centre, "Feral Camel," PestSmart Connect

web page, accessed November 17, 2015, http://www.pestsmart.org.au/pest-animal-species/camel/.

54. Northern Territory Government, "Feral Camel," Department of Land and Resource Management web page, accessed November 17, 2015, http://www.lrm.nt.gov.au/feral/camel.
55. Logan and Smith, foreword to *Intangible Heritage*, xii.
56. Frederick T. Macartney, introduction to *The Collected Verse of A. B. Paterson: Containing "The Man from Snowy River," "Rio Grande," "Saltbush Bill," "J. P."* by A. B. Paterson, 16th ed. (Sydney: Angus and Robertson, 1967), v.
57. Ibid., v.
58. See the video montage made by Leisa Caldwell for the Snowy Mountain Riders Association: https://www.youtube.com/watch?v=zKq2luOD4O0.
59. Nimmo and Miller, "Ecological and Human Dimensions," 408.
60. Ibid.
61. Ibid.
62. Anne Crawford, *Great Australian Horse Stories* (Crows Nest, AU: Allen and Unwin, 2013), 6; Ernie Masky interview transcript, *Report of the Heritage Working Party on the Horses of the Guy Fawkes River National Park to the Minister for the Environment*, vol. 2 (Sydney: New South Wales Department of Environment, 2002), 5; Dianne Thompson, interview, November 5, 2015.
63. Young, "Protect the Snowies: Videos."
64. See Jed Smith, "Discredited Class-War Fable or Priceless Promotional Asset? The Duality of Rugby Union's William Webb Ellis Foundation Myth," in *Sport, History, and Heritage: Studies in Public Representation*, ed. Jeff Hill, Kevin Moore, and Jason Wood (Woodbridge, UK: Boydell Press, 2012), for an example of how the myth that William Webb Ellis invented the sport of rugby has proved singularly impervious.
65. Cubit, "Tournaments of Value"; Caldwell, "Protect the Snowies: Videos"; see also the Carlyon family as depicted in the documentary film *The Man from Cox's River* (Empress Arts Film, 2014).
66. Cubit, "Tournaments of Value," 398.
67. Caldwell, "Protect the Snowies: Videos"; see also Caldwell's video montage for the Snowy Mountain Riders Association.
68. Caldwell, "Protect the Snowies: Videos."
69. Ibid.
70. Leisa Caldwell interviewed in Alex Blucher and Bill Brown, "Shooting Brumbies in Kosciuszko," ABC Rural, April 1, 2014, accessed July 1, 2014, http://www.abc.net.au/news/2014-02-27/shooting-brumbies-in-national-parks/5267898.
71. Catriona Elder, *Being Australian: Narratives of National Identity* (Crows Nest, AU: Allen and Unwin, 2007); Peter Pierce, *The Country of Lost Children: An Australian Anxiety* (Cambridge: Cambridge University Press, 1999); Welberry, "Wild Horses"; Lisa Slater, "Anxious Settler Belonging: Actualising the Potential for Making Resilient Postcolonial Subjects," *M/C Journal* 16 (2013), accessed July 1, 2014, http://journal.media-culture.org.au/index.php/mcjournal/article/viewArticle/705.
72. Pierce, *Country of Lost Children*.
73. Smith, "Howl and the Pussy," 298.
74. Welberry, "Wild Horses," 23.
75. Lowenthal, "Nature and Cultural Heritage," 86.
76. Welberry, "Wild Horses," 25.
77. Ibid., 24–25.

78. Cubit, "Tournaments of Value," 400.
79. *The Man from Cox's River.*
80. Caldwell, "Protect the Snowies: Videos."
81. Ann Brower, John Page, Amanda Kennedy, and Paul Martin, "The Cowboy, the Southern Man, and the Man from Snowy River: The Symbolic Politics of Property in Australia, the United States, and New Zealand," *Georgetown International Environmental Law Review* 21 (2008–9): 455.
82. Ibid., 458.
83. Hansard, "Environment, Communications, Information Technology and the Arts Legislation Committee, Estimates Committee," Senate, May 26, 2006, accessed November 19, 2015, http://parlinfo.aph.gov.au/parlInfo/search/display/display.w3p;adv=yes;orderBy=customrank;page=0;query=Dataset%3AcomSen,estimate%20Decade%3A%222000s%22%20Year%3A%222005%22%20Month%3A%2205%22%20CommitteeName_Phrase%3A%22environment,%20communications,%20information%20technology%20and%20the%20arts%20legislation%20committee%22%20Questioner_Phrase%3A%22senator%20ian%20campbell%22;rec=1;resCount=Default.
84. Brower et al., "Cowboy," 488.
85. Hansard, "Environment, Communications, Information Technology."
86. Brower et al., "Cowboy," 491.
87. For examples, see ibid., 485; Smith, *Uses of Heritage*, 162–92; Caldwell, "Protect the Snowies: Videos."
88. Smith, *Uses of Heritage*, 191.
89. Caldwell, "Protect the Snowies: Videos."
90. Brower et al., "Cowboy," 485.
91. Smith, *Uses of Heritage*, 175–76.
92. Ibid., 174–78.
93. Ibid., 184.
94. Natasha Fijn, personal communication, February 13, 2014.
95. Ann McGrath, *Born in the Cattle* (Sydney: Allen and Unwin, 1987).
96. David S. Trigger, "Indigeneity, Ferality, and What 'Belongs' in the Australian Bush: Aboriginal Responses to 'Introduced' Animals and Plants in a Settler-Descendant Society," *Journal of the Royal Anthropological Institute* 14 (2008): 640–41.
97. Mantle, *Horse and Rider*, 59–60.
98. This idea has now acquired cliché status. In the episode "Summit Attempt" of the satirical comedy *Utopia*, the marketing team suggests the blatantly ridiculous "Summit on the Summit," envisioning delegates on horseback, wearing Akubra hats and Driza-Bones and holding stockwhips, atop Mount Kosciuszko (series 2, episode 8, Australian Broadcasting Commission, 2015).
99. Tim Flannery, "Beautiful Lies: Population and Environment in Australia," *Quarterly Essay* (Melbourne, Black Inc.), 2003 (e-reader edition).
100. Mantle, *Horse and Rider*, 3.
101. Forbes, *Australia on Horseback.*

CONTRIBUTORS

SINAN AKILLI is assistant professor of English literature and British cultural studies at Hacettepe University, Ankara. Since completing his doctoral work on late Victorian imperial adventure fiction in 2005, he has published research and review articles, book chapters, and book translations on a variety of research interests including adaptation studies, travel writing, imperialism in literature, early modern astrology and prophecy, ecocriticism, and, most recently, animal studies. His Turkish translation of Donna Landry's *Noble Brutes: How Eastern Horses Transformed English Culture* (2008) was published with the title *Asil Hayvanlar: İngiliz Kültürünü Değiştiren Doğulu Atlar* (Istanbul: E-Yayınları, 2015). His research and teaching concentrate on cultural theory and British fiction of the eighteenth century and the Victorian period. Currently he is working on a book on equine agency through mortality in Victorian fiction.

MAGDALENA BEYREUTHER is a historian who recently completed her PhD at the University of Bamberg; her dissertation, "Horses and Princes: The Art of Riding and Keeping Horses at Early Modern Courts in Franconia (1600–1800)," has been published as *Pferde und Fürsten* (Würzburg: Ergon, 2014); she has also worked at the Stable Museum in Nymphenburg Castle, Munich.

CHARLOTTE CARRINGTON-FARMER is associate professor of history at Roger Williams University, Rhode Island. She specializes in early American history and the early modern Atlantic world and received her PhD from the University of Cambridge (Trinity Hall) in 2010. Her dissertation, "Dissent and Identity in Seventeenth Century New England," is now a book project. Carrington-Farmer's research centers on framing dissent, deviance, and crime in early America in a wider Atlantic world context. She is particularly interested in Thomas Morton, who founded the Ma-Re Mount settlement (modern-day Quincy, Massachusetts), and she has written a biography of Morton for *Atlantic Biographies: Individuals and Peoples in the Atlantic World* (Leiden: Brill, 2013). Carrington-Farmer has reviewed a number of books for *History: Reviews of New Books* and is currently a reviewer for Bloomsbury Press. Her new research project deals with horses in the Atlantic world in the seventeenth and eighteenth centuries. Carrington-Farmer has presented her initial research findings on the Narragansett Pacer at several conferences and academic gatherings, including the British Group in Early American History Annual Conference (Edinburgh, 2014) and War Horses of the World (School of Oriental and African Studies, London, 2014).

JESSICA DALLOW is associate professor of modern and contemporary American art history at the University of Alabama at Birmingham. She received her PhD from the University of North Carolina, Chapel Hill. Her current research focuses on human-animal relationships in American equine and equestrian sporting imagery, and she is also working on a larger study of the nineteenth-century painter Edward Troye. Her other interests include contemporary African American art, feminist art, self-taught artists, and families of artists. Her work has appeared in the journals *Nineteenth-Century Art Worldwide* and *Feminist Studies*, the anthologies *Reconciling Art and Motherhood* and *Sacred and Profane: Vision and Voice in Southern Self-Taught Art*, and in the exhibition catalog *Family Legacies: The Art of Betye, Lezley, and Alison Saar*.

SUSANNA FORREST studied social anthropology and modern languages at Trinity College, Cambridge, and writes about the cultural history of horses as an independent scholar, author, and journalist. Her first book, *If Wishes Were Horses* (London: Atlantic Books, 2012) dealt with horse-crazy girls in Western culture. Her second book, *The Age of the Horse* (London: Atlantic Books, 2016), explores six themes with wide-ranging geographical and historical arcs: wildness, culture, power, meat, wealth, and war. She has written for the *NYTimes.com, Guardian, Telegraph, Times, Spiegel Online, New Statesman*, and other publications and has appeared in BBC documentaries on sidesaddle riding and women's remount depots in World War I. In 2012 she was awarded a Society of Authors Authors' Foundation Grant for research in Mongolia.

RUNE GADE is associate professor of art history at the University of Copenhagen, specializing in contemporary art. His research areas include theory of photography, museum studies, visual culture, and gender theory. He has published and edited several books, mostly in Danish but also some in English: *Symbolic Imprints: Essays on Photography and Visual Culture* (Aarhus: Aarhus University Press, 1999); *Performative Realism: Interdisciplinary Studies in Art and Media* (Copenhagen: Museum Tusculanum Press, 2005); and *Performing Archives/Archives of Performance* (Copenhagen: Museum Tusculanum Press, 2013). Gade's latest Danish publication was the edited volume *Cybermuseologi—kunst, museer og formidling i et digitalt perspektiv* (Aarhus: Aarhus University Press, 2015), on museology and digital media. Gade was a member of the board of PSi (Performance Studies International) from 2006 to 2010 and is the editor (with Edward Scheer) of the series In Between States, which is being published in collaboration between PSi and Museum Tusculanum Press. His current research explores alternative practices in art history that challenge the prevalent ideals of objectivity still dominating the discipline. Besides his academic practice Gade has also for more than twenty years worked as an art critic for the Danish national newspaper *Information*.

KRISTEN GUEST is a professor in the Department of English at the University of Northern British Columbia, researching and teaching Victorian literature and animal studies. Her publications include *Eating Their Words: Cannibalism and the Boundaries of Cultural Identity* (New York: SUNY Press, 2001) and an edition of Anna Sewell's *Black Beauty* (Calgary: Broadview Press, 2015).

DONNA LANDRY is professor of English and American literature at the University of Kent and a fellow of the Royal Asiatic Society. She is the author, coauthor, or coeditor of six books, including *Noble Brutes: How Eastern Horses Transformed English Culture* (Baltimore: Johns Hopkins University Press, 2008), translated into Turkish by Sinan Akıllı as *Asil Hayvanlar: Ingiliz Kültürünü Değiştiren Doğulu Atlar* (Istanbul: E Yayınları, 2015). Her work on horses in history includes "English Brutes, Eastern Enlightenment," *Eighteenth Century: Theory and Interpretation* 52, no. 1 (Spring 2011): 11–30, and "Learning to Ride in Early Modern Britain, or The Making of the English Hunting Seat," in *The Culture of the Horse: Status, Discipline, and Identity in the Early Modern World*, ed. Karen Raber and Treva J. Tucker (London: Palgrave Macmillan, 2005), 329–49. She is one of the founders of the Evliya Çelebi Way project: http://kent.ac.uk/english/evliya/index.html.

MONICA MATTFELD is assistant professor coappointed in the Departments of English and History at the University of Northern British Columbia. She is coeditor of two collections: *Performing Animals: History, Agency, Theater* (University Park, PA: Penn State University Press, 2017), and *Cosmopolitan Animals* (Palgrave Macmillan, 2016) and has written a monograph, *Performing Centaur: Eighteenth-Century Maculinity and English Horsemanship*, in the series Animalibus: Of Animals and Culture (University Park, PA: Penn State University Press, 2017).

ISA MENZIES holds a master of arts (museum studies) from the University of Sydney and is currently completing her PhD through the Australian National University's Humanities Research Centre. Her research centers on representations of the horse within the museum context and the horse's place in the Australian national imagination. Isa has spent almost a decade working in collections management, exhibition development, and public programs associated with cultural heritage, both in Australia and internationally. She has published on Phar Lap's remains; the influence of the horse on the pastoral mode in Australia; and the history of prisoner art in Western Australia's heritage-listed Fremantle Prison.

TATSUYA MITSUDA is senior assistant professor of economics at Keio University in Tokyo, where he researches the social and cultural history of veterinary medicine in Germany from 1750 to 1930. He currently holds a research grant for the project "Medicalization of Meat in Modern Germany: Animals, Food, Veterinarians," and his work has appeared in such journals as *Medical History*, *Food and History*, *Japanese Journal of Human Animal Relations*, and *Hiyoshi Review of English Studies*.

CHRISTINE RÜPPELL is an art historian who is currently at work on her dissertation, which focuses on the original interiors of early modern princely stables in Germany. She is also a scientific collaborator at the German Horse Museum (Deutsches Pferdemuseum) in Verden/Aller and has published in German on the Pommersfelden stable: "Ein Salett von oben bis unten mit Architectur, Figuren und Pferden: Der Stallsaal von Schloss Weißenstein in Pommersfelden," in *Marburger Jahrbuch für Kunstwissenschaft* (2004).

KARI WEIL is University Professor and director of the College of Letters at Wesleyan University, where she teaches courses in nineteenth- and twentieth-century European literature and philosophy, animal studies, feminist theory, and theories of autobiography. She earned her PhD in comparative literature from Princeton University with specializations in nineteenth- and twentieth-century France and feminist theory and has published numerous essays on feminist theory, questions of gender, and, more recently, theories and representations of animal otherness and human-animal relations. She is the author of *Androgyny and the Denial of Difference* (Charlottesville: University Press of Virginia, 1992) and *Thinking Animals: Why Animal Studies Now* (New York: Columbia University Press, 2012) and coeditor of a special issue of *Hypatia*, *"Animal Others"* (*Hypatia* 27, no. 3 [2012]). She is currently completing *Meat, Mobility, Magnetism: Horses and Their Humans in Nineteenth-Century France* (Chicago: University of Chicago Press, forthcoming).

INDEX

Page numbers in italics indicate figures and tables.